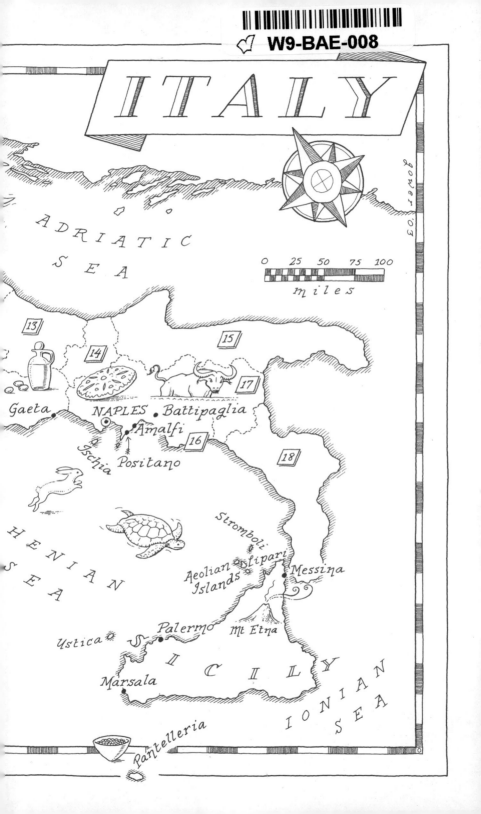

al dente

www.**booksattransworld**.co.uk

Books by William Black and Sophie Grigson

TRAVELS À LA CARTE

FISH

ORGANICS

al dente

The Adventures of a Gastronome in Italy

WILLIAM BLACK

BANTAM PRESS

LONDON · NEW YORK · TORONTO · SYDNEY · AUCKLAND

TRANSWORLD PUBLISHERS
61–63 Uxbridge Road, London W5 5SA
a division of The Random House Group Ltd

RANDOM HOUSE AUSTRALIA (PTY) LTD
20 Alfred Street, Milsons Point, Sydney,
New South Wales 2061, Australia

RANDOM HOUSE NEW ZEALAND LTD
18 Poland Road, Glenfield, Auckland 10, New Zealand

RANDOM HOUSE SOUTH AFRICA (PTY) LTD
Endulini, 5a Jubilee Road, Parktown 2193, South Africa

Published 2003 by Bantam Press
a division of Transworld Publishers

A catalogue record for this book is available from the British Library.
ISBN 0593 04942X

Typeset in 12.5/13.5pt Perpetua by
Falcon Oast Graphic Art Ltd.

Printed in Great Britain by
Mackays of Chatham, Chatham, Kent

1 3 5 7 9 10 8 6 4 2

To my brothers, Nick and Andrew.
And to the memory of Carlo Giuliani, and the
Fratelli Rosselli who all died too young.

CONTENTS

CONTENTS

RECIPES

RECIPES

ACKNOWLEDGEMENTS

With thanks to everybody who put up with me and my endless questions, but particularly to Maria Teresa Salis, Mary Taylor Simeti, Luigi Pomata, Gennaro Contaldo, Peppe and Gennaro d'Urso, Debora Protti, Gian Domenico Rinaldi, Assunta Lo Schiavo, Francesco Cecchetti, and Andrea Bocchi in the Domus Mazziniana, as well as Aldo and Silvia Rosselli in Rome. Thank you all.

I have to mention also Michael O'Leary, the genius who created Ryanair and enabled us all to travel without being millionaires.

Thanks too to Doug Young, who got so excited about worms full of cheese and donkey recipes, and to Linda Evans, both at Transworld.

And also to Mari Roberts who wielded the scissors with tact, speed and an awesome efficiency.

al dente

PROLOGUE

I SPENT TEN YEARS DRIVING A TRUCK STUFFED FULL OF FISH, weird mushrooms, the odd chicken and even a cheese or two from Paris to London and back. I was a mobile restaurant, and the French customs officers in Boulogne got so used to me that they would suggest I let them taste something exquisite lest they make my life a misery and search the truck.

I loved food. I loved fish, I loved eating, and I loved the sea. Over the years, I used to buy from further and further afield, which appealed to my other great passion: standing in queues at airports. Dealing with fish took me far and wide, to Cape Verde, to the Amazon, to the Galapagos.

The one country in Europe I barely visited was Italy. For fish reasons it's hardly surprising since they export very little. I put Italy in a neat beribboned box to be opened at a later date. Then one day I began to work on a project that meant that I simply had to go to Italy and eat as much pasta as I could. I checked out the cheap flights, and began to plot. It seems ridiculous now, but I decided to fly to Nice. Well, it was near Italy after all, and I knew the language. Dodging the poodles, and the blue rinses, I headed due east, and crossed the border into Italy at Ventimiglia. I drove on, deviated, climbed inland and stopped for lunch. I was in a small village called Molina di Triora, with only one restaurant. I pushed the door open and sat down. Part of me felt that I'd come home at last.

In a sense, part of me had. A story, a little vague to be sure, had surfaced every now and then that the family on my mother's side, the Rossellis, were related to Mazzini. Or was it Garibaldi? No one seemed to be certain, and no one really knew anything more than that. On balance, it was Mazzini's name we heard more often, but I had very little idea who he was. For all I knew, he could have been the great Mazzini, circus master extraordinaire, or Mazzini, purveyor of *gelati* to the royal family. But not at all. This man, I learnt, was one of Italy's greatest heroes, a devoted Republican who spent his life plotting and scheming and trying to nudge and bludgeon his homeland into unity and independence. Giuseppe Mazzini was born in Genoa in 1805 and died in Pisa in 1872. Closely involved with the Italian Risorgimento, when Italy eventually emerged as a united country for the first time, he and the great soldier Giuseppe Garibaldi provided the drama and much of the energy behind this extraordinary period of Italian history. Much of his life was spent in exile, and most of that in London, a city he eventually, somewhat grudgingly, came to love. And just to set the record straight we weren't related to him at all.

And so began two years of blissful investigation: a series of trips, no-frills hops, to Italy, hours of reading about the Risorgimento and, of course, an exploration of Italy's finest offering – its food, a fantastic variety, where dishes change from town to town and where almost without fail a story is lurking. This perhaps rather bizarre mix of personal history, political history and food was at the heart of my quest to discover all I could about my new *amore*, Italy.

My big break came one day in Turin. I walked into Turin's Palazzo Caragnon and climbed up the stairs of the Subalpine Parliament to take a look at the city's Risorgimento museum. And on that cold and grey September day, I saw to my utter amazement a picture of a rather haughty-looking woman called Giannetta Rosselli. It seemed too good to be true. Here was a Rosselli, who appeared to have been among Mazzini's most fervent supporters. Was she anything to do with my Rossellis? All I had to do was to follow a few leads.

A museum in Pisa had the original photographs. Giannetta's mother, an even more matronly figure, was also one of Mazzini's close friends. Was this the missing link, as far as my family was concerned? I called my brother in London, who seemed peculiarly unexcited by the whole thing, but then it was 12 September 2001, and the world was still in shock.

PART FOUR

MAINLAND

PART ONE
MAINLAND

TURIN

I CAN'T IMAGINE ANYONE SAYING, 'OH GOD, I LOVE TURIN!' It's not that it's an actively unpleasant city. It's just that Turin doesn't seem to grab you by the *coglioni* in that almost physical way that some of the more exquisite Italian towns and cities do.

Flying off to this centre of financial rectitude for my regular fortnightly dose of cheap travel, I had booked into the cheapest hotel I could find that had at least a vague recommendation, but I became a little concerned when neither my contacts in Turin nor the taxi driver had ever heard of the place. Driving in late on this autumnal day, past the vast empty space of the Porto Palazzo market and down through the Piazza San Carlo, I looked at the glittering, satisfyingly comfortable caffès where the next day – in a matter of mere hours – I was to be taken around to be pumped full of caffeine. Turin's caffès are in the Premier League: the Caffè Torino, Caval'd Brons, San Carlo, all cheerfully brimming with wealthy Torinesi, chatting away and nibbling on cakes and *gelati*. But I had promised the hotel on pain of death that I would check in as soon as I possibly could, for they seemed a little anxious, and I didn't want my bed given away to another penny-pinching writer.

The hotel I had chosen was right opposite the station. Outside every mainline city station in Italy there is, almost without fail, a Rabelaisian world at your feet. Hotels, three-star, two-star and even the unmentionable one-star, cluster around the mother station, greedily waiting for tourists searching nervously for a name they recognize, trying not to look too vulnerable. It is difficult to blend into the local landscape while pulling a suitcase around on wheels and you are easy meat, so I tend to stride off as purposefully as possible even if I haven't got the faintest idea where I am going. The darker it gets the darker is the atmosphere. Child pickpockets greet you at Roma Termini, pimps, junkies, desperados, Africans ululating, and cheap hotels. Turin, I have to say, wasn't quite this exciting. The massively modest entrance to the hotel was up a rickety lift to the first floor, and I was greeted by a man who looked like he was about to walk around the Lake District, possibly the most unfashionably dressed Italian I had ever seen. With his shorts, sandals, knobbly knees and, horror of horrors, white socks, this gentleman had perhaps spent his formative years in darkest middle England.

He was keen to tell me that the hotel was *quiet*, and woe betide me if I was to come back after midnight. I should not, I was told, ring the bell, but should (giving me a set of jangling keys with unease and suspicion) lock this and unlock that to gain access to my room. I must add that his desire for quietness sat uneasily with the fact that the rooms were quite the noisiest I had ever found in Italy. The busiest road in Turin seemed to echo endlessly around the S bend. Bravely I escaped into the outside world, back to the street-sellers and the Africans flogging dodgy watches. But I hadn't forgotten that it was the autumn. It was time for some fungus fun.

Whole generations of Italians are brought up with every antenna focused on the deep joy of wild mushrooms, and in particular *porcini*. Stubby, solid and utterly delicious, the cep has a warm chestnut, almost phallic top, smooth and hard to the touch. Earthy to the nose but meaty when cooked, *Boletus edulis* should be on everyone's must-taste-before-I-die list. The Italian section will be voluminous and unmanageable. The English will include Marmite, Cheddar, apples off the tree and turbot.

Buying fresh *porcini* is like a game of gastronomic Russian roulette. At particular moments in the lunar cycle the mushroom is liable to be riddled with worms, which, however broad-minded you are, seldom add to the gustatory experience. An honourable mushroom dealer will often cut his *porcini* in half, but logic suggests that he is unlikely to do so to all his specimens, so if you should see the slightest hint of worm tracks in the white, solid flesh of the stem, beware. A hint of warmth in the air — technically possible in autumn — and the more likely the worms are to have spat and chewed their way through your precious mushroom. Feel the stem, and if there is a little give, it could be that the worms have beaten you to it. You could, of course, take the easier route and buy dried *porcini*. With their intense luscious perfume, they truly grace any larder.

Dried *porcini* can be made into dishes of sublime excellence. Ligurians add *porcini* to their *baccalà*. Tuscans add them to beef. The Piemontesi to pasta, meat, fish — just about anything edible. And for my dinner, liberated from the man with the golden sandals? I ate *vitello albese*, raw veal with raw *porcini*. Then *taglierini* and *porcini*. (The next day I ate unctuous risotto with *porcini*. By then I had overdosed on them.)

Luckily raw food and pasta called for little cooking, and I hurried back to my two-star solitude moments before the curfew struck and I was turned into a *zucca* as the dark gates clanged shut for ever. But I completely blotted my copybook by buzzing *and* then trying to open the door with the keys provided. By the time morning finally came, I had been deprived of deep sleep all night long by the noise of sirens and cars, and was the ideal candidate for hefty doses of caffeine.

You can thank the wily Venetians, who would have been happy to trade in mongoose droppings had the opportunity arisen, for introducing coffee into Italy in the early seventeenth century. With their well-established links with Constantinople, where coffee-drinking had been popular for some time, they were well aware that this powerful drink was an excellent candidate for trade: long-lasting, valuable and, at the time, novel. The Turkish authorities were never very fond of the idea of having so many of the city's population gathering together in coffee houses chit-chatting, so much so that one Grand Vizier took to sewing up deviant coffee drinkers in sacks and having them tossed into the Bosphorus. But such zeal wasn't the sort of thing the Venetians went for at all, and by the latter part of the eighteenth century over 250 caffès graced the city alone. Pope Clement VII, when asked to ban the demon drink by a band of Christian fanatics, sipped the devil's cup and actually liked it. Benedict XIV went as far as having a coffee house built for his own use. Coffee-drinking boomed all over Italy. And where Venice led, Genoa often followed, and from there, using the trade routes that were originally based on wheat and salt, coffee first appeared in Turin in the middle of the eighteenth century.

Originally, coffee was a drink for the rich, or the rich at heart, drunk in what was at first called the *bottega del caffè*, the coffee shop, which soon became the *caffetteria*, whose finest evolutionary expression must be the British transport caff, temples of grease where a Gaggia machine would be laughed out of court.

A coffee cruise around Turin should start with the Caffè Torino. Notice the shiny and well-worn bronze bull on the pavement outside with a distinct indentation around its nether regions. The locals say that a quick rub on its brassy erogenous zone will infuse you with lust and fertility and indeed I barely restrained myself from calling the whole tour off and hotfooting it back to the hotel in search of other entertainments. Sadly no scenes of Felliniesque merriment greeted me inside the Torino, but rather the usual collection of neat businessmen galloping through their breakfast, standing up at the counter, smoking, reading *La Gazzetta dello Sport*: the true Italian *prima colazione*. It isn't the done thing to sit for breakfast in Italy. Stand, be uncomfortable. Sitting is for namby-pamby foreigners and people of a certain age. I sat.

At the other end of the piazza you will see another caffè with history oozing from its every pore. The Caffè San Carlo is famous for being the first to use gas lighting, and the first to sell out to Häagen Dazs. This is a little ironic to say the least, for Italy takes its *gelati* very seriously indeed. Italians are also, at certain levels, ardent anti-globalization enthusiasts, and I was told somewhat darkly that young people didn't go to the San Carlo any more. Since most of the clients were under twenty, I wasn't too sure what was meant by this. Opposite these two is the Caval'd Brons, named in Piemontese after the sculpture of a bronze horse in the middle of the square. Piemontese is fairly close to French, indeed it was French rather than Italian that was the lingua franca of the House of Savoy, and Cavour, infamous local schemer and statesman, was always more at ease in French than Italian. The caffès go through a regular evolutionary cycle as the day goes by. The early-morning shift for the smart and busy moves into the late-morning shift for those who are smart but no longer busy plus the odd tourist looking desperately for somewhere to sit down.

Tucked away close to the Porto Palazzo market is Il Bicerin, a caffè that is geographically and conceptually a little apart from the others. Before you go there, think wigs, powdered faces and women. Whereas the Torino and San Carlo are slightly flouncy and verging on the vulgar, the Bicerin is tiny, almost, you might say, perfectly formed. It has low ceilings in a rectangular salon with neat little seats waiting for its natural clients who died long ago. Now, poor caffè, it has to put up with the curious and the well-intentioned, tour guides and food writers. When I went there, there were two of us and a family of Swedes. But, *tant pis*, we ate and drank with suitable reverence.

The drink for which the Bicerin (oh, by the way, it is 'beech-er-rin' for those who like the phonetic crutch) is famous is called, unsurprisingly, *bicerin*, and it is undergoing a sort of renaissance in Turin. There is no finer drink with which to start a winter's morning, for not only does it have a dose of coffee but a dollop of the city's finest chocolate, and cream too. Originally called a *bavareisa*, this has morphed into *bicerin* over the years, called after the glass in which it was served. This caffè is and always has been run by women, slightly fearsome ladies at that, who dispense the drink with efficiency and a touch of *froideur*. When the Bicerin first started trading back in 1763, caffès were mostly for men, but since this one was set apart from the centre it attracted clients who could slip in and out without being noticed, useful for women on account of the social opprobrium attached to their drinking coffee.

To prevent *ennui*, you can drink a *bicerin* in one of three ways. As a *pur e fiòr* (caffè e latte), *pur e barba* (caffè e cioccolato) or *pò' d'tut'* (a bit of everything), which is what most people seem to drink. To keep the locals happy it was decided that the *bicerin* should have its price pegged at 15 centesimi, and so it was from 1850 right through to 1913 when the scandal of a *bicerin* price hike to 20 centesimi got Turin's tongues a-wagging. To mollify the population it was proposed that for a mere 5 centesimi extra you could have a minuscule nibble to go with it.

There is a whole world of nibbles out there, some sweet, others savoury, and most have unctuous-sounding names in dialect. *Brioche* becomes *brioss*. *Poppe di suora*, nun's tits, becomes *pupe d'monia*. Political snacks hark back to Turin's golden days in the 1860s: *Garibaldin, democratich, savoiardina.* So, when you're bored with shopping and bored with the museums, hurry on down to the Bicerin, the best place in the world to nibble a nun's tits.

In England a Piemontese friend had told me not to bother asking the Torinesi any questions. 'They won't tell you anything,' he said. 'They are secretive and like only two things, making money and talking about making money.' Not my favourite topics of conversation, nor an area where I have any expertise. Turin seems to be going through a middle-aged identity crisis, trying rather desperately to create a funkier alter ego. Step one seems to be to instruct the minions in the Ministry of Disseminating Marginally Useful Information to create pamphlet upon pamphlet to get the visitor's juices flowing. It's true there is quite a lot to see in Turin. There are, for example, over eighteen kilometres of covered arcades where you can shop in all weathers. You can pop into the museum of marionettes, 'with over 10,000 pieces'. When you've finished, hurry along to the Carlo Biscaretti di Ruffi National Car Museum, with over 150 vehicles. And why not round off your day with a visit to the Martini Museum of Oenological History, 'more than 600 pieces', or the GAM, the Gallery of Modern Art, with its magnificent 15,000 pieces. That makes 25,750 pieces, surely enough to keep you busy for a few days.

It is a particularly easy city for ramblers, its streets laid out on a rigidly uniform grid, superimposed on the ancient Roman streets of the original town they called Augusta

Taurinorum, which was in its turn built upon the ruins of Taurasia, the mythical capital of the Tauri. But you could go really wild and follow your nose, particularly to the one building you simply cannot avoid, which characterizes the skyline as completely as the Twin Towers did in New York twenty-four hours before my Turin visit. To the north-east you will see a strange dome topped by a long metallic prong. This is the *Mole*, which houses the National Cinema Museum and looks like a curious hybrid of the Eiffel Tower and St Paul's Cathedral. It is distinctly out of place, almost exuberant, in staid Turin. Originally it was destined to be the city's synagogue but the architect, Alessandro Antonelli, fell out with the local Jewish community as the building costs escalated. They eventually handed it over to the city and washed their hands of the project entirely. Turin was left with a lasting oddity, which gives it a little dose of wackiness. You can understand the clients' concern when, after thirteen years, the building was still being built; it was finally finished in 1875.

You cannot go to Turin without expecting to see its greatest attraction: the *Sindone*, or as we call it in English, the Shroud. The problem is that the Turin Shroud is kept well and truly shrouded in the Duomo, the rather subdued Renaissance cathedral. Enclosed in a Hogwartian trunk behind a sheet of plate glass, bulletproofed in case anyone wanted to assassinate it, the shroud's appearances are strictly controlled. The most recent was when Pope John Paul II came to pay his respects in 2000.

The best place to get to grips with the mysteries of the shroud is not in the Duomo itself but in the nearby church of Santa Cristina. Since the matter is rather difficult to prove, a whole industry of speculation has grown up trying to establish whether this was indeed Christ's burial shroud or not. We can be certain about one thing: that we cannot be certain. Endless debate rages, and there is quite a lot of rage. If you follow the evidence from the carbon-

14 tests carried out in the late 1980s, the shroud seems to be dated between 1260 and 1390. Other tests indicate traces of human blood, but of course it is impossible to say whether this is Christ's. Yet more tests have come up with traces of pollen from flowers found only in Palestine, which was after all Jesus' 'hood, even if you call it Israel.

Christian lore goes something like this. Records dating back to CE 525 describe a cloth bearing 'the true likeness' of Christ being seen in the Byzantine city of Edessa (Urfa in present-day Turkey). The connection with Byzantium is important, for the image of a Christ-like face, an image 'not made by hands' or an Acheiropoieta, has deep significance in Orthodox Christianity, hence the importance of icons. Every year on 29 August, far away in central Europe, the Ukrainian church celebrates the Third Feast of the Saviour, the time when the Mandylion (the original name for the image of Edessa) arrived from Palestine. A blind local king called Abgar was said to have written to Christ asking for help in restoring his sight. The reply was that he, or He, depending on your state of belief, was too busy to sort out the man's vision but that he would send an emissary. Later we hear that St Jude Thaddeus arrived bearing a cloth with the image of Christ, which, when touched to Abgar's face, restored his vision.

Then nothing much is heard about the shroud – this was the Dark Ages after all – until in 1349 a French knight called Geoffrey de Charny built a church in Lirey, France, to honour what was claimed to be the shroud. How it got there isn't exactly clear either. The next few centuries see the shroud being shunted around Europe, at times exhibited to the faithful, at times used to generate cash by de Charny's descendants, who were keen to keep this nest egg within their grasp. We know that in 1453 Duke Louis I of Savoy had it in his possession – though he took some time to pay for it – and thus came the shroud to the House of Savoy. It was recorded at Vercelli, Ivrea and even Mons in present-day Belgium. The shroud was intended to be given a permanent home in the Royal Chapel in Chambéry, but it turned up in Milan on 14 September 1578, when it was taken there to enable crotchety but saintly old Cardinal Charles Borromeo to give thanks for the city's delivery from the plague.

Turin's fortunes rose in 1560 as the House of Savoy moved their capital there from Chambéry under the successful aegis of King Emmanuele Filiberto, starting the dynasty that survived right through to Italy's independence, when they became Italy's very own, very second-rate royal family. Although the first king of Italy was Vittorio Emmanuele, he liked to call himself Vittorio Emmanuele the Second, King of Italy, rather than King Vittorio Emmanuele the First. He preserved his Piemontese title for sentimental reasons, which shows you, in the immortal English phrase, where he was coming from. What might seem confusing is that the kingdom was for many years called the Kingdom of Sardinia. The Treaty of Utrecht in 1713 gave Sicily to the House of Savoy, but the king, realizing Sicily was too far away to exploit, swapped it for Sardinia in a twist of the global power game of the time.

Nineteenth-century Turin was inextricably tied up in the whole business of making Italy into a single, unified country. The city buzzed with intrigue and political passion, the scene of a complex dance between Monarchists and Republicans. By the end of the nineteenth century Turin was to become the first capital of a united Italy but to the utter disgust of many of its citizens promptly lost the title, first to Florence and then to Rome. The struggle to keep control over events long before this dénouement called for someone of special talent, and only one man was up to the job: arch-manipulator, political chameleon Camillo Benso Conte di Cavour, the third man of the Italian Risorgimento, a shrewd, utterly devious politician who fought by fair means and foul to undermine the growing importance of Mazzini, Garibaldi and the Republicans.

Cavour was born in Turin in 1810, spoke French as his mother tongue, and was a successful minister of agriculture, and later of finance. His politics were liberal, and he was genuinely committed to the idea of a written constitution in the kingdom, which when granted gave Piedmont an aura of democratic respectability lacking elsewhere in the peninsula. When he became prime minister in 1852 he

The devious Cavour celebrates his success in gaining control of both the foreign affairs and financial portfolios.

became closely involved with the machinations of the Risorgimento and played a subtle game of trying to be all things to all people. He well knew how important it was to keep the Emperor Louis Napoleon of France happy while slowly trying to create a rich, powerful monarchy around King Vittorio Emmanuele, who ironically was far more sympathetic to Garibaldi, in his post-Republican stage, than Cavour ever was. Cavour's subtle scheming outwitted everyone, including himself, but he didn't live too long, shuffling off his mortal coil at the very unripe age of fifty-two. He was, however, ultimately effective, and managed to hijack the creation of an Italian republic on behalf of the House of Savoy, and the Kingdom of Sardinia.

So, in respect to the memory of my ancestors, and Mazzini, may I add, with complete historical objectivity, that he was an unappetizing little creep who loathed Mazzini and looked down on Garibaldi – a classically Machiavellian figure of the first degree.

A suitably rounded man, we are told, with a pompous air and a high squeaky voice, he is the one figure among the Risorgimento greats whose greatness did not perhaps help Italy at all in the long run. In mitigation, though, he was fond of his food. Cavour ate regularly at a restaurant in Turin that still stands little changed from the days when the city was at the centre of so much scheming and tension.

So after I had stumbled upon, to my utter amazement on that cold and grey September day, the picture of the haughty-looking Giannetta Rosselli, who at long last held out the promise of providing the missing link between my family and the Risorgimento, I decided to reward myself with a little gastronomy in Cavour's favourite restaurant, del Cambio, conveniently placed right opposite the museum. No surprise, since the museum is in the old Subalpine Parliament building where Cavour saw his schemes evolve into something far greater than he ever expected. Actually, Cavour was originally keener on the idea of annexing Lombardy and the Veneto for the kingdom and neither wrote nor spoke of the greater unification of Italy until Republican fervour started gaining ground. So, while tucking into a plate of the most exquisite *agnolotti*, I mused. From his favourite table, Cavour noted the comings and goings into Parliament with interest. It was said that if he spoke in Italian, he thought like a Frenchman and ate like a Piemontese. I was happily following him in the last of these. Spooky.

Agnolotti

This serves six.

FOR THE FILLING AND SAUCE
50g unsalted butter
2 cloves garlic, finely chopped
50g finely diced pancetta
1 onion, finely chopped
200g minced pork
200g minced veal
1 sprig rosemary
1 bay leaf
150ml red wine
150ml meat stock
200g finely shredded cabbage or spinach
200g freshly grated Parmesan
5 egg whites (use the yolks in the pasta)
salt, pepper and nutmeg
Parmesan or reduced meat stock, to serve

FOR THE PASTA
500g type 00 flour
5 egg yolks

In a flameproof casserole, melt the butter and cook the garlic, pancetta and onion for 5 minutes. Add the meat, rosemary and bay leaf and cook for another 20 minutes. Meanwhile heat the oven to 170°C. Add the wine and stock to the casserole, cover and transfer to the oven to cook for 30 minutes. Then remove and set aside to cool. When cool, add the cabbage or spinach, Parmesan and egg whites, combining well and making sure the meat is not in clumps. Season with salt, pepper and nutmeg.

To make the pasta, tip the flour into a mound on the work surface and put the egg yolks into a crater in the middle. Combine the flour and egg yolks to make the dough and work it well. Divide it into two equal halves and roll each one out into a thin sheet. Place teaspoons of the meat mixture 3cm apart over one sheet of pasta. Cover with the second sheet of pasta, press down and cut into squares around the little mounds of filling. Cook as for any pasta, and serve with fresh grated Parmesan or a little reduced meat stock.

I had walked through the door of del Cambio slightly hesitantly, being rather scruffy, and had expected to be greeted by a sniffy waiter who would ask if I had booked and then show me the door even if I had. But not a bit of it. Turin has a Ruritanian alter ego, a cosier side to it that I grew to respect. Just as the Bicerin is snug, if a little powdered and unworldly, so del Cambio is smart, a showpiece, a gastronomic museum, well-oiled, efficient but welcoming, and I like that. I was shown to my table.

The menu is dotted with classic Piemontese dishes, and classic Piemontese cooking is among the world's very best.

But if any dish had to become Cavour's own particular favourite then it had to be *la finanziera*; fitting, since he was highly effective as a minister of finance, and this is Turin after all. In fact, the dish is more rural than it sounds. A wild and wacky mix of unmentionable parts of animals cooked in a broth (*brodo*) with a little Marsala and vinegar, and perhaps a glass of Barolo. Most of these unmentionable parts are these days considered so illicit that a good and true *finanziera* is hard to find. Once, not long ago, you could have found, nuzzling next to your kidneys, tidy slices of calf's brain, sweetbreads, cock's crests and bull's testicles, and while this sort of food now creates gasps of disgust, it is sad that this is so, for even the moderate, modern versions I ate were truly excellent. How daft that we have become so restricted in our repertoire that the only way we now eat these bits and pieces is as delightful mechanically rendered meat washed from the skeletons of intensively reared animals. We call it the sausage.

And then there's *fritto misto*. Sounds simple. It isn't. It calls for lamb. Veal. Brains. *Lacetti* (sweetbreads). *Filoni* (veins). Liver. *Batsoà* (pig's trotters). Sausage. A few ceps. Some *frisse*, which are themselves made from lungs, hearts, *coscia di maiale* (pig's thigh), liver. It is a truly gestalt dish made from many bits that together create a formidable whole, and in the days when pigs were slaughtered on the farms of the Piemontese hills and valleys, these bits were ready to hand.

Del Cambio is typically Torinese. Comfortable, bourgeois, self-assured. You can imagine why Cavour liked it so. It is the only restaurant in Italy I visited that has tablecloths, and I would be happy, immensely happy, to powder my nose, wear breeches, and be either scheming or gallant to get a table there. I really would.

Finanziera alla piemontese

This calls for a good butcher, or a farmyard. Serves six.

100g cock's crests
100g prepared veal sweetbreads
100g chicken liver
100g beef entrecôte
80g veal rump
flour
salt
80g butter
50g fresh porcini or 10g dried porcini, reconstituted
100ml dry Marsala
100ml red wine vinegar

Cut all the meat, apart from the crests, into equal-sized slices about 1cm thick. Flour and season lightly with salt. In a pan, melt the butter and brown the meat on all sides for a few minutes, then add the cock's crests, cover and cook over a low heat for 20 minutes. Add the porcini and cook for a further 20 minutes, still over a low heat. Add the Marsala and vinegar, turn up the heat and allow the liquid to reduce to a sauce consistency, then serve immediately.

* * *

Piemontese cooking is also full of impossibly large-scale, complex dishes that call for at least fourteen people to eat them at a time, a challenge for a writer eating mostly solo in this particularly appetizing part of the world. There is, for example, *bagna caôda*. Essentially a simple combination of raw vegetables, olive oil, anchovies and butter, its apparent simplicity can be easily ruined by using crappy second-rate ingredients. Restaurants, and families of fewer than fourteen, i.e. everyone, have had to learn how to tone down, or at least adapt, these dishes to modern times. In Italy, it is the nuclear family that now rules, and whereas grannies were once lovingly kept within the family fold they are now often left to be looked after by a combination of Eastern Europeans and the state.

However, old dishes die hard, and almost every Piemontese I met was still charmingly committed to the idea of eating *bagna caôda* in the chillingly cold autumn as the vines are harvested, and especially at Christmas time. It is still a very sociable dish. The word 'Barolo' inevitably passes their lips: this ravishing wine from the Langhe is when young a perfect combination with *bagna caôda*.

Bagna caôda means warm bath in Piemontese, the bath usually being a clay dish, kept hot, into which you put the sauce. The idea is hardly radical. You dip the vegetables into the sauce. *Basta*. And if you look at the ingredients they are unfrightening, almost mundane. Olive oil. Butter. Garlic. Anchovies. Some of the ingredients were carried into Piedmont across the mountains from Liguria along the ancient salt trails. As far as anchovies are concerned they were one of the few fish to swim off the sharply sloping, rather fish-poor Ligurian coast, and have been salted and preserved for centuries, although these days many Piemontesi don't actually use anchovies at all but seem to prefer using cheaper salted sardines from Spain, packed tightly into glorious multicoloured tins. Ligurian olive oil is ideal, far milder than Tuscan, which can be mouth-splutteringly *piccante* at times and isn't suitable. The Tuscans tend to pontificate about being at the northern limit of olive growing, but they seem to have forgotten about Liguria, and probably have even less idea that olives are also grown along the shores of Lake Garda.

The classic *bagna caôda* uses vegetables that can be found in winter. So, although you could use a bit of celery and even a carrot or two, what you really need are Jerusalem artichokes, cardoons and, if you can find them, some sweet peppers. That said, it's not quite that easy.

First, the Jerusalem artichokes. You can make a version of *bagna caôda* using these alone: see page 25. You might be wondering why we call these knobbly tubers artichokes at all, when we know full well that the artichokes that aren't said to come from Jerusalem are the buds of a thorny Mediterranean thistle. In Italian, Piemontese and French, Jerusalem artichokes are known as *topinambur* or *topinambour*, named after a tribe in South America who had nothing at all to do with the plant but happened to be 'visiting' Europe at the time, so that some clever soul thought their name would be ideal for what was in reality a North American tuber. An explorer named Samuel de Champlain reported in the early seventeenth century that these edible tubers tasted like artichokes. He never mentioned Jerusalem, or the South American tribe called Tupinamba. As for the 'Jerusalem', this comes, we are told, from a corruption of the Italian for sunflower, *girasole*, for science tells us that the Jerusalem artichoke is in fact a member of the sunflower family. Phew! Phew indeed. For eating *topinambur* in any form invokes an immense amount of wind, so *bagna caôda* evenings would obviously not be the ideal setting for either romance or solemnity, though ideal for post-harvest Piemontese celebrations.

Jerusalem artichokes will always remind me of the time I was hauled over the coals by British Customs for failing to provide a Meat Health Certificate for what they thought were Toppinham boars, i.e. some weird sort of wild pig, a name they had gleaned from a pile of French invoices I had faxed across, as one had to do in those days. I spent some time trying to convince them that, despite appearances, the tubers I held in my hand were not pigs at all, and eventually, and most generously, they conceded the point and let me through. This is one of the reasons why I personally felt so happy when the European frontiers finally came down. *Vive l'UE!*

Jerusalem artichoke bagna caôda

Serves four.

500g Jerusalem artichokes, washed and thinly sliced
(peeled if you like)
175ml extra virgin olive oil
cloves from 3 heads of garlic, thickly cut
15 to 20 salted anchovy fillets
50g unsalted butter

Heat the oven to 150°C. Place the Jerusalem artichokes in a thin layer over a wide ovenproof dish. Pour the oil over the top; it should just cover them. Add the garlic, then lay the anchovies on top. Cook in the hot oven for 90 minutes, checking after the first 30 minutes that the garlic isn't burning. If it is, turn the oven down. At the same time, stir so that the anchovies melt and mix with the oil. After the full 90 minutes, add the butter and return the dish to the oven for a final 10 minutes. Serve.

The cardoon element of classic *bagna caôda* is more challenging. I once grew some cardoons, but they were so beautiful I didn't have the heart to eat them, and by the time I plucked up the courage I was told by a local cardologist that they were far too big. So I left them, and let them happily fill up a quarter of the vegetable garden that was out of control anyway. Ironically, cardoons are a type of artichoke, technically a thistle, of the species *Cynara cardunculus*, but it is the stem rather than the bud that is eaten, which is thick, slightly rough and has to be protected from the light to prevent it becoming too bitter to eat. This is mostly done by judicious use of a sack or paper. Here in Piedmont, particularly around the town of Nizza Monferrato, grow the finest cardoons of all: the Ferrari of the thistle family, which they call *cardi gobbi*, or hunchbacked cardoons. And the best of these are the variety called Lo Spadone. The plants thrive on the sandy alluvial soils of Monferrato and every September, just as the frosts are beginning, expert cardoon growers, *cardaroli*, gather round to cover the plants with mounds of soil. Naturally the plants try to get out of this unnecessary piece of human folly and grow towards the light, and in the process become crooked. Hence 'hunchbacked'. *Bagna caôda* purists insist that it is only this variety that is sweet enough to eat raw. So, item two on your checklist are *cardi gobbi di Nizza Monferrato*.

As far as peppers, *peperoni*, are concerned, bell peppers to Americans, we in the UK have to put up with endless amounts of tasteless peppers from Holland, perfect, shiny, but quite magnificently bland. For peppers at their very best, you should go wild one day and trek off to Cuneo, only 50km to the north of Turin, deep in the heart of *bagna caôda* land, and where my *bagna* journey began. Cuneo is yet another of those places with a special affinity to one particular crop. You know this to be the case for Cuneo peppers have little stickers telling you why you are about to pay double for them, but they really do taste. Do they taste!

Bagna caôda

Many versions can be found, but all share certain principles. These are:
- *to cook the* bagna *at a low temperature, in a terracotta dish if possible;*
- *to soak or cook the garlic in milk;*
- *to use the freshest winter vegetables;*
- *to avoid the stronger-tasting vegetables such as fennel and celery, if possible;*

• *to serve the* bagna *hot.*
The vegetables are dipped into the hot sauce and eaten raw,
so a plate warmer or fondue set would come in useful. Serves
eight.

FOR THE BAGNA
cloves from 6 heads of garlic, soaked in milk overnight,
or cooked in milk until tender for an even milder
version
250ml olive oil, preferably Ligurian
50g unsalted butter
12 fillets of salted anchovies or 5 salted sardines
a selection of fresh vegetables that should include cardoons
(*cardi gobbi di Nizza Monferrato*, Lo Spadone variety is best),
sweet peppers from Cuneo or Carmagnola, Jerusalem
artichokes, cauliflower, carrots and cabbage
juice of 1 lemon
1 tablespoon cream, optional

Put the garlic, 150ml of the olive oil and half the butter
in a large flameproof terracotta dish (or a saucepan) over
a low heat and cook for 30 minutes, stirring occasionally
with a wooden spoon. The garlic must not fry but rather
steam in the heat of the oil and butter. Then add the rest
of the oil and butter along with the anchovies or sardines
and continue to cook over a low flame until they have
melted into a relatively homogenous sauce.

Meanwhile, prepare the vegetables by cutting them into
strips. The cardoons should be trimmed and cleaned of
any hard bits, then put in water to which you have added
lemon juice to prevent them from browning. Serve with
the *bagna* (to which you have added, if you like the idea,
the cream), which should be kept hot over a flame – this
is where a fondue set can come in handy. A bottle of fine
young Barbera or Barolo goes down well.

Being a bit of a market queen, I had read on more than one occasion that the *mercato* at Cuneo, home of the peppers and more besides, was one of the finest in the area. Keen to bring home the usual pack of gastronomic hostages, I booked into a hotel right on the square where it was due to begin the next day.

The market was being talked about almost as soon as I got to Cuneo.

'You mustn't park your car outside tonight, sir. It's the market tomorrow. It starts in the morning.'

Unusual, I thought. 'I've read that the market here is pretty good. Will I be able to buy everything I need for a *bagna caôda*?'

'Oh yes. You can buy anything. Wait until tomorrow.'

Just about able to sleep despite the excitement, I hurried downstairs in the morning to see the piazza trans-formed. Endless rows of white vans – rears turned outwards, tents pinned to their sides – stretched right around the piazza. It was quite impressive. I imagined a Piemontese cornucopia opening up before my very eyes. Piles of cheeses. Sumptuous barrows full of Cuneo peppers. Cows spurting milk into churns. Wonderful.

I pushed my way eagerly towards the white vans and the riches before me, then gasped in horror. Row upon row, yes. But of shell suits, enormous panties and curtains. It took me a while to discover that the food section was stuffed into a covered market on the other side of the square, where I did at least find my *cardi*, my *topinambur* and even my Cuneo peppers.

When I arrived back home, while the kids asked me what sort of pasta I had brought this time, Sophie, who seemed to have lost track, asked me where I'd flown in from.

'Turin,' I said.

'Oh God, I love Turin!'

ALBA

SLIM, SLEEK, MUSCULAR, TOBY WAS, DESPITE HIS NAME, 100
per cent Italian. He, like me, was on the trail of the
elusive white truffle *Tuberosum magnum*, a strange subterranean fungus that gourmets and gourmands travel
hundreds of miles to find and spend small fortunes on.
Unlike me he had a fine tail and wagged a lot, and was
happy to be fobbed off with crusts of bread soaked in a
mere hint of truffle oil. Toby's mission was simple. To
sniff, perchance to wag and maybe dig a little in the humic
leafy soils of the woods around Canale, a little town in the
Langhe in Piedmont, and to bring to us rapacious humans
as many truffles as he possibly could. And all for a measly
truffled crust.

I needed Toby, but I'm not entirely sure that Toby
needed me. For a start I spoke a bastardized tongue. He
spoke patois. And then I had an odd habit of stroking his
head, which his master rarely did. Even odder was the fact
that I apparently wanted to look for truffles in the middle
of the day. Now everyone but everyone, even the
humblest mongrel, knows that truffles come out at night.
Toby had cost his master £4,000,000, which may strike

you as a little excessive unless you know that the £ sign
was also used to indicate the lira, once upon a time anyway, for the lira has slipped away into history, largely
unloved and unmourned. Expert *trifolau* Stefano Grosso,
a.k.a. Merlot – pronounce the 't' please – has spent much
of his life, his autumnal life at least, in search of truffles,
and he knows how to train a good truffle hound. Before
Toby, not the best of his hounds by his own admission,
were a long line of canine super-heroes. We humans with
our profoundly underdeveloped sense of smell are sadly
not well adapted to scampering around on all fours and
sniffing, the sort of activity we mainly confine to the bedroom. Dogs are far less bashful.

Stefano had a wizened face and a wizened sense of
humour, perfect for a *trifolau*. We were due to meet outside the Enoteca Pubblica in Canale, a little way from the
world's white truffle epicentre, Alba. Let me say, without
further ado, that this will be disputed. In Tuscany, fine
truffles are unearthed around San Miniato. In the Marche,
there is Sant'Agata Feltria, and truffles are found in the
remoter parts of Molise, and even as far south as Calabria.
So don't believe the story that Alba has a complete
monopoly on white truffles and don't necessarily believe
that all truffles you buy in Alba are dug from its very
woods. Neither is it a matter of science that their truffles
are the best, but where there is belief and the full weight
of tradition, then truth tends to be assumed.

There is no foolproof way of knowing whether your
truffle truly is Albese, apart from relying on reputations
and trust. I was told that the best *tartufi* have a reddish
tinge to them, but others dispute this completely. In 1954,
the world's biggest truffle, a colossal 540-grammer, was
offered to President Truman by the community of Alba.
The tradition had been started as a rather unsubtle
marketing ploy, to offer a chosen global worthy the biggest
truffle of the harvest, a tradition that seems a little risky

given that many of the recipients were probably expecting a box of chocolates rather than a fungus. But was Truman told, I wonder, that the truffle was actually found in San Miniato, Tuscany, and sold on to an Albese truffle dealer? The year 2001 had been absolutely terrible for truffles. The yields were pathetic. For the hours, the nights, that Stefano had spent in the hills the financial rewards were pretty scant; don't imagine that this is a quick path to immense wealth.

So here we were in broad daylight looking for something that we knew we would never find, but what fun it all was. For a start, Stefano had ample time to fill me in on his own very personal path to being a *trifolau*. It started long ago, when he was fourteen. The war had ended. Piedmont had suffered enormously. Turin, the industrial heart of Italy, had been smashed and bombed. Reconstruction began quickly and it was the Fiat factory, the huge Mirafiore works in Turin, that drew in thousands of workers from the countryside, among them Stefano. In the truffle season, Stefano's contribution to the Agnelli family business lapsed into automatic mode. In the morning the bus would pick him up to take him to the factory gates. Time to sleep and dream a little for he had often been up all night long, truffling. Time also to keep well away from the other *trifolau* who worked at Fiat, all rather keen to know where their rivals had been that night, wondering what they had found. Being secretive in such a tight-knit community is tricky. Ancient enmities pepper the soil.

When he was telling me all this with a gentle smile on his face, my mind wandered and thought of all those abysmal Fiats that were once turned out from the Mirafiore factory. The gruesome 124 that became as famously socialist as the Lada and valiantly broke down for everyone. The Mirafiore, a car of such inspired ugliness that it made the Austin Marina look as elegant as a Gucci handbag. Was their renowned unreliability anything to do with the lack of sleep of some of the workforce, perhaps?

By now, Stefano had been hanging around autumnal woods for fifty-two years. There was little he didn't know about the habits of the truffle. Armed with his main weapon, Toby, and his truffle pick, or *zappino*, he told his misty-eyed story, not, I suspect, for the first time.

Just as man and dog have such a well-developed symbiosis, so do the truffle and the roots of a tree. For the truffle is the fruiting body of a fungus that sends out a network of ultra-fine hyphae through the ground around the foot of the host tree, which feeds off the sugars that are found in the plant's root system. And in addition, the tree benefits from having a wider network of capillaries that increase the water supply to its roots, and from the extra microbial activity in the soil. The best truffles are said to grow around oak, but hazel, willow, even poplar will do. Whatever the tree, the life cycle of the truffle is essentially the same.

At the beginning of the truffle season, in September, the tubers can grow quite close to the ground, which is about the only time that a human might stumble across one. As does *Helomyza tuberivora*, the truffle fly, which treats the truffle as a nursery for its maggoty offspring to eat and digest. If you see a group of flies dancing over the roots of a tree, a truffle might just be underfoot. But don't dig frantically with a spade like a hysterical gold miner. Bring a *trifolau* along with you. And his dog. But not his pig. This is considered to be a French habit. Pigs are, after all, notoriously greedy and despite their sensitive nostrils they are not deemed to be suitable here in Italy. The possibility that they might not be content with a mere bread crust is just too awful to bear.

I suspect that one day soon some fool will invent an electronic truffle sensor that scans underground and beeps at any growing mass of truffles. Smell is after all closely connected with taste, so there is little point in buying a truffle unless it has that particular pungency, which science has kindly told us is akin to the smell of arousing, sexy things like sweaty armpits and stale crotches. Ah! The mysteries of human cooking!

Of all the stories I heard about where *tartufi bianchi* came from, I liked this the best. A Piemontese friend was told by his father that *tartufi bianchi* grew where the moon-beams shone through the forest on cool autumnal nights and struck the ground, slipping through the soil to touch the trees' roots. And looking at a truffle, you can begin to see what a fabulous idea this is. There in your hand sits this magical minuscule moon, pitted with craters, utterly mysterious. Bah to the symbiosis humbug. And the earth is flat too.

There are slightly muckier, less romantic versions. One says that these earthy lumps are born of drops of stag semen, so if you walk through the Piemontese woods at night and come across piles of lurid magazines of naked deer, with painted antlers and pouting lips, that could be the definitive proof we need. And then there's the classical interpretation: that the truffle comes from thunder where it strikes the autumnal ground. Science, mundane and sadly irrefutable, has brought to us the facts of symbiosis, and dampened our ardour still further by informing us that the truffle is sexless. Yet the truffle is still considered to be an aphrodisiac. Food and sex have a long history, and while we might not get excited by an avocado, the Aztecs did, and called it *auhacatl*, or testicle.

But the truffle? Is there something deeply and atavistically sexual about its perfume? Truffles smell for a reason. Which isn't to excite strange foreigners into pay-ing ever-increasing amounts of money for the substance and then furtively grating it over pasta, but to lure an animal to dig it up – the fruiting spore, remember, of the invisible microscopic mycelium – and to eat a chunk and drop bits off here and there while snacking so regally. And the spores, if they land in the right place, get on with the job of spreading the mycelium elsewhere. One of the reasons why the Langhe is so rich in truffles is down to the paucity of the wild boar, which elsewhere, in Calabria in particular, are keener and more capable trufflers than *Homo sapiens*. How better to attract animals (such as ourselves) than being all basic and sexual?

Elena was an Albese through and through, and figuratively held my hand in Alba's busy and rather famous autumn truffle *fiera*. Although I was expecting people with furtive, weathered faces to sidle up to me holding out a truffle in a gnarled hand, the *fiera* is rather elegant and courteous. With truffles sitting respectfully under glass on sheets of rice paper, the only slight hint of vulgarity is the price, which at times will make you laugh.

It is inevitable, in this country that celebrates almost anything with a *sagra*, that there would be a truffle fair. Alba devotes no less than three weeks to the Fiera Nazionale del Tartufo Bianco, which was exactly why I was here, along with more than a smattering of Austrians, Swiss and Germans, all exuding their own version of Teutonic human warmth, bonhomie and wealth.

Let me offer you a few hints, a few truffle do's and don'ts. If you feel the need to splash out on a white truffle, go for as round a truffle as possible: they are much easier to grate. If you haven't got a truffle grater, an *affetta tartufi*, immediately cancel all social interaction and buy one. Truffles, like all mushrooms, abhor plastic, which makes them sweat and rot. One of the best ways to keep your truffle is not to keep it at all, but to go home and cook it straight away. But truffles can voyage a little if you don't happen to live in a truffle zone. They can be packed in a glass jar, surrounded with kitchen paper, and kept in the jar, in the fridge. Some like to keep truffles surrounded by eggs or rice – superfine Carnaroli or Arborio for preference – which take on the truffle's strange perfume. But as the days go by your truffle will simply fade away, desiccate, and you will be a severely disappointed gourmet if you base your truffle experience on this feeble ground. For those of you brave, rich or greedy enough to risk a kilo or two, truffles can be packed in woven-reed boxes, which suit them perfectly, but each day you store them they gradually lose weight and finesse, so realistically you have to eat them as soon as you can.

And then there is the small matter of what to do with your truffle. Firstly, and most importantly, you don't really need to cook it. Unlike France's finest – the Black or Périgord truffle, *Tuberosum melanosporum* – *tartufi bianchi* are at their best when eaten raw, grated or shaved onto a simple, fairly anodyne base. Stefano ate his truffles grated over baked eggs, which is how many of the Piemontesi I asked said they preferred theirs, utterly simple. For me, the most sublime way to eat *tartufi bianchi* is grated over freshly made *tajarin*, ultra-thin egg-based pasta. It is my – OK, one of my – desert-island dishes, quite exquisite. Go to Alba before you go to heaven. Or hell.

Tajarin with truffles

Serves four.

FOR THE PASTA
500g type 00 flour
4 egg yolks
salt and olive oil

FOR THE *SUGO*
1 onion, chopped
2 cloves of garlic, chopped
1 tablespoon olive oil
250g chicken livers, chopped
3 large tomatoes, skinned and seeded
1 sprig rosemary, leaves stripped and chopped
60g butter
salt and pepper
60g white truffle

Place the flour in a mound on the work surface and put the egg yolks in the middle so it looks like an eggy volcano. Mix the flour and yolks together, with a little salt and a splash of olive oil, to make the pasta dough. Work well. Leave to rest for an hour in a cool place. Pass the dough through a pasta machine ten times, decreasing thickness at each turn. Then either pass the dough through the machine's finest cutter to give something like *tajarin* or *tagliorini*, or roll it up and slice through it to create thin ribbons.

Prepare the *sugo*: fry the onions and garlic in olive oil until the onions are translucent, then add the liver and tomatoes and cook for 5 minutes. Add the rosemary and butter and cook for 10 minutes more. Season.

Cook the pasta in salted boiling water, drain and transfer to serving dishes. Pour on the *sugo* and cover with finely grated fresh white truffle.

* * *

Sadly I had missed Alba's annual palio. Not as fierce or as tribal as Siena's medieval horse palio, nor as dangerous as bull-running in Pamplona, the Alba palio is special for using those well-known speedy quadrupeds, donkeys. In a calculated snub to nearby (loathed) Asti, the Albesi decided to reinvent their palio after the Astigensi refused to allow anyone from Alba to ride in their own equine palio, which had been won once too often by a citizen of Alba. In 1932, with the Albesi still being refused entry to Asti's palio, they decided to start their very own donkey palio, which was an immediate, rip-roaring success.

Topping all this medieval revivalism are the *sbandieratori*, the flag throwers, and if you think this sounds a banal occupation, you are wrong. If ever you have a chance to see a *gruppo sbandieratori*, hurry along down. They are mesmerizing. Well, I thought they were anyway. Even better than synchronized swimming, although that might be hard to believe. Wearing tights, typical medieval clothes for a medieval man, multicoloured and meaningful, they strut and throw their flags with admirable precision.

The division into communes is something you find in almost all of Italy's old cities, particularly where they have managed to avoid becoming industrialized. You see it in Genoa. In Pisa. In Siena, most famously. And here in Piedmont. Flags, gaudy tights and hats, songs and rivalry are all part of the way that the cities have kept their sense of . community, while ours are famous for their very lack of it. So, don your tights, Basildon. Don your tights, one and all, and choose your quadrupeds wisely.

I once had the misfortune to be invited to a polenta fair in Switzerland, only a few weeks after an arduous cod festival in the Lofoten Islands of northern Norway. I hope this doesn't sound too snotty, for I do appreciate these quirky, anthropological events, but the cod festival was in Lofot, a dialect of an incomprehensible language (to me, that is, please note, Norwegian readers), and at the polenta fest, high up in the Graubünden, they spoke and sang in Romansh. Surrounded by well-meaning and friendly Swiss, and huge vats of polenta, we tucked keenly, at first, into plates of this golden-yellow stodge. There was polenta with cheese, polenta with cream, grilled polenta. It was, as my daughter would say in her own very expressive way, 'blerk'. The vision of endless bowls of thick yellow polenta and cream stayed with me for years. It would loom up as a ghostly thought when I was bobbing around on a cross-channel ferry in a force-8 gale, just waiting for the twinkling lights of the home port to appear.

In Italy, polenta is one of those quintessentially mamma-ish foods, very much part of home cooking. Made simply from ground maize, it is, like the tomato, Italian by distant adoption, but unquestionably Italian all the same. In far-off times Romans would tuck into bowls of *puls*, a dish made of ground barley, a precursor to the real thing, or else a millet and sorghum mush, which thankfully has gone the way of the archaeopteryx. Hannibal would almost certainly have been a polenta eater, but his *Puls punica* would most likely have been made from an ancient form of exceedingly hard-husked wheat called emmer, which preceded our own dearly beloved *Triticum* species by many centuries but was often combined with wheat in Roman times to make *alica*. Another dish that called for few teeth.

Chestnuts were also used to make polenta, doubling as the food of pigs and the food of the poor. Buckwheat, *Grano saraceno*, the grain of the Saracens, made its way into Italy, especially into the Lombardy valleys, where it is still used to make *pizzoccheri*. Millet, sorghum, ancient spelt or farro, all were given the same treatment and all had but one culinary mission, to make as satisfying and cheap a base food as possible for a population that needed its stodge.

When maize finally burst onto the scene, brought into the country by the ever-industrious Venetians, the culinary ground had already been well prepared. In the sixteenth century, the population of Europe was entering into one of its periods of rapid expansion, which called for an equally rapid increase in the area of land under crops. Imports, and trade, thrived. But so did famine. When maize was first introduced into Europe by the Spaniards, it had already been used for thousands of years in Central and South America, and was barely recognizable in its original genetic persona, *Zea mays* ssp. *Parviglumis*, or teosinte. It is one of the most thoroughly humanized of all plants, originating in the western Sierra Madre of Mexico over four thousand years before the Spaniards arrived to wreck the social structure so comprehensively. The cobs exist in blues and blacks, long and short. Some are excellent as cattle feed. Others make popcorn, and flour for tamales. And yet other varieties make polenta.

Somewhere along the line, we in the old world seem to have forgotten where maize came from. Tuscans call it *gran turco*, grain from the Turks; in the Veneto it is *sorgo turco*, Turkish sorghum. The Turks have been known to call it Egyptian grain, and the Egyptians to call it Syrian. In the French Pyrenees it is Spanish, and in the Vosges, Roman. No one seems to have opted for Mexican, or American, which would possibly have had too much of a hint of 'uncivilized' for us civilized Europeans who had just destroyed a whole series of civilizations with such speed. The Piemontesi tend to use a version of the old Latin word for sorghum, *milica*, which becomes *meliga* in Italian, *meira* in Piemontese.

It was for a while considered to be the great yellow nutritional hope, but Europeans soon discovered that a diet based on maize is unbalanced and results in pellagra. In Central America they had already learnt to avoid this by adding beans to the corn, as the Chinese had done with rice and soya. But we Europeans were not so well advanced in matters nutritional, and the northern Italian polenta-eaters, the *poltroni*, of Piedmont, Lombardy and Friuli in particular, often suffered from a long-term dose of pellagra.

I had spontaneously wandered off among the valleys of western Piedmont to look, not for polenta, but, for reasons of curiosity, for the source of the Po, and it was there that I finally lost my heart to polenta. An odd thing maybe, but I like the idea of seeing rivers dribbling from the ground. And the Po does exactly that: it dribbles from the ground. Above are a few tranquil lakes that get gawped at en masse by a Babylonian babble of ramblers doing the almost spiritual trip to the source of the Po, high up in the valley. And as the very molecules coalesced, splattered on the rocks around the source under the clear Alpine skies, I could hardly fail to notice the words 'Padania Libera', the catchphrase for Italy's odious Lega Nord, Northern League, painted there on the rocks in its own characteristic green. What a depressing first sight of Italy this must be – the sign of the most inward-looking, xenophobic group of agitators, politicians who bleat endlessly about how diligent they are and how the country is being ruined by the corrupt politicians in Rome, all the while appealing to the baser side of humanity by promoting a movement that flirts with racism and practises a finely honed intolerance.

Luckily, no one seemed to be inspired to pull out their microphone and huskily harangue the locals, as Signor the Honourable Umberto Bossi, the Lega's leader and devolution minister in Berlusconi's second government, is so fond of doing. I slipped off to the warmth of the nearby Baita della Polenta, keeping my knowledge of the delights of pellagra (a red tongue, a sore and ulcerated mouth, brown and scaly skin on the neck, chest and back of the hands, nausea, diarrhoea, insomnia, depression, dementia and death) to myself.

This is one of those hurried, busy restaurants that cope with wave upon wave of Italians, Swiss, Germans and French, and possibly even the odd group of wayward British ramblers. However, everyone was being very chummy and merry, and as you would expect quite a lot of polenta was on the menu. The waitress came and spouted for the zillionth time the words that began to merge into each other: . . . polenta . . . polenta . . . polenta . . . polenta . . . on and on and on. I decided to go for the polenta. On the next table to mine were a family of Lombards, a veritable picture of disharmony. They were already wading into a plateful of prosciutto and other porcine derivatives when the waitress scooped the plates away and brought a magnificent bowl of steamy polenta. And more bits of pig.

The kids plainly disliked the stuff, picked solemnly, and eventually escaped outside, much to the relief of their grandparents, who relaxed a little, smiled at me and asked where I was from, and of course whether I liked polenta.

'Well, I'm not too sure. Let's say I'm ambivalent about it,' I said, guessing correctly that it was *ambivalente* in Italian.

'But have you ever eaten real home-made polenta? When we were young there wasn't any instant polenta around at all. It hadn't been invented. My mother used to make it . . .'

Of course she did. It's compulsory in northern Italy for everyone's mother to be adept at making polenta. My new friend told me how her mother used to sprinkle it from on high, onto the water in a copper pan, and stir and stir and stir.

'How long did it take?' I asked.

'She would go on for about thirty or forty minutes, and when it was ready we used to pick off the dry bits on the outside of the pan.'

Which is the purest way to make polenta. Given that it was the staple food for so long, I can only assume that most Lombard, Friulian, Venetian and Piemontese *contadine* closely resembled Sylvester Stallone. Stirring polenta (it is alleged) is highly physical, demanding work. With this image before me of robust, stocky women, their muscles rippling, I tucked into my polenta.

We have been liberated from polenta drudgery by the

arrival of the instant version. But this does nothing for the subtleties of fresh polenta, its particular flavour and texture. I am told that the cornmeal once made from local cobs of eight rows, called, appropriately, *ottofile*, was far tastier, though rougher, than today's mixes, but you rarely find *ottofile* these days since it has been replaced by modern hybrids of fifteen or more rows.

With my own plateful steaming in front of me, I had to admit to something definitely appealing about polenta. Its colour, for a start. Its scent. But what you don't need is something bland and creamy to eat with it, as I had done many years before in the land of yodelling and cuckoo clocks. If you look at the long list of polenta dishes of the world, you can pick out a dominating theme of utter stodge: polenta and milk, polenta and breadcrumbs, polenta and cheese, although there are cheeses, those with a little spark, such as Castelmagno made in a valley a little further to the south, that work well. But try the Bergamasco dish, *polenta e pica sö*, which uses salt herring, and you begin to see a little of the charm. Or try a piquant sausage or two. Or a tomato. Anything with sharpness. Or try it with game. With rabbit, hare. Anything but mountains of Swiss cream.

LIVORNO

THE TRATTORIA ANGELO D'ORO LIES ON THE EDGE OF THE
dusty Piazza Mazzini, which I thought was peculiarly
fitting. Shipworks lurk in the background. It is in all
respects totally unpretentious, with a television in the
corner and no-smoking signs stuck on the wall. Inside
the *clienti* smoke and don't watch television, but the
owners' grandchildren do, watch television that is; they
might even smoke. With a dark, blustery wind kicking up
the dust and the leaves outside, pushing the door into this
warm, smiling trattoria was magic. I had spent a little time
earlier in the day talking to the family who owned the
trattoria, explaining that I was on an arduous journey, trying to get to the soul of my ancestral past by immersing
myself in food and a little history. By special request – that
is, I had pleaded – they had agreed that if I came back at
eight o'clock sharp, I could eat *cacciucco*. I pushed through
the door bang on time.

All along the Mediterranean coast, fishermen have
grappled with the problem of making a living, and while
slavering fish merchants waited on shore for the most
valuable catch, the basses, the rock lobsters and the red

mullets, the fishermen were left with the piscine riff-raff, a peculiar mix of grizzled, often hideous, spiky fish. Well acquainted with the fine art of making fish soup, few seaside-dwellers fall for the temptation to throw the whole lot away. And while the French have their *bouillabaisse*, the Greeks their *kakavia*, the Spaniards their *zarzuela* and the Portuguese their mighty *calderada*, the Livornesi have *cacciucco*. (By the way, show your street cred by spelling it with five Cs.) All of these fish soups have somehow managed to make the seamless leap from being the cooking of piscatorial detritus, a dish eaten to keep fishermen's hunger at bay, to gastronomic icon. *Bouillabaisse* is now served in ludicrously expensive French restaurants to tourists in awe of the momentousness of being allowed into a smart French restaurant, where they sit embarrassed by their ignorance of where to smear their *rouille*.

Quite whether it is true to say that *cacciucco* is a purely Livornese dish depends on where you are when you eat it. Up the Tuscan coast in Viareggio, they swear blind that it is theirs. But if you reflect for a moment on the word, you might feel that the multicultural Livornesi rightfully claim it as their own. '*Cacciucco*' is believed to be derived from the Turkish word *cuzuk*, meaning little, relating conveniently both to the little fish that were used after the main part of the catch was sold and to the little pieces of cut fish that went into the soup itself. There's another less convincing explanation, that it is derived from the Spanish for a particular type of fish, the *cachuco*, an unlikely etymological source for a dish whose contents vary as the seasons move on.

What characterizes the soup is simple: fish, of course, and as always the fresher the fish the better the soup, and a touch of piquancy. So, there could be a mollusc or two, a cuttlefish or squid perhaps, or a crustacean, a prawn maybe, in the mix as well. The other sine qua non of a genuine *cacciucco* is this: a slice of Tuscan bread, oh, and a dash of chilli. Tuscan bread is a little special in that it is made without salt, the reason perhaps being that they wanted to make a type of bread that no one would dare copy, i.e., it's oddly tasteless. And they have succeeded magnificently. In truth, it is said that the parsimonious Tuscans wished to avoid paying excessive salt tax, but even if you find Tuscan bread a little unexciting, its adherents say, with some reason, that it goes well with salty salami, pecorino and prosciutto, of which the Tuscans are inordinately fond. And it suits the saltiness of the fish in *cacciucco* as well.

Specific fishy must-haves are needed to make any fish soup true and gutsy, but the fact that most of the fish can be caught close to the shore, and relatively easily at that, has meant that as the summer hordes have descended seawards for so long to satiate themselves on this wonderful dish, the fish that were once plentiful and cheap have now become rare and expensive. The star of the fishy firmament is undoubtedly the scorpion fish, the *scorfano*. This fish has a Yeatsian terrible beauty about it. Its army of poisonous spikes can cause you some discomfort if you happen to handle it carelessly, so wear a suit of armour and pay attention when preparing it. Its head is broad, swollen no doubt with poisonous pride for the generations of people it has spiked. At times magenta, at times scarlet, it is a beautiful, slightly alarming fish, whose charms are only obvious when you cook it and get to taste the indescribably concentrated, fresh pungency of the flesh. Sadly, if you are eating *cacciucco* as it should be eaten, that is, simply and cheaply, you will be lucky to get any *scorfano* at all. You could, however, go native and cook it yourself, which you would find easiest in a small Mediterranean fishing port, lost to the outside world. And there aren't too many of those left.

Slices of Tuscan bread sit in the bottom of the dish with the fish. Mine did have a little cuttle among its many pieces. The sauce, based on a slowly cooked *battuto* of onion and tomato, gets its pungent twang from the *peperoncino*. It does not need to be served with awe, nor brought to the table to a gasp of applause. I tucked into mine very humbly, and, observed from on high by my lapsed English self, I found myself saying that I was descended from an old Jewish Livornese family. It sounded rather odd. My suburban Essex roots were miffed and willed me to talk about sausages and lager. About Epping Forest and standard poodles. I was riven in two.

Since neither driving nor walking under the influence of fish is an offence, I left the trattoria distinctly happy and fell into bed, not quite dreaming of *cacciucco*, but impressed by the Angelo d'Oro, and depressed that such a place is impossible to find in England.

Cacciucco livornese

This serves six.

500g frozen octopus, thawed
500g squid, cleaned
300g fresh dogfish
100g scorpion fish
100g red mullet or gurnard, scaled and gutted
300g live mantis shrimps or langoustines
12 large mussels
2 cloves garlic, chopped
1 medium onion, chopped
200ml good extra virgin olive oil, preferably Tuscan
4 sage leaves, torn
1 small chilli, not too *piccante*
1 sprig rosemary

200ml red wine
500g good quality tomatoes, or equivalent tinned, drained
1 teaspoon tomato purée
salt and pepper
8 slices Tuscan bread (or white farmhouse loaf)

Clean the fish and seafood and cut it into equal chunks (there is no need to fillet the fish) of about 2cm. Cook the garlic and onion in the olive oil over a moderate heat until golden. Add the sage, chilli and rosemary and cook for 1 minute. Add the octopus and cook slowly for 20 minutes. Add the wine and the tomatoes, tomato purée and squid, and cook for 10 minutes. Add two glasses of water and all the rest of the fish, including the live shrimps/langoustines, apart from the mussels. Season, increase the heat and cook for a further 10 minutes at a fairly brisk boil. Add the mussels and cook until opened. Take the pan off the heat and set aside for a few minutes. Place slices of bread in the bottom of warmed bowls, pour the *cacciucco* over and serve.

* * *

Most families quite like the idea of being interesting. For me, there has always been this tense ideological battle between Chingford and Kensington. My father's family was good solid Essex, suburban and comfortable, fond of golf, Methodism, fusty cars, Empire and chrysanthemums. Sadly, they always struck me as seriously dull. Maybe they had their wilder moments but, well, somehow I doubt it. On my mother's side, there was slightly less of this tweedy worthiness. My grandparents lived in a mansion block near Holland Park, within earshot of the peacocks whose cries used to create horrible visions of strangulation and desolation when I was an impressionable, young, pre-hormonal thing. The flat was full of ticking clocks and luscious velvet chairs. Downstairs there sat a hall porter, uniformed and deferential, who would open the accordion lift door for us and wish us good afternoon, even in mid-morning. My mother had four uncles, all with good solid English Christian names: Reggie, Charles, Hugo, Jack. But what wasn't so English about them was their family name, Rosselli. Before coming to Livorno I spent days poring over letters in the Mazzini museum in Pisa, guided by that chance encounter with a photograph in Turin, reading books about the Rossellis and their Livornese roots and their habit of marrying anyone called Nathan, and of course endless tomes about Mazzini. The flawed hero of the Italian Risorgimento, Mazzini had died in 1872 in the Casa Rosselli, the house that Giannetta Rosselli bought with her husband, the delightfully named Pelligrino, when they were free to leave Livorno after unification, and that had now become the Domus Mazziniana, the Mazzini museum.

I had found records of Rossellis in Livorno dating back to 1819, and many of them had been deeply involved in the Risorgimento. I had also found out that the family was Jewish, probably exiled from Spain, forced to leave at the end of the fifteenth century. They were eventually to settle in Tuscany, which was mostly, under the Medicis, exceptionally tolerant of Jews.

The expulsion of the Sephardim by the Spanish monarchs Ferdinand and Isabella in 1492 caused demographic turmoil in Europe. The whole of the Jewish population in Spain, and later Portugal, was given four months to leave. They took with them very little but their talent and a strong sense of community. The intolerant royal duo also called for all New Christians or *marranos*, Jews who had agreed to convert to Christianity but who were considered by the Church to have remained faithful to their original religion, to be expelled as well. Many of these people were rich and well connected, and with no choice but to leave the Iberian peninsula they settled where they could. Many went to Amsterdam and Antwerp, some to Italy, some even to London. The Rossellis moved to Livorno to become bankers, arms dealers, explosives manufacturers, mercury miners and coral merchants, which suggests there was at the very least a streak of entre-preneurial creativity about them.

Livorno was always unique, a thriving Renaissance Milton Keynes. There is a hand-written document, still visible in Florence, called the *Legge Livornina*, the Livornine Law, signed by Grand Duke Ferdinand de' Medici of Tuscany on 30 July 1591, which decreed that 'Levantines, Ponentines, Spaniards, Portuguese, Greeks, Germans and Italians, Turks, Moors, Armenians, Persians and people from other states are invited to reside and to frequent and to trade in our delightful city of Pisa and the port and slipway at Livorno.' The Medicis reasoned that it was all very well to create an idealized Renaissance city but what it really needed was a population that was both energetic and capable. So they decided to make Livorno a free port, open to all. Even criminals were made welcome, all that is except usurers and heretics. Given the climate of intolerance in Europe at the time, Livorno's population exploded. It soon became the foremost port of Tuscany, and it remained so for three hundred years, a unique and extraordinary *città*.

The city was divided up into various *nazioni*, all of whom were freely allowed to practise their religion and marry whom they wanted; Jews were even permitted to employ Christian wet nurses and cleaners, unheard of else-where. The Jewish community flourished. By the nineteenth century, the synagogue was the biggest in the country and the community was some 6000-strong. Livorno became a seat of learning and theology, and for a time was the only city in Italy within whose walls Jews were allowed to move freely without wearing an identify-ing badge. Medicean tolerance was pragmatic, and out of step with the situation elsewhere. In March 1516 the

Venetians had instructed all Jews to live in a specific quarter of the city (called in dialect the *geto*, or foundry, from where we get the word 'ghetto'). Other cities followed. All over the peninsula Jews were enclosed and persecuted. So not only was Livorno particularly attractive to the Sephardim, but also to the Jews who had been living elsewhere in Italy for hundreds of years, even, in the case of Rome, for over a thousand years. The exclusion of Jews was justified on two grounds: first, to protect them from unwarranted aggression, and second, as an expression of the blame that the Christian establishment heaped on the people they held responsible for the murder of Christ.

And so Livorno thrived on trade both legal and illegal under the benevolent gaze of the authorities. Naval ships which might be blasting each other to bits one day could happily drift into Livorno and berth side by side, while pirates, fed up with the difficulties of their *métier*, negotiated with the Livornesi to sell their boats to gain citizenship. Some Livornese Jews later settled in Tunisia, where they bought wheat, coral and even ostrich feathers to ship off to Livorno. The Tunisian Livornesi arranged for pirates' ransoms to be paid and for the release of any Jewish hostages. They also became a class apart, and to this day Tunisian Jews often refer to themselves as Livornesi to distinguish them from the indigenous Jews or *tuns*. All in all it sounds a pretty happening sort of city.

As the Livornese Jews grew wealthy and their population expanded, an elite developed. Among them were the Rossellis, who grew up in Livorno in a climate of liberalism and religious freedom, which they must have cherished dearly, given that Italy was not exactly over-burdened with tolerant cities. In the early nineteenth century, one Ricca Rosselli of Livorno married Angelo Levi, and one of their children, Sarina Levi, an ample-bosomed woman who married a German, Meyer Moses Nathan, moved to London, where the Rossellis became part of the banking fraternity and were to meet Giuseppe Mazzini, who first arrived in London in 1837.

Maybe what really distinguishes Livorno is that while America or Australia welcomed their huddled masses, they largely tried to make them into Americans or Australians. I'm not entirely sure that anyone ever thought so clearly about creating the Livornesi; they have evolved from their peculiar past, the richer for it. The *nazioni* of Livorno kept their cultural identities remarkably intact until the late nineteenth century at least, when Livorno became just another Italian seaport after unification. Dutch, Armenian and Greek churches still stand upright, and there is even an English cemetery. But where the glorious synagogue once stood, the most beautiful, the most grandiose in all of Italy, there now stands an astonishing example of 1960s brutalism, a building of colossal ugliness.

Livornese food reflects the city's cultural hotch-potch. From the Jews came a love of couscous, or *cuscussù*, from the English came punch, called *ponce* in Italian, and then there are the strange, rather unappetizing biscuits called *roschette*, distant cousins to the Spanish *rosquetes*. I struggled to find these anywhere, and when I did, I dramatically overbought and hastily binned the lot, for they really were the driest, dullest biscuits I had tasted for years and made even Rich Teas seem interesting. You can buy them in sweet and salty versions, each as dull as the other.

My hotel was dusty, but close to the trattoria. It looked dead to the world, with its balconies and blinds firmly closed, but inside the receptionist seemed unusually happy for a hotel receptionist, a breed of person for whom I have developed a deep respect over the years, particularly while writing this book. He was surrounded by cigarette-smoking compadres who were telling each other what appeared to be uproariously funny jokes. It's wonderful how the sound of laughter can make you forgive fumigation.

The next morning, slipping out quietly to avoid any chance of being molested by a hotel breakfast, I walked towards the canals and Livorno's Quartiere Nuova Venezia, built to emulate the elegance of Venice. It doesn't quite manage it. The canals that once served as the main artery for this part of the city run alongside tall, substantial buildings, now full of banks and solid financial institutions, insurance companies and hairdressers. I was due to be joined by two Livornesi from the local tourist office and, by now gagging for a coffee, I met them in the city's Piazza Cavour. Well briefed, Andrea and Francesco had planned a gastronomic mystery tour about which I knew absolutely zilch, this being the essence of a good mystery tour. Doing it this way takes away the fun of being disappointed and overcharged, and I was energized by the arrival of a cappuccino, Livornese style, which is served the wrong way up: froth down. To no great advantage, it has to be said, but an excellently anarchic way to start the morning.

Off to the market. This unreasonably cavernous structure, called by the locals with due lack of deference the Louvre, is a working, functional market, and an excellent place to stock up for your *cacciucco*. The fish section was, as usual, tucked away like a leper colony so as not to offend the delicate vegetable-sellers and their dew-scattered herbs. But it is here, among the fish, that the colour and the bustle reach a perfect balance. The Livorno coast isn't the world's greatest fishing ground, or Italy's, but there is goodness beneath these waves.

Each stall tries to pull you into its fishy vortex. Tiny little octopi, *seppiolini* (little cuttlefish), exquisitely coloured Moray eels, and what we call in English mantis ray shrimps. These hard-shelled crustaceans are impossibly difficult to eat, but you find them here as well as on the other side of Italy, from the Abruzzo right up to Venice. Beige and mantis-like, they not only give good head but body as well, but if you try to cook them yourself I advise you strongly to have an expert to hand, for they have an exoskeleton of chainmail toughness that requires fingers of steel.

Another fish the Livornesi have taken to their hearts is the red mullet. I have a long-standing love of this fish, which in its Mediterranean form reaches heights of tastiness never quite achieved by its chubbier Northern European counterpart, which just lacks finesse. You might see two types of red mullet: the *triglia di scoglio* and the less classy *triglia di fango*. With the smaller fish magnificently helping along a *cacciucco*, the larger are often served as *triglie alla livornese*. This is said to be a Jewish dish, and has become another of Livorno's signature dishes. When served correctly it is extremely red. In the 1980s this might have been called 'symphony of red mullet with a jus of tomato'. But let us stick to the Italian. One Livornese said to me: 'Of course we welcomed the Jews. They gave us *triglie alla livornese!*' The story goes that the Jews were among the first to bring tomatoes into Tuscany from Spain, too, and it might even be true, but it is impossible to prove.

Triglie alla livornese

This serves four.

8 red mullet of about 100–120g each, gutted and scaled
handful of parsley, chopped
2 cloves garlic, diced
flour
7 tablespoons olive oil
500g tomatoes, peeled and chopped

1 mild chilli, chopped
salt

Wash the fish. Divide half of the parsley and all of the garlic among the fish, stuffing it into the gut cavity. Dip the fish in flour and fry them in the olive oil in a large pan for a maximum of 5 minutes each side. Add the tomatoes, the remaining parsley and the chilli, and cook for 5 more minutes or until done. Season with salt and serve.

As an added bonus, outside the covered market is a piazza full of vegetable-sellers singing verbal challenges to each other. Artichokes *dieci per tre mila lire*, soon to be *dieci per un'euro 50*. Piles of tomatoes, endives, lettuces, rocket, and *mandarini* spurting juice from their unmolested skin. Permit me to rant a little, but why is it that we are sent the dullest, least ripe citrus fruits every year? Why can't someone wake up to the fact that pipless wonders with flabby skin are so abysmal?

And then I noticed it again. Laughter. Here and there, among the stallholders, the customers, people just talking, I was struck by a curiously high incidence of laughter. I struggled to find a miserable face until I spied a *carabiniere*, shiny but dim, fingering his weapon in the corner.

It was intriguing. Were people laughing because they were happy at that very moment or was this odd city perhaps a happy place? What makes a city a happy place to live in anyway? Are people happy if they live among streets and houses of real beauty? This is not Livorno's case. In the Second World War Livorno was bombed by both the Americans and the Germans in a monstrous double-whammy. And let's face it, achingly beautiful cities are often full of thoroughly miserable people. Londoners say they would be a lot happier if the city simply functioned and you could get from A to B in less time than it takes to walk. The Parisians have practised the art of being surly for so long there is no chance of change there. Take Stockholm: a classic case of a beautiful city where everyone walks around with a long face and drinks too much.

Could it be that Livorno, with its radical multicultural past, has acquired a sort of social cockiness? As relative upstarts in the Tuscan history books, the Livornesi love to have a good laugh at their neighbours, particularly the long-suffering Pisans whose great claim to fame is to have built a tower that is permanently on the point of collapse. Tuscany, possibly more than anywhere else in Italy, is riven by what's called *campanilismo*, which used to mean roughly the feeling everyone got when they heard their church bells ringing. The feeling of belonging, rather than irritation, that is. This helped everyone develop long-standing traditional enmities that kept communities, and even districts within communities, at permanent and not always good-natured loggerheads.

We were chatting about this as we passed a funky bit of graffiti painted on the wall. *www.gagarin*, it said.

'Come. We're going inside. I'm hungry!' said Andrea.

The door opened onto a small, perfectly rectangular space with a counter at one end and a glowing wood-burning oven behind it. It's easy to tell a place that's run by a family when the person at the till reflects a little of the mamma behind the stove and the papà sitting at the counter. And so it is in the Gagarin.

The speciality here is *torta di ceci*, but to call it chickpea tart does it no justice. There is musicality in the word *ceci*. 'Che-chee', it's pronounced. This *torta* has been adopted by the Livornesi as their very own. It isn't really Livornese, but who cares? In truth, *torta di ceci* is none other than the Genovese *farinata*, or *fainâ*, which moved along the coast both eastwards and westwards. In Nice it is called, somewhat mysteriously, *socca*. But however dull you might think it sounds, it certainly doesn't taste it. (And if you are after dullness you've always got those *roschette*.) This thin crisp *torta* should be nibbled searingly hot from a sheet of white waxed paper. Its heart is warm and comforting, and, being Ligurian in origin, it is almost embarrassingly cheap to make. *Torta di ceci*, baked hard and fast, is made from chickpea flour, water, olive oil and a little salt. Nothing more. The dough needs to be quite liquid, and left a while before being poured thinly onto a well-oiled red-hot *taglio* and cooked in a wood-fired oven. In Liguria and here in Livorno, a *taglio* is a special heavy round dish, but you can cook your *torta* in just about anything, so long as it has an element of non-stickiness about it. It is the quintessential Livornese snack, and fortified us all for a walk around Livorno's fortifications.

'*Dammi un' cinque e cinque!*' said Francesco.

'Give you a what?' I asked.

'A *cinque e cinque*. It's a sort of sandwich, with some *torta di ceci* in the middle. Give me two, *signora!*'

A *cinque e cinque* is an excellent way of beefing up a slice of chickpea *torta*. Stuff the *torta* into a well-oiled doughy roll, a kind of *focaccina* called a *francese*. Calling it a *cinque e cinque* dates back to the days when soldi were around, and a slice of *torta* costing five soldi was placed in a *focaccina* also costing five soldi. Simple really.

Chickpeas deserve a place of honour in the history of what is called *la cucina povera*, providing countless generations of Italians with a source of flour when wheat was too expensive or the crops had failed. Much the same could be said of chestnuts, and alongside piles of piping hot *torta di ceci* you will often see, particularly here in Tuscany, a slice of *castagnaccio*, a sweet and rather unctuous *torta* made from chestnut flour. But I cannot really wax lyrical about *castagnaccio*, for apart from committing the culinary faux pas of being rather too brown to be appealing, it is dense, unsubtle and frankly the last thing you will probably feel like eating after a slice of *torta di ceci*. But it is cheap, and it should be.

During the morning's wander around Livorno, I was shown the site of the old, rather grand-looking Palazzo Rosselli, where the family had once lived and where Mazzini in his endless wanderings had stayed. Livorno had been a hotbed of a very particular kind of radicalism, and took to the idea of the Risorgimento with enthusiasm. But the palazzo, like the Rosselli home in Pisa, was bombed flat in the war and absolutely nothing, not the merest brick, remained. Nor does, as far as I could ascertain, a single Rosselli.

We shuffled off to Il Sottomarino, another Livornese trattoria that serves food of real class. The owner, true to Livornese form, laughed endlessly, and told us to sit back and relax. Everything was arranged. Out came the food in dribs and drabs. *Riso nero*, a jet-black risotto made with cuttlefish. A brilliantly red *triglie alla livornese*. *Taglierini di sugo di mare*. Multicoloured Livornese dishes that challenged us all to shout: No more! But none of us did. Oh, that looks so good. I'll just try a little. And a little more. And a little more . . .

Oiled by wine, I encouraged a new bout of mirth, and we started a round of Livornese jokes. (Wine, by the way, of some excellence. I should point out that the province of Livorno is home to some of the world's finest wine, super-Tuscans and non-super-Tuscans.) With something almost approaching bashfulness, unusual for a Livornese, the restaurant's owner said, sotto voce, 'Have you heard this one? What did Osama bin Laden say when he went to the Torre Pendente in Pisa?'

This was in a place from which New York was just about distant enough to be able to tell a joke about it all.

'Tell us, what did Osama bin Laden say when he saw the Leaning Tower of Pisa?' we said.

'He looked it up and down, and whispered to his one-eyed mullah: *"Dilettanti!"* Beginners!' Well, I laughed.

Pisan jokes erupted from their mouths when I told them that I had been warned by the Pisans that the Livornesi were descended from whores and criminals. Had I heard that the only good thing to come from Chernobyl was a genetic mutation that had created the world's first intelligent Pisan? And this: Better a death in the house than a Pisan at the door.

Their humour doesn't rest with mere verbal abuse of Pisa. Back in 1984, three local students took on the whole pretentious world of art criticism in a brilliant coup de théâtre. One of Livorno's greatest sons was Amedeo Modigliani, who spent most of his life in Paris, an archetypical poor artist who died, his body riddled with drugs, drink and tuberculosis, at the early age of thirty-five. Famous for his reclining, stretched and spindly nudes, he developed a love for sculpture, and created a series of heads and busts of almost African simplicity. On the centenary of his birth and with local interest in the artist still strong, a group of Livornese students miraculously found some lost sculptures that had allegedly been thrown into the canal by Modigliani in a fit of pique. The art world was fascinated and approved largely of the style and content of these marvellous new finds.

It was a complete scam. Some seventeen years later the originators were awarded a Laurea Honoris Causa by the highly esteemed Università degli Stupidi di Livorno. An institution that keeps Livorno at the cutting edge of silliness, and an honour emphatically well deserved.

I had fallen for Livorno. I loved its ability to laugh, and its lack of staggering beauty. It almost seemed like a Utopian city, lost now in the present but still exerting immense appeal. This was an excellent city for the Rosellis to come from: slightly wacky, interesting. I was proud of the odd Livornese corpuscle making its way through my veins.

To suddenly find out that you have Jewish blood is peculiar. I found myself thinking more deeply about the Israel–Palestine conflict, and changed my support, twitched it a little Israeli-wards. But it tended to fluctuate while the suicide attacks and reprisals continued with gruesome inevitability. The Jewish community in Livorno now numbers hundreds where once it was in its thousands. Its synagogue had been the most beautiful in Italy, housing the learned works of scholars and rabbis written over the centuries. Little remains of the Jewish *nazione* in Livorno. You can visit the modest Jewish museum, tucked well away from the main part of the city, but it's a sad and forgotten place where tombstones lie haphazardly, broken and forlorn.

During the Risorgimento, Livorno was one of the most revolutionary cities in Tuscany. Their fight against the Austrian occupation was courageous. The Rossellis, split between Livorno and London, were in an excellent position to help Mazzini and the Republican dream, and it seems only too obvious that support for the Risorgimento would come from a secular liberal Jewish family from Livorno, for their dream was in a sense Mazzini's: to live in a land free of prejudice, and to be free to worship as they wished. Sad that history proved to be such a massive disappointment to both.

GENOA

A LOMBARD FRIEND TALKED ANIMATEDLY OF A HOLIDAY IN Calabria as if she were spending time on the planet Ug. 'The Calabrians are as thick as the earth they stand on,' she told me. So long as it is all low-key and amusing, I am quite partial to a bit of bias and unreasonableness. But, hey, I am a *Guardian* reader and will not allow any sinister xenophobic tracts in these pages. Wait until we look at Mussolini for that. However, there is this on-going 'misunderstanding' between the north and south of Italy, the idea being that one is stupid and the other virtually perfect. I'll leave you to work out which is which.

Italians are also of the opinion that anyone from Genoa is miserable, penny-pinching and tight-fisted. But could there be just an element of truth in it? There's a joke that goes something like this. A recently widowed Genovese goes to the local newspaper office to arrange for an announcement to be printed on the death of her dearly beloved husband.

'All I want,' she says, 'are the words "Mario Dead". That's all I can afford.'

'But, signora, that's so little to say. And after such a long life. Surely you can add a little more? Listen, as a special offer we'll let you add three extra words at no extra cost.'

'For nothing? Absolutely free? You're sure? *Senta*. OK then, add this: "Fiat For Sale".'

Trying objectively to assess whether the Genovesi are as mean as they are made out to be would be challenging. A city survey would in any case cost far too much. I was reminded of this when I traipsed all the way down to the old port looking for the local tourist office. Now, generally they are a fount of wisdom, manned or more often womanned by a local who is both young and enthusiastic, and far more fluent in English than I am in Italian. But here the tourist office is tiny and for the two days I was trying to make human contact with it, during a very cold Ligurian December, the shutters remained resolutely closed. I could peek through the glass and see tempting piles of leaflets about mountain biking in Piedmont and boat trips down the coast but, frankly, it looked as if someone was being a little – how can I say it? – ungenerous with the resources here.

Liguria is a small coastal province with mountains that rise steeply from the sea and soil that is thin, and whose sea, to cap it all, is particularly unproductive. Ligurian cooking inevitably has a teeny hint of the infamous meanness – no slabs of meat and creamy sauces here – but paradoxically it is also one of the richest and most astonishingly well adapted to be found in Italy. The Ligurians became the Italian first-division ekers, and although they are all much wealthier now, they still remain sentimentally attached to the concept of eking. To this day, Liguria's one great speciality, *fainâ* or *farinata*, is made from nothing more than chickpea flour. The origin of the Livornese *torta di ceci* is here in Genoa. The *torta* uses the simplest of ingredients, while its one dash of excitement, *cappun magro*, is an elaborate and rather exquisite culinary joke. *Cappun* is Ligurian for scorpion fish and *magro* means lean, which makes the dish sound ascetically simple. In reality it is served as a mound of the most incredible variety of ingredients, from ship's biscuits to rock lobster, and is the most exuberant dish you will find in Liguria.

If you walk along the edge of the old part of Genoa, there is a line of venerable arches, the Sottoripa, where you will find some of the city's last remaining and finest *sciammadde*. These tiny bustling spaces specialize in food to be eaten quickly on the hoof or, in the style of the Italian breakfast, animatedly, surrounded by a gaggle of your closest *sciammadda* buddies. Some *sciammadde* are almost clinical when empty, with white tiles and fluorescent tubes, a simple counter and little else. On the counters sit piles of slightly battered metal trays stacked full of *torte*, salads and obscure edible bits and pieces. But in the true *sciammadda* there is definitely something farinaceous in the air. A wood-fired oven glows in the background – *sciammadda* means 'flamed' in Genovese – and if you look closely inside you might see an enormous metallic dish sizzling in the oven's heat, full of a golden yellow *fainâ*.

The chickpea is about as unglamorous a pulse as you can find. Yet another plant that arrived in the distant past from the Middle East, it has been given the Latin name of *Cicer arietinum* for the highly improbable reason that one of Cicero's ancestors had a wart in the shape of a chickpea. And, rather neatly I think, the Italian word for chickpea, *cece*, can also mean wart. As for the *arietinum*, this comes from the seedpod, which is said to resemble a ram's head, *aries*. Its real value is that it grows on poor soils and pulls most of its nitrogen from the air, so it doesn't exhaust the soil like some crops do. And even better, when the pulses are dried they are easy to store, and although not exactly a nutritionist's dream they have been given the honorific 'aphrodisiac' in Sheikh Nefzaoui's titillating Arabic tract, *The Perfumed Garden*.

Torta di ceci

This makes enough for six people.

500g chickpea flour
750ml mineral water
pinch of salt
200ml extra virgin olive oil
crushed black pepper, and red onion and/or rosemary
to serve

Mix the chickpea flour, water and salt to a smooth, liquid paste. Leave for 2 to 3 hours, then add the olive oil. Heat the oven to 250°C. Heat a baking tray (with edges) in the oven until it is very hot. Pour the chickpea liquid into the hot tray to a depth of about 2cm, then bake the dish until it looks brown and cooked. This should take no more than 10 minutes. If you cook it in batches, you will soon see how efficient your oven is and how much cooking time you need. Cut, top with crushed black pepper and finely chopped mild red onion or rosemary, serve and eat at once.

And then there are the *torte*. Or more precisely, *torte salate*. It's not easy to use English here. If I say savoury tarts, it sounds too much like a drinks party in Cheam to get the full everydayness of these ancient dishes. And salty tarts are even more problematic. In fact, the saltiness of these tarts is quite subdued: they are *salate* to distinguish them from *dolci*. But it's the vegetables that really make the variety. The *torta* could be made from chard or artichokes, great Genovese and Ligurian favourites, or leeks, pumpkin, even *cardi* (cardoons). Whatever is used the principle is the same: you roll out a shortcrust pastry made from flour and olive oil as thinly as possible. I must honestly admit that I have great difficulty in doing this successfully, and have twice sweated away to try to make the finest *torta* of all, *torta pasqualina*, but with dismal results as far as the pastry was concerned. Bread I can master, but I think I have the touch of the Gorgon, and thin pastry defeats me. So instead I use frozen filo pastry, and while this might be laughed out of court in the back streets of Genoa, it seems to go down all right in the back lanes of middle England.

Torta pasqualina

Enough for six.

600g chard
500g ricotta
40g pecorino, grated
80g Parmesan, grated
4 eggs

FOR THE PASTRY
200g type 00 flour
200g plain white flour
3 tablespoons olive oil, preferably Ligurian
salt

Cook the chard in a little salted water until tender, then cool under running cold water and squeeze dry. Chop finely and place in a mixing bowl along with the ricotta, pecorino and Parmesan. Set aside.

Make pastry with the flour, olive oil, a little salt and enough water to combine – in the usual way – and divide into 6 to 12 balls, depending on how thin you can roll the pastry. Keep them damp and cool while you work. Roll each one into as thin a sheet as possible. Line a lightly oiled 25cm round baking tray with half the number of sheets of pastry. (In theory you should have thirty-three sheets but this is probably beyond most of us. It certainly was beyond me. You can always use filo pastry instead; the results are quite acceptable.)

Place the chard and cheese mix on the pastry sheets, leaving four dips at the four compass points. Break an egg into each dip. Cover with the remaining pastry layers and bake in a medium-hot oven (about 170°C) for 50 minutes.

Much tradition surrounds the *torta pasqualina*, a dish that as its name suggests was originally eaten at Easter. But so good is it that it can now be found all year round, envied by the piles of Christmas pudding and turkey that await their very short seasonal moment of joy. Tradition once had it that the *torta* should have no fewer than thirty-three layers of ultra-thin pastry, one for every year of Christ's life, but these days such subtleties are largely forgotten. However, layers there must be. And chard there must be, a Genovese favourite, which becomes the bulk of the filling of the *torta*, and eggs too, a nicely pagan Easter touch, neatly positioned so that when the cooked *torta* is cut through they positively glow against the light green of the stuffing. It is seductively beautiful. To eat any of these *torte* or a slice of *fainâ* along the Ripa in Genoa's harbour seems more than appropriate. It is as near to medieval bustle as you'll get.

But if *fainâ* and *torta pasqualina* seem remote, at least we have all heard of focaccia. After all, the word has finally been granted admittance at the hallowed portals of the *Oxford English Dictionary*. Few of us, however, can say we *know* focaccia in its purest and finest form. The focaccia, or *fugassa* in Genovese, is leavened bread made with a lot of olive oil, dressed with more olive oil and sprinkled with sea salt. That, at least, is *focaccia classica genovese* and in its simplest form that is how it is made. But, as always, the devil is in the detail. When *fugassa* was first baked in the wood-fired ovens of Genoa, olive oil was cheap, positively oozing from barrels stored around the port. There wasn't much room to grow wheat on the steep slopes behind the city so flour was probably more difficult, at least until the fourteenth century when trade with Sicily, so often called Italy's bread-basket, brought shiploads of wheat into Genoa. Salt, sea salt, was shipped and stored; it was also a key item in trade, taxed at times to excess.

In those times the focaccia would have been made to the rhythm of the day. Last thing at night, using the warmth of the dying fire, the dough would have been prepared, and first thing in the morning, as the fire was built up, the focaccia would be quickly baked and served to the passing Genovesi. At one time, so popular had the focaccia become that the Church threatened anyone with excommunication who dared to snack on it during services. Slow rising allows the dough more time to develop its complex taste, so as progress arrived and created short cuts and quick tricks, focaccia, like so many other breads, lost its perfection. Cheaper versions are now made using vegetable oils. Commercial ovens use characterless blasting heat. What was once simple, but gloriously so, has in no time at all become flabby and dull. This, sadly, is the focaccia we are more likely to know.

But, as we shall see so often, the cavalry is at hand. Slow Food, the estimable, gallant international organization that is fighting hard to preserve so many of the world's fine culinary traditions and obscure specialities, has created one of its beloved presidia, and has written as law the following guide to making a great focaccia.

FOCACCIA LAW

The whole process of making focaccia should take a minimum of eight hours, including the rising of the dough.

The flour used should be type 00.

There should be a minimum of 6 per cent extra virgin olive oil used [I should add, Ligurian by choice].

The focaccia should be soft yet crunchy on the top, should smell intensely of olive oil and bread, and should be of a golden hazelnut colour with white eyes.

It is fascinating to watch focaccia being made and to see the baker's fingers hurriedly march up and down the dough making the dimples or 'eyes' that help collect the olive oil you sprinkle on the freshly baked bread.

More complex than this but just as addictive is *focaccia al formaggio*, which comes from a little further down the Levante at Recco. The name 'Levante' gives you some idea of the absolute primacy, in the past I hasten to say, of Genoa over the rest of the Ligurian coast. The Riviera di Levante is to the east of Genoa, where the sun rises, and the Riviera di Ponente is to the west, where it sets. All very Genocentric.

Sadly, if ever a place was well named it was Recco. Brutally bombed in the war, its new look is functional and charmless, but it has bravely pinned a *focaccia al formaggio* to its culinary mast to give it something to sing happily about. There is a famous restaurant, Manuelina's, which is, allegedly, a fine place to eat *focaccia al formaggio*. I have to admit that I failed to find out if this was true, for the simple reason that it was closed when I tried to visit; disappointing, particularly because I had dragged an Australian friend to eat there, tempting him with juicy stories of focaccia-to-be. On the way down, he spied and bought a military jacket with German armbands that made him look like a demented Fascist, so when we arrived at the door we might have been refused permission to eat there anyway. Who knows? I was also a little alarmed to find that Manuelina's had tinted doors, brassy plaques and, horror of horrors, tablecloths. Focaccia is rough and ready food, to be eaten in rough and ready places. So we hurried away, mightily pissed off and hungry but secretly quite relieved that it was closed.

We had taken the train from Genova Brignole (Brignole was the last doge of Genoa, by the way) and cruised in a leisurely fashion along the coast, marvelling at how very closely, almost intimately, the train seems to run above the sea. You half expect to push through the crowds like a roller-coaster, shoving tourists on their chubby legs out of the way, and to be harangued by slick Ray-Banned boys zipping alongside the tracks on their Piaggios.

What really makes Recco's focaccia so special is the cheese. The purest of the pure would suggest using what is called in Genovese *prescinseua*, a hyper-fragile fresh curd cheese still made in the hills of the Ponente and around the Gulf of Tigullio but nowhere else. Or *formagetta*, which is even more obscure, no longer made in Liguria in anything but the tiniest quantities. However, you can use, and indeed the Ligurians themselves do use, a soft, slightly tangy cheese called *crescenza*. This is a particular variety of a group of cheeses called *stracchino*, but beware, for there are two kinds. *Stracchino* is a Lombard cheese, made traditionally with milk – and I love this idea – from tired cows: cows that are brought in from summer pasture as the winter approaches, cows not necessarily tired of summer grass, but tired from walking to the valleys from the mountains. *Stracch* in Lombard means *stanco*: 'tired' in English. There is a winter version, rindless and almost tart, and a rinded version, blander and almost sweet. *Crescenza* resembles the runnier, tarter version, and is often available under the brand name Inverninizza. But if you've travelled hundreds of miles with the wrong sort of *stracchino*, and there's an embarrassed hush when you admit this to your immensely knowledgeable dinner-party guests, just persevere. Life's too short to get your knickers twisted over such detail. The principle, however, is important: that the focaccia should be studded with a sharp rather than a bland cheese.

Focaccia al formaggio
Fugassa cö formaggio

This was originally made in Levante for the giorno dei morti, the Day of the Dead (All Souls' Day: 1 November).

25g fresh yeast
mineral water
500g strong white flour
150ml extra virgin olive oil
350g *stracchino, taleggio* or *formagetta* cheese, in small chunks
sea salt

Mix the crumbled yeast with about 150ml warm mineral water and allow to foam. Combine the flour, yeast, half the oil and a little extra mineral water into a dough. Knead the dough until it is supple and stretchy, then cover and leave for an hour. Knock back the risen dough and divide into two uneven pieces: one-third and two-thirds.

Heat the oven to 200°C and oil a square baking dish. Roll out both pieces of dough and use the larger one to line the dish. Cover with the cheese pieces then place the remaining dough on top. Sprinkle with sea salt, and dimple with the fingers or prick with a fork. Bake in the hot oven for half an hour.

Back along the Sottoripa you might notice the *friggitorie*, which fry just about anything they can find. Fish, yes, but not exclusively so. And you will be hard put to spot greasy sausages, meat pies, soggy chips or even a saveloy in this city once ruled by the House of Savoy. This is a classier version of fried food altogether, but served to and eaten by all Genovesi, as no doubt it has been since the days when the street was built far back in the twelfth century. In the Friggitoria Carega, at 113 Via Sottoripa, piles of prawns and freshly cooked steaming octopus sat alongside *baccalà* and *fritto misto*. The octopus, a strange snack if ever there was, my friend and I ate feeling proud and Jules Verne-ish.

Some *friggitorie* serve what in English we would call vegetable fritters but in the more sing-song tones of *zeneize* (Genovese) are called *frisceû*. Chard, borage, courgettes, spinach, even lettuce leaves are coated in a light batter and fried in olive oil. Simple stuff. But oh so good.

Higher up, behind the Sottoripa, rises the city's old quarter. Meander and you will come across a whole world of weird and ancient specialists who still serve this city with its slightly melancholy air. The Antica Tripperia in Vico Casana sells a product it is almost impossible to imagine anyone in England buying these days, let alone eating. But here tripe is slopped and slurped and washed and cooked with insouciant love.

All of Italy's great maritime cities have their own idiosyncratic ways with salt cod (*baccalà*) and Genoa is no different. Salt cod, and its ancestor dried cod, is a food that fascinates, but we in Britain have lost our appreciation of it. We eat cod frozen and sometimes fresh and often fried but never salted. A small shop in Via Macelli di Soziglia called Stoccafisso Valle has been selling pungent pieces of salted and dried cod for over fifty years. Dried cod, *stoccafisso*, is even more venerable than salt cod. Fresh cod are caught in the spring in the icy seas off northern Norway and hung on endless lines of wooden frames around the shore, dehydrating until they become stick-like, solid and almost imperishable if kept dry. The name *stoccafisso* is derived from the Dutch word for stick, the Dutch at one time being the main merchants to trade the fish with the northern Italians. To reconstitute stockfish requires time and a lot of water, so in Italy you mostly see ready prepared fillets of *stoccafisso* for sale, to be cooked in one of a thousand ways all over the country.

Italy was once full of *trattorie* run by ancient, wise and welcoming old women. These days most have retired to their second homes in Portofino. In England we have an equally threatened species, *Trattoria phallocratica*, where the genial Neapolitans who popularized the suggestive pepper mill, the itchy crotch and the leering look are having trouble adapting to modern times, unsure where to put their black and white signed photos of Roger Moore, Pavarotti and someone from *EastEnders*. Others are quite sure where they should put them. Both species should be protected by an EU department or two.

In Genoa, I found the perfect version of the former: Da Maria, which still has a Maria, who smilingly told us that she'd been working there since 1947. Maria has a beatific air about her – happy, I can only assume, in this place where eating well seems to be only part of what people do. Tucked up one of Genoa's narrowest alleys, Da Maria's has a touch of the medieval about it, in the very best sense of the word of course. I have never knowingly been to a restaurant where people seem to dress down, but as we sat, innocent and eager, being lovingly introduced to samples and dishes of utter deliciousness, I spied at the end of a table a man who looked desperately miserable, fingers stained by nicotine, racked, thin and ill. He sat, was served equally lovingly, and chewed slowly, smoked a lot and left. The next day, walking along a street nearby, we both saw him again, the same rake-thin face and piercing eyes, but this time city-clothed and busy on a mobile phone.

I developed a fantasy that Maria supported a whole net-work of destitute people and had become a sort of gastronomic Mother Teresa. Da Maria's has the oddest selection of customers I have ever seen. There are the young, poor immigrants who have found work and like everyone else rush in at lunch-time, without thinking of changing, with dust on their jeans and hard hats on their laps. Then there are the regulars, the old, the couples, and the food groupies who are likely to be a little bemused by the pace and intensity. The orders, ours at least, were taken by a cousin, old but not yet ancient and entirely unfazed.

But the menu. Oh the menu! Never have I become so entranced. Hand-written Post-It notes were stuck hap-hazardly all around, giving the trattoria the air of a busy office. It was all resolutely low-tech, with the menu hand-written and copied for each table. So many of the dishes I had read about were here, making it fiendishly tricky to choose, until we noticed the delicate marks of a red pen that had crossed out almost all of them. Moral: get there early.

This is some of what was on offer: *Minestrone all' genovese. Trenette al pesto. Lasagne al forno. Pastasciutta col sugo. Ravioli al sugo. Ravioli in brodo. Salsiccia con fagiolini. Seppie con piselli. Polpettone alla genovese. Stoccafisso accomodato. Torta pasqualina.*

It was, it had to be, the *trenette* I chose; we both chose, I think. This dish deserves a closer look, for if there is but one gastronomic icon Liguria has given the world it has to be pesto. So popular has it become that there is probably someone in deepest Cornwall planning to launch a pesto pasty. Pesto's origins are truly Ligurian. It evolved as an admirably practical way of preserving the basil that once grew only during the summer, that is, long before much of the Ligurian coast was given up to glasshouses devoted to squeezing as many crops of flowers, basil and tomatoes as possible from the coastal zone. Off to the east of Genoa is a little suburb called Pra. Not the most exquisite part of Italy, but it does have a reputation for growing the finest of Liguria's basil. And why? Basil is one of those odd self-denying little plants that does best under stress. It might be the constant rumble of the motorway or the brutal overcrowding of the basil plants in the rows of green-houses, but Pra's basil is ultra-fine.

Pesto needs basil, of course, and olive oil – Ligurian, naturally – pine nuts gathered from the pines that grow along the coast, and Sardinian pecorino. Some mix this with Parmesan. There are a hundred minor variations, but basically all the recipes share those ingredients. As to how it is made, that's another matter altogether. Purists insist not merely upon the use of pestle and mortar, but on the use of a marble mortar with a wooden pestle, and certainly not a food processor that would heat up the mix and burn off the fragrant oils that are to be found in Ligurian basil. Whether you take all this seriously or not is entirely up to you. But pesto is a serious business in Liguria.

As lunch ended, Da Maria's slowly ground to a halt and quietened down. The hard hats left. We breathed more slowly, and Maria still smiled. It will have a permanent place in my memory, to be drawn upon when I find myself in silly restaurants with silly prices, tablecloths and snotty waiters. It was what eating out should be all about.

Infinitely more comfortable and bourgeois is one of Genoa's most comforting food shops, the Villa di Profumo on the corner of Via Garibaldi, not far from Da Maria. Unrushed and unperturbed, it is stacked full of chocolates, *marrons glacés* and *torrone*, all neatly wrapped and subdivided into zones of sweetness. Here I saw the very same rectangular balsawood boxes stuffed with candied fruit – mandarins, plums and slices of pineapple all glazed with an opaque sugary coat, brilliantly coloured and deeply enticing – that my maternal granny used to buy years ago from Fortnum and Mason and send to us at Christmas, along with huge tablets of soap.

And this is when *pan dolce* muscles in over the chocolates. Often said to be the Genovese version of the Milanese *panettone*, it is possible to take *pan dolce* as an aberration, a rare example of the Genovese people luxuriating. A moment of weakness, perhaps, or maybe an outsider who looked at the riches that moved in and out of the port and had an uncontrollable rush of creativity. It is now ubiquitous. *Pan dolce* can be found in two forms, a lower, denser version and a higher, breadier, yeastier version, but both use the same basic ingredients: flour, eggs, local raisins, candied fruit – particularly the citruses, *cedro* and *limone*, from Napoli and the Amalfi coast and Sicily – orange-flower water and Marsala, all of which would have found their way into the entrepôts around the harbour and into the shops that fed the wealthy. We have, in our own inimitable way, reduced, anglicized and bastardized this cake as Genoa cake, which once was probably a fine thing to eat, but these days is an excuse to plonk a few glacé cherries into a boring sponge.

Pan dolce

Adapted from La Cucina del Bel Paese *(Accademia Italiana della Cucina 2002). Serves four. This is the breadier version.*

25g fresh yeast, crumbled
150ml warm milk
500g white flour
75ml Marsala
1 teaspoon orange-flower water

75g unsalted butter, softened
125g golden caster sugar
10g fennel seeds
20g shelled pistachio (Bronte Reds if possible)
25g Tuscan pine nuts
50g sultanas
50g candied citrus or lemon
50g candied orange
salt

Stir the yeast into the warm milk along with a spoonful of the flour, and leave for an hour. Then rub the butter into the remaining flour and mix in the Marsala and orange-flower water. Add the yeast and all the remaining ingredients, combine and knead well. Make into a round loaf shape and leave to rise in a warm place, covered with a damp tea towel, for at least an hour. Heat the oven to 200°C. Cut a cross shape onto the loaf's surface with a sharp knife. Bake for an hour or until cooked. Serve warm.

* * *

The city of Genoa is a very particular place. It's not a flouncy, oooh-look-at-me sort of city. In fact, it's rather subdued. During the war it was blasted and bombed by the Allies and it's a miracle that there's anything left from the past at all, but there is, and it retains much of its original grandeur. But the port has gone bankrupt and the city has become somewhat despondent about its future. The five-hundredth anniversary of Genoa-born Christopher Columbus's little excursion across the sea gave the impetus for some urgently needed renovation, resulting in the weird modern structures you can see in the old port. More recently – during the G8 summit in 2000 – Genoa became the centre of the world's attention. With neo-fascists in the ascendant, in the police and on the street, tensions were high, and what was to have been Berlusconi's brief moment on the world stage was eclipsed by incomprehensible brutality. The net result was the entirely avoidable death of one young Italian, Carlo Giuliani, shot dead by a panicky and inexperienced Sicilian *carabiniere*, a timely reminder perhaps that Italy might not be quite as benign a country as it seems.

Old Genoa is somewhat amphitheatric. The old port is its stage and the old quarters of the city the tiers. Its heart is full of dark and gloomy passages called *caruggi* that draw you down towards the sea and the *porta antica*. And since you are almost bound to get lost on your journey down, you begin to expect to stumble into a huge medieval scene: a port full of noise, seagulls, barrels of salted fish and olive oil. Toothless drunken sailors carousing with slutty, smutty whores. But sadly the ancient thrum is no longer there. Any thrumming is more than likely to come from the flyover that runs right across the old port. It is breathtakingly disfiguring. So prepare to be mildly disappointed, for the port has almost, though not quite, lost its soul. You pay now for minor amusements. The aquarium. The Pavilion of the Sea. A lousy sandwich. The weird arachnoid construction that offers tourists a ride vertically to nowhere, and a stupendously difficult-to-find museum that discreetly relishes the city's maritime past.

Genoa was once a great port. La Superba, they called it: the Proud. Its golden age was back in the sixteenth century, when the shrewd Genovese admiral Andrea Doria forged a pragmatic alliance with the Spanish in 1528, switching support rather dramatically from their traditional allies, the French. Genoa had been a significant player in Mediterranean trade since the twelfth century and the Doria family was part of the noble elite that had governed the city for centuries – with the odd, almost democratic blip. If ever there was a miserable-looking famous Genovese, this must be he. Doria's portrait shows his long sinuous hands and a pointed face that simply gushes misery.

Given his enormous wealth, maybe it was merely an air. But this man was known, as it has to be said were many Genovesi, to be a dealer in slaves, who powered his galleys with these unfortunates on ten-year rowing contracts. He in turn was legally bound to supply galleys to the Spanish Crown. Both Genoa and the Doria family were to profit vastly from this arrangement.

This was the age when gold and unimaginable riches flowed into the kingdoms of Spain and Portugal from the new world revealed by Columbus and his companions. Like many Genovesi, Columbus had left the city when young, making his fame and fortune by working for the Castilian monarchs. The Genovesi had always been highly mobile. Having practically no hinterland to speak of, they had learnt to look seawards and knew that trade rather than empires would make them wealthy. Their trading tentacles reached throughout much of the eastern Mediterranean and to the North African coast – their very own version of the world-wide web – and they played the elaborate game of merchants and alliances for a long time with great success.

Historically Genoa was one of the four great maritime republics, along with Pisa, Amalfi and Venice. The Pisans were for many years their greatest foe, vying for influence in Sardinia and Corsica in particular, but in 1284 the Genovesi inflicted serious and long-lasting damage on them in the Battle of Melora. One Sunday in August of that year, a powerful fleet of ninety-three Genovese galleys appeared off Porto Pisani and dared the Pisans to come out and fight. They didn't, and chose to stay within the harbour walls, but the Genovesi pressed on and managed to destroy much of the fleet, killing over 5000 Pisans and filling their vessels with some 9000 prisoners, who were to languish in Genoa's jails for many years.

Much of Genoa's early trade was carried on with the Byzantines in the east, and they established a series of commercial outposts built in the Genovese style and manned by them, looking after their city's interests from far away. They had one in the Black Sea at Caffa, and another on the island of Chios, where alum was bought from nearby Phocea, sent back to Genoa and then on to Antwerp, a city that was to work closely with Genoa for centuries.

Genovesi were to be found in Constantinople and Alexandria, in Cyprus and in Sicily. Many moved with the prevailing political winds, but one institution became almost supranational, the overmighty financial heart of the Mediterranean: Genoa's bank, the Casa di San Giorgio. Rich with the gold that flowed from the New World, the bank flourished on the Spanish connection and had real power throughout the Mediterranean.

Despite all this, surprisingly perhaps, there was a hint of democracy in the way the republic was organized. The *popolo*, the broad mass of the population, was quite capable of rising up and overturning the elite that ruled in their name. This they did famously in 1257 when, angry and overtaxed, they elected Guglielmo Boccanegra as captain of the people and threw out the ruling nobility to the cry of '*Fiat Populus!*' (meaning power to the people, rather than small Italian car). Boccanegra seems to have believed in spending his way out of an economic crisis, and began the works on the harbour which gave the old port its present form, as well as the glorious Palazzo San Giorgio on the waterfront.

Behind this, the city developed a network of *alberghi*, a word which originally meant groups of families and neighbours who nurtured their own identities and community spirit, as well as the usual fierce rivalries to keep them on their toes. This is one of the reasons why Old Genoa has few grand civic squares but rather a collection of smaller ones with a number of quite modest churches. The *alberghi* provided the *popolo* with a degree of organization that was used in their long generational battle against the nobility.

Of course, some of the *popolo* became nobility, turn-coats and traitors to the cause, but the idea that the people could elect their rulers, although not entirely novel, took root in Genoa, as it occasionally had elsewhere in Italy. Another famous Boccanegra, Simone, was eventually to become the city's first doge. In 1335, more discontent and much public clamour pressured the authorities to call on the crowd to suggest who they thought should run Genoa's affairs. 'Let it be Boccanegra!' a silversmith allegedly called out as a joke. It wasn't taken as such by Boccanegra himself, who, conveniently close by and thrust forward by the crowd, took on the mantle of power once held by his grand-uncle a century earlier. Refusing the religious office of *abate*, he was said to have boldly suggested that what the city needed was a doge, and that was what he became. This system was borrowed from the Venetians, who had proved that elected representatives ruling for set periods could, with proper checks and balances, provide a remarkably effective form of government. And it worked well in Genoa too, lasting for hundreds of years. Some four hundred years later, John Adams, looking for organizational inspiration for his native America, visited Genoa and made the following observations on how the system worked:

> The legislative authority of Genoa is lodged in the great senate, consisting of seniors, or the doge and twelve other members, with four hundred noblemen and principal citizens, annually elected. All matters of state are trans-acted by the seniors, the members of which hold their places for two years, assisted by some other councils; and four parts in five of the senate must agree in passing a law. The doge is obliged to reside in the public palace the two years he enjoys his office, with two of the seniors, and their families. The palace where he resides, and where

the great and little council, and the two colleges of the *procuratori* and *governatori* assemble, is a large stone building in the center of the city. At the expiration of his time, he retires to his own house for eight days, when his administration is either approved or condemned; and in the latter case, he is proceeded against as a criminal. At the election of the doge, a crown of gold is placed on his head, and a sceptre in his hand, as king of Corsica; he is attended with life-guards, is clothed in crimson velvet, and styled Most Serene, the senators Excellencies, and the nobility Illustrious.

The nobility are allowed to trade in the wholesale way; to carry on velvet, silk, and cloth manufactures; and to have shares in merchant ships: and some of them, as the Palavicini, are actually the greatest merchants in Genoa.

John Adams, 1786

By the beginning of the nineteenth century, however, Genoa was a city in decline. The Genovesi had ditched the doges and gone all revolutionary *à la française* in 1798, but as far as trade was concerned, the city was losing out badly to upstart Livorno. Napoleon Bonaparte, ex-citizen of an ex-Genovese island, Corsica, briefly became both Emperor of France and King of Italy. And in June 1805, in a solid bourgeois Genovese house, emerged our hero, Giuseppe Mazzini, born to a principled, intelligent mother and an equally principled, honourable father. By all accounts, they, like many Genovesi, were committed Republicans, anti-French, and in Mazzini's mother's case anti-clerical.

The Republic of Genoa was to be utterly shafted by the Congress of Vienna, called in 1815 after the defeat of Napoleon. The great powers, Britain, post-Napoleonic France, Austria, Russia and Prussia assembled in Vienna and proceeded to carve up Europe and many of its colonies to their mutual satisfaction. From it emerged, among other changes, a German federation, and the restoration of the monarchy in France and Spain. With Italy barely in its uterine stage, some of the old micro-kingdoms were re-instated, such as the Duchies of Parma, Piacenza and Guastella, together with the more important Duchies of Modena and Tuscany. But it was the Kingdom of Sardinia that gained most out of this. The island of Sardinia, as we saw, became part of the Piemontese House of Savoy by power manoeuvrings in the eighteenth century, creating what became known as the Kingdom of Sardinia, although most of its kings never went to Sardinia at all. And, at the Congress of Vienna, by dint of artful politics, the kingdom was awarded indisputable sovereignty over the Republic of Genoa, and the once mighty independent maritime republic was consigned to the historical rubbish tip for ever. It was a pretty sad and ignominious end, to become a historical adjunct without the merest gesture of consultation, and the events stimulated the intellectual energy that was behind the Risorgimento, driven by two subjects of the Genovese republic: Mazzini and Garibaldi.

If the Ripa has a proletarian twang still in the air, the higher you go the more bourgeois it all becomes. Walk down the glorious, comfortable, sixteenth-century Via Garibaldi in the early evening and you can see just how the extremes of Genoa cohabit, apparently quite happily. I suspect they have done so for hundreds of years. Indeed it seems that the Via Nuova, as it was called before Garibaldi was so honoured, was built on one of the port's redder-lighted districts. It's hard to believe that these enormous chunky buildings were originally residential. But that's precisely what they were until the eighteenth century, when the street, which had been enclosed and protected from the nasty world outside, was opened up to traffic. Slowly the residents moved out, and the banks moved in. It was a Renaissance version of Millionaires Row. The

Dorias were there. The Spinolas too. Rubens, delighted by the lush architectural apparition before him, drew the Via Nuova in detail and marvelled at its riches. A tradition grew up that the more important visitors to the city would be entertained in some of these private *palazzi*, which were divided up into specific *rolli* or lists of households that could be called upon if needed.

Step down to the side of Villa di Profumo on the Via del Portello, follow the ribs of the Garibaldi spine, and the world rapidly changes. There is a sense of danger and a generous dose of prostitution. Dodgy dealers, depressed tarts and a few happier souls who perhaps never nibbled at this sort of candied fruit at all scurry in the shadows. The Via Garibaldi is about as un-Garibaldian as you can get, with the rich and the louche living cheek by jowl. The old man must be wriggling in his tomb, looking in horror at all the *piazze* and *vie* in his name. But walk to the end, deviate a little down and a few alongs, and then you'll come to Via Lomellino, which is in a sense the why and the wherefore of this chapter, for this is where Giuseppe Mazzini was born, and where he spent his early years. The house has become a museum, a slightly gloomy one at that, for poor old Mazzini, for all his dedication to the cause, has never quite managed to morph into a popular all-Italian hero. Garibaldi most definitely has, which would no doubt have irritated Mazzini considerably for their relationship ultimately became tense, with Mazzini accusing Garibaldi of selling out to the royal family, and Garibaldi accusing Mazzini of being unworldly and incapable of understanding what Italy was really about. Both these extraordinary people owe much to their Genovese blood.

VERCELLI

IT IS FIVE O'CLOCK IN THE MORNING. THE ODD FROG PLOPS
desultorily into the water. *Zanzare*, irritating swarming
mosquitoes, irritate and swarm. In the name of authenticity
– and insomnia – I have driven out under a pallid April
sun to reflect a little on tales of exploitation and lust
among the rice fields of Vercelli, in deepest dampest
Piedmont. And I was thrilled to see real Italian lust
occurring beneath my very feet. A pair of copulating frogs
looked at me unconcerned, and carried on copulating.
Forza, rani, forza!

There was but one place to go: the Cascina Ventura,
within sight of Vercelli's high cathedral tower. This
neglected and run-down farm once positively exploded
with noise as the itinerant rice-weeders, the *mondine*,
arrived every year for a biblical forty days and forty nights
to keep the rice fields clear of weeds, travelling from near
and far to work in the slushy, muddy water. This *cascina*
was where one of the most famous films ever to be made
about rice-weeders in Piedmont was filmed: *Riso Amaro
(Bitter Rice)*, directed by Giuseppe de Santis in 1949. It's a
fantastic piece of Italian neo-realism and I spent weeks

trying to get my hands on a copy of it, which I did eventually, and reverentially, over the hills from Vercelli in sophisticated metropolitan Genoa. The plot centres on a stolen necklace, and the *mondine*. There's much singing and meaningful gazing. Walter (Vittorio Gassmann) is severely out-sleazed by the delicious Silvana Mangano, whose triangular cleavage looks as if it were designed by Jean-Paul Gaultier. It's extremely atmospheric, but most notable is the emphatic dominance of the women as a group, and even as individuals, which wasn't always a popular theme for Italy when the film was made. Even if you speak not a word of Italian it is worth seeing for the sheer spectacle of rice fields absolutely stuffed full of people. Thousands, it seems. The dormitories are full. The fields are full. The noise must have been quite deafening.

Women were not only cheaper but better at the back-breaking work required to keep the rice fields weed-free. Their presence was eagerly anticipated by the locals for reasons that had little to do with discussing the merits of arborio rice. They came from the hills of Monferrato and from as far away as Emilia and the Veneto, arriving with the regularity of a migratory flock of birds to decamp into the *dormitorio*. The heart and soul of the rice-growing business was the *cascina*. These rather abrupt, enclosed farmhouses were built around a courtyard, and the outer buildings were divided into houses for the families of the full-time workers and the managers. The *mondine* were housed outside, in huts that together looked suspiciously like a POW camp.

So here I was, ready for work, only fifty years too late. In the distance were the towers of Vercelli. But don't get it out of proportion. Vercelli is a modest town, an odd place that seems to have developed a mild identity crisis. I had the impression that deliberate attempts to confuse visitors were afoot. I had failed to find the time for the

ritualistic trawling of the web for information, so I had no
idea of the stark reality that would face me. There aren't
very many hotels in Vercelli. One, I was told, was closed
'for works'. The other wasn't. So, to the one that wasn't.

I thought I had followed instructions explicitly but I got
lost, and lost again, within the space of 200 metres, tricked
by a one-way system that provocatively confused you at
every turn. I asked someone else. The town had a touch
of the *Alice in Wonderland* about it. Round and round in
circles I went and returned to where I was before, and the
hotel miraculously appeared.

I walked in and asked wearily whether they had a room.
The signora looked like a practitioner of the dark arts.

'For how many people, signore? How many nights?'

One and one, I answered.

'One person. One night.' She studied the book closely.
'No, I am sorry, I think we are full. You could try the
hotel on the piazza. No, I think it's closed. I am sorry . . .
ah, just a minute. There's always room twelve.'

Room twelve? I felt like asking. Not the one where the
murder took place?

'Well, I'll take it if I may,' I said. 'Thanks.' I felt relieved
and uplifted. I wouldn't have to wander the streets after all.
I had a bed. And the room was perfectly clean, perfectly
unpretentious and perfectly free of bloodstains.

I was exhausted. I had left my permanent suite at
Stansted before dawn, flown to Turin and driven straight
out to the flat Vercelli plains. I had first tried to make this
trip late in the autumn of the previous year, when it was
kindly pointed out to me that there would be precious
little to get my teeth into since rice was planted in the
spring and grew quickly to be harvested in the autumn and
I had already missed the harvest. I postponed, and jammed
in a few other trips while biding my time for the rice.

'Come back when the fields are flooded,' I was told.
'Or better still, come back when the plants are just

growing through the water. Then everything is green. Beautiful.'

Well, it was nearly May. I had done as requested. But there seemed to be precious little that was verdant around Vercelli. The landscape had indeed been flooded and stretched endlessly to the rigid, wet horizon, divided up into fields that were entirely empty but for the water and the odd machine. Not a brilliant green sprout to be seen.

Vercelli is a one-crop town. It has a rice bourse. An experimental rice station. And lots of agricultural machinery that does things to rice: threshers, cutters, desiccators and milling equipment, all with lovely shiny new mechanical bits specially designed to make you even less reliant upon human beings and even more reliant upon your bank manager. You feel that if you stopped anyone on the street to talk, the conversation would soon slip back to rice. (My faux pas on this trip was to admit that I liked canned rice pudding. My hosts looked genuinely shocked.) I would have liked to see the rice bourse in action, but it was Liberation Day and all the rice-sellers had been liberated.

I had an out-of-body experience that afternoon. I'd developed a fairly well-tried formula for these trips. Arrive early if possible. Get a bed and bearings. Find decent caffè for morning cappuccino. Then find bookshop to stock up on scented pens for the kids and esoteric books on local food for me. Rest. Eat. Gear up and go for it. I was at the bookshop stage. I found one stacked with the usual guides to diving off Indonesia and new classic low-fat *trattoria cucina*, marked it as probably the best in town, and set off to look for another. But I simply couldn't find the bookshop again. Either I was developing a severe case of absent-mindedness or it had quite blatantly moved. Or perhaps I was just losing my grip.

Later, as the sun was setting and the ice-cream sales rocketing for the evening *passeggiata*, I noticed how many groups of old men there were happily talking away in Vercellese, a variation on Piemontese. Despite constant claims of mutual incomprehensibility, there is a pattern to Italian dialects. They have all evolved from the golden days of crazy emperors when Latin was the Roman Empire's lingua franca. Very roughly, those in the north-west – Ligurian, Piemontese, Lombard, Emilian Romagnan – are tarred with a touch of the Gallic brush, while those in the north-east are variations of Venetic. To the south lies Tuscan. Florentine Tuscan is considered to be the granddaddy of modern-day Italian, with a special place in the linguistic history of the country. Dante and Boccaccio wrote in mellifluous Florentine dialect, and it was really only in the eighteenth century that this evolved from an essentially written language read widely throughout the peninsula to become what we now call Italian. Its progress was inevitably quickened by the political moves for unification. Meanwhile, the dialects of Umbria, the Marche, Molise, Campania and the Abruzzi also have similarities to each other, as further south do those of Calabria, Basilicata and Sicily.

These are the dialects. But then there are the languages. In the Süd Tirol, or the Alto Adige as the Italians like to call it, a variation of German is spoken. In the Dolomites are Ladino speakers. In the Val d'Aosta a curious language called Walser is spoken. In Friuli there are remnants of a Romance language called Friulian, and Sardinian is most definitely a language apart. On the French Provençal border Occitan is still just about a living language and is being revived, with a bizarre linguistic pocket in the Aspromonte right down in Calabria. Weirder still are the Albanian-speaking communities, widely dispersed among the southern provinces, who speak a language they call *arberisht*. Their prospects look a little bleak, for this is another linguistic anachronism that most people consider to have no future. And there are Griko and its close relation Graecanic, spoken in pockets of Apulia and Calabria respectively, which predate the Roman Empire, linguistic leftovers from the days when the area was ruled by Greece and called Magna Grecia.

I was beginning to suspect that Vercelli was far more interesting than it had first appeared to be, but that it didn't quite know what to do about it. One of its endeavours was to produce a host of multicoloured publicity brochures that vary from 1950s socialist exhortatory style to the gloriously lyrical. Of Vercelli's food we are told: 'These flavoury products deserve to be tasted while touring around a fascinating land.' A simple statement, but, as if to keep you mentally alert, the tourist buffs have come up with this memorable non-sequitur: 'Vercelli: you are like a land that nobody has never mentioned.' This is supposed to be a quote from one of Italy's greatest poets, Cesare Pavese, but I suspect something was lost in the translation.

Vercelli was once on the pilgrim route to Rome and has in its firm civic grasp a few startling historical gems as a result. The star attraction is the Vercelli Book, *Codex Vercellensis*, probably brought here from England by one Jacopo Guala-Bicchieri who had been a papal delegate there, though no one can be quite sure. It might also have belonged to a wealthy pilgrim who died en spiritual route to or from Rome in Vercelli's Scots Hospice, leaving behind this exquisite tenth-century book written in Anglo-Saxon. It is an anthology of the most soul-searingly depressing kind, written presumably to remind good Christians of the horrors that await in the afterlife anyone who transgresses: i.e., everyone. This is the earliest known writing in Anglo-Saxon, so I was genuinely surprised to see it here in Vercelli, so far from the damp northern climes where the language was spoken. And what better to read when tucked up in your damask cotton late at night than these words from a passage in the Address of the Soul to the Body:

Then it calls out sadly with a cold voice, the soul speaks harshly to the dust: 'So, you bloodstained clod, what did you torment me for? Earthly filth, all shrivelled up, effigy of clay, little did you remember what the state of your soul would come to, once it had been taken out of the body. What can you blame me for, damned thing? So, food for worms, you certainly didn't think much, while you were following all your terrible pleasures, about how you will have to be a banquet for the worms, in the earth. See, in the world before you little thought how long it will be here, like this. And look, it was the angel who sent you your soul, by his own hand from heaven above, it was the almighty Ruler in his majesty, and he paid the price for you with his holy blood – and you bound me with a fierce hunger, made me a slave in the torments of hell.'

from *Poems of Wisdom and Learning in Old English*, edited and translated by T. A. Shippey (D. S. Brewer, Cambridge, 1976)

Far more inspiring than Stephen King. By the time dusk had fallen and I had experienced the deep joy of Vercelli cathedral's treasury, it was time to go and eat copious amounts of pig fat, for Vercelli has found a brilliant way to combine the best rice with the best lard in town. It is their beloved dish *panissa*. This is Debora Protti's recipe, cooked nobly for me one Saturday lunch.

Panissa

Serves four.

1 shallot, finely chopped
60g *lardo d'Arnad*, finely diced
350g risotto rice
150g salami *sotto grassa* or *salam d'la duja*, chopped

1 litre hot vegetable stock
1 sprig rosemary
2 bay leaves
150g canned or fresh cooked borlotti beans
1 squeeze tomato purée
50g unsalted butter
150ml red wine
salt and pepper

Fry the shallot in the lard in a large pan for 5 minutes. Add the rice and stir for a further 2 minutes over medium heat. Add the salami. Then pour in a ladle at a time of hot stock. Stir, and add more as the liquid is taken up by the rice. Add the rosemary and bay. After 10 minutes, add the borlotti beans and the tomato purée. When the rice is *al dente*, finish it off with the butter and red wine, and allow the red wine to be absorbed. Check the seasoning and serve.

Now, a word about *panissa*. In the food business you pick up the odd dribble of information here and there, and I had foolishly assumed that Vercelli's *panissa* was one and the same as Ligurian *panissa*. But no, that would have been too simple. While that *panissa* is nothing more than chickpea chips, Vercelli's *panissa* is a particular type of risotto much loved by the Vercellesi. My diligent contacts had already arranged a bout of rice wandering for the next day, and Debora Protti, whom I had contacted in an entirely wholesome way over the Internet, had promised that she would cook me some *panissa*. She had even promised me a recipe, and without my asking, too. So obviously I was keener than the hottest mustard to find out what this dish was. This is called background eating.

So, my first night in Vercelli and I had asked various innocent bystanders where was the best place in town to eat and the answer came back not once but three times that it was the self-same hotel I had chosen to stay in: the Giardinetto. Since I had earlier asked the noble lady whether I should reserve a table, and since she had quite clearly said no, I felt comfortable slipping unannounced into the dining room, although I anticipated nothing more than dullness and emptiness. But no. A miraculous transformation had taken place. The good lady was smart, smiling and solicitous. And she protected me womanfully when it was almost suggested that I couldn't eat there because I hadn't booked. The bustle was truly amazing. A Liberation Day party was in full swing, and well-heeled Vercellesi were sipping Prosecco and chatting amiably among themselves.

I have to admit that *panissa*, with its main ingredients of rice, lard and *salam d'la duja*, a stubby sausage that was traditionally kept in a terracotta pot (called in Piemontese a *duja*) filled with lard, doesn't sound a particularly appetizing dish. However, I had found myself in the excellent position of being able to sample it without having to walk very far afterwards. And I also discovered that lard, that bland, unctuous, white greasy stuff, a.k.a. rendered pig fat in English, can in the right hands become something surprisingly tasty. Lard has had a bad press. Lard is fat and fat is instant heart attack and a short lifetime of chest-clamping misery. Say no to lard, kids! But there are two lard love-zones left in Italy, and there is more to what the Italians call *lardo* than perhaps meets the English eye.

Lard was once widely used almost all over Europe, anywhere the pig ruled, at least. This most supremely utilitarian of all farm animals, giver of leather, hams, sausages, bacon and, yes, lard, inspired an enormous number of regional dishes wherever it went. Lard was spread on bread when butter was too expensive, and used as a medium in which to fry food. Pigs have fat on their backs, around their loins, and in layers surrounding their internal organs, and it is the last of these that was once rendered down to make joyous lard. But as Britain became industrialized, so did lard, and its taste became increasingly neutralized. These days spreading lard on your bread would be considered reckless, antisocial, almost suicidal, as we are all too well aware of the damage an excessively fatty diet can cause. But for those who are happy to take their future into their own hands, an occasional nibble of *lardo* might reawaken an ancient awareness that fat can taste, that fat has great subtlety.

One of the great joys of food in Italy is its healthy sub-culture, its artisan-made food, which has escaped the industrial process and, despite all the gloom that comes from certain Italian quarters, is to an interested outsider like me alive and very much kicking. Among this marvellous food is *lardo*, a long way away from what we now know as lard.

As to who produces the finest lard in Italy, well, that's a regional thing and the subject of heated debate. Perhaps the Rolls-Royce of lard comes from Tuscany: *lardo di Colonatta*, where the fatty loins are laid on a bed of the purest sea salt in brilliant white marble containers, for Colonatta nestles among the marble quarries of Carrara. This *lardo* was once called the food of the anarchists: the marble-quarry workers, devotedly independent-minded, were active supporters of the Risorgimento, taking to the hills in the later part of the nineteenth century and helping to foment discontent wherever they could, all fuelled by lard. We must also mention the estimable lard from Aosta, known as *lardo d'Arnad*. This is again a local food for local people, made from good-quality pork and the mountain herbs that are used in the maturation of the pork. Instead of marble, the traditional containers, called *doïsls*, are made of chestnut. It was this lard that I ate thinly sliced in Vercelli, and it is said that it makes the finest *panissa*.

A plate of lovingly sliced pure white lard is perhaps not the most tempting sight, but this writer is made of sterner stuff, and, oh joy, as the lard reached my tongue I knew that this was the moment to proudly jettison all those years of lard humour and join the growing fan club of lard lovers, for it was divine, delicate, herby – yes, OK, slightly fatty, but I had only to get upstairs before my veins silted up and I departed to the world of eternal vegetarianism.

And to round things off, might I encourage you to seek out the forgotten cinematic masterpiece set in the lard-ripening caves of Tuscany and starring Amedeo Nazzari: *La Fossa degli Angeli* (*The Ditch of the Angels*)? It is one of the world's most prestigious lard classics.

'Excuse me. Have you got any salami *sotto grassa*?'

With a knowing, if surprised, look, he slipped away from the counter and brought back a plastic bucket: anonymous, very white, and perfectly clean. He slipped his hand gracefully into the fat. 'How will you be cooking it? Do you want me to pack it for you? Are you travelling far?'

I said yes, I was off back to Oxford, and entreated him to pack my sausage tightly, and as far as cooking was concerned, why, I was going to make *panissa* of course. Perhaps he thought I had flown straight in from London to shop in his neat, serious little *macelleria* in the heart of Vercelli. Or perhaps he just had that natural politeness of the artisan, proud to initiate the stranger into the finer points of his art. Anyway, he was the very model of politeness.

I watched him pull out the salami, trapped in its bath of the purest-looking soft fat. He laid it in front of me, stroking it, talking to me, wiping away the remains of the lardy old grease. I love this sort of thing. I used to stroke fish, dead ones, as they were about to be chopped up and cooked. I can still wax lyrical over fish, beauteous, tasty creatures. And he, I knew, loved his meat. Even though the plastic bucket has replaced the *duja*, the salami still has its devotees.

I nosed around the *macelleria* and my eyes fell on something extraordinary. *Bouillon* cubes of chamois, *camoscio*. We were not far from Val d'Aosta and the mountains, but I imagined vats of these beautiful little antelopes, already on the outer margins of existence, and railed at the idea. There are limits after all.

'*Camoscio?* As stock cubes? I have never seen that before.'

'It's the trademark.'

I laughed. So did he. And carried on with the business of the sausage.

Every year, in the first weeks of September, Vercelli opens its doors to the frantic world of frog cookery. Their annual *sagra* is remarkable in that local frogs are not eaten at all; instead, they are imported from far-off places such as Indonesia and distant France. During this exciting frog weekend, the mighty pantheon of Piemontese frog cookery is wheeled out. Frittata of frog. Brodo of frog. Frog risotto. The locals drink and dance. And games of football are played in honour of this much-loved amphibian.

You might be surprised to learn that eating frogs isn't exclusively a French culinary thing and that the northern Italians are just as fond of them. Their rice fields were once an ideal place for frogs: wet, insect-rich and full of nice slow-moving water. In the days when I used to sell just about anything edible to some of London's finest restaurants, a Greek fish merchant tried to talk me into a major deal over frogs. The frog, by the way, being a creature of the water, is the domain of the fish merchant rather than the butcher; as is the snail, less understandably perhaps.

I arranged to meet my Greek fish merchant, whose

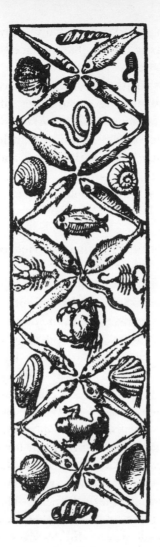

*The frog, as a creature of the water, is the domain
of the fish merchant.*

frogs were so cheap I felt I had at least to take a look, and
listened half-heartedly as he tried to sweet-talk me into
buying them. Usually frogs are presented impaled on a
stick, bodyless, skinned, just a row of little legs tucked up

like mutated ballerinas. He drew me towards his giant walk-in fridge, slid open the door and showed me pile upon pile of orange boxes full of live, whole, rather chilled Greek frogs. Fool, I said to myself. No wonder they were cheaper. This was a challenge too far, and although I reluctantly bought a box or two I felt miserable about the whole thing. A classic piece of hypocrisy, I might add, for I had never once flinched at buying the dinky little *baguettes* of frog's legs.

Frogs have a reputation for making an excellent, fortifying brodo. In fact, it seems to play, around Vercelli at least, a role not too dissimilar to a Jewish mother's chicken soup. Feeling under the weather? Sip some *brodo di rani*. A cure-all. The great, and very late, Pellegrino Artusi, Romagnol by birth, and author of one of Italy's finest nineteenth-century cookbooks, *La scienza in cucina, e l'arte di mangiar bene* (*Science in Cooking and the Art of Eating Well*, translated by Kyle M. Phillips (Random House Inc. 1996)), wrote a vigorous defence of the frog while slagging off the Florentines for dubious practice on the market stalls. 'Why,' he wrote, 'if you don't keep an eye on them while they're cleaning the frogs they throw away the eggs, which are the best part.' In his little homily to the amphibian he also points out, and this is the science side of him, that the reason why salamanders are thought to be immune to fire is that they have an inordinately thick layer of protective mucus. Remember that when you plan your next salamander roast. On frog brodo, Artusi wrote: 'Since frog broth is both refreshing and invigorating, it should be included in the diet of those with chest diseases or low-grade intestinal inflammations. It is also good for those recovering from an illness, and in all cases in which a person requires nutritious, soothing food.'

In the rice fields of Vercelli, where once trod the feet of a thousand *mondine*, also trod the feet of rather fewer *ranate*, the frog-fishers, the professionals who joined the amateurs, the kids, the old men and those who liked to go a-frogging for the fun of it and for the food. Armed with a rod and an acetylene lamp, the *ranate* used the age-old art of deception and croaked, drawing the frogs out to look at who was responsible for this aberration of frog language. Another way was to trap a frog, a loud, vociferous specimen, let it croak and then sweep up any other frog that came to check out the poor trapped amphibian. The habit was then to break their legs to stop them escaping; *skrusi*, they called it in dialect. And the Vercellesi still manage to wax lyrical about the frog. It remains a part of the bucolic past of the *risaia*, the rice field. And this despite the fact that no one I spoke to would dream of eating them from the fields these days.

During the 1950s, agriculture was seduced, or quite possibly violated, by the idea of becoming big, macho and industrial. Gone for ever were the days of mass fertilization with good old animal manure. Chemical fertilizers, sacks of innocuous nitrogenous pellets, became the norm, to the delight of the country's giant chemical plants. Chemicals were brought in to do the job of a thousand *mondine*. Pesticides, defoliants and herbicides cascaded from the wonderful metallic creations of the agricultural engineers. The *mondine* disappeared. So did the frogs. And the fish. The birds. In fact, the whole delicate web of biodiversity was fundamentally altered.

And you could say that it was being altered for the second time, though in a slightly different way. In 1872, the Piemontese government opened the Cavour Canal, which allowed huge new areas of land around Vercelli, further up towards Novara and in the Lomellino to be developed as rice fields. Cavour had cut his political teeth in the nearby town of Grinzane, now reverentially renamed Grinzane Cavour, and had been a highly effective minister of agriculture, who supported the idea of developing the flood plain for rice cultivation.

Today, there is an air of more than a little gloom about the business of growing rice. One source of concern is political. As subsidies are no longer thought to be justifiable, how can Italian rice, with its costs so much higher than those of the developing world, remain competitive? Some put faith in organics. Trekking around the endless rice fields, you do sort of wonder about this land of excessive monoculture. I almost jumped for joy when I came across a field where they had been practising the ancient art of crop rotation. So don't moan too loudly when you pay a little more for your organic risotto rice please.

There seems to be a somewhat resigned agreement among rice growers that their rice will feed the risotto-hungry niche markets of Europe and America, and that's about it. Italy itself isn't one of the greatest consumers of rice in Europe, but here in the north at least, in the three provinces of Lombardy, Piedmont and to a lesser extent the Veneto, rice is still widely eaten, and rice cultivation leaves its mark on the landscape. The countryside is flat, dead flat, but the colours of the rice fields move with the seasons from earthy brown after the autumn's harvest to the mirror-smooth, water-covered time of early spring. This is when the young rice shoots begin to pierce the water's surface and colour it with a vibrant green. But even if the plants look similar, hundreds of different varieties are in fact grown, although only a few are high profile. A few years back it was Arborio or nothing for anyone making a risotto, but this is not the best variety. Even Carnaroli, now assumed by many to be the best because it is the most expensive, is thought by the locals to be nothing like as good as Sant'Andrea. Cheaper varieties such as Baldo and Roma are also good enough for risotto, and you might see a variety called Vialone Nano, which is mostly used in the Veneto for their classic dishes, such as *risi e bisi*.

And when it comes to making the perfect risotto there are, as you would expect, a few crucial do's and don'ts. Make sure that the pan you use has a thick enough base to distribute the heat evenly. And it goes without saying that you will need a good variety of short-grained Italian risotto rice, which holds its shape during cooking. First prepare the *soffrito*: finely chopped onion gently fried in butter or oil, or a mixture of both, until slightly translucent; this should take no more than 3 to 4 minutes. Then on to the *tostatura*, when you add the rice (70–90g per person depending on hunger and greed) to the *soffrito*, cooking it over a higher heat to seal it. This takes about 4 minutes, during which time you stir continuously, making sure that all the grains are coated with butter and/or oil. Then begin to add the stock, a ladleful at a time, in whichever form your recipe suggests but scaldingly hot no matter what so that it doesn't stop the risotto from cooking. Leave the stock to bubble away on the adjacent hotplate to keep it scalding while you are adding and stirring. And you do need to stir vigorously and continuously, using a wooden spoon and making sure that none of the rice sticks to the bottom of the pan. At the end you will probably be asked (by the recipe, that is) to finish the dish off with a little butter – Alpine and Italian, if possible – and some freshly grated Parmesan. Serve immediately, on hot plates. And that is the method. Simple really. The liquid can be as luxurious as champagne or as mundane as vegetable stock. The variety is endless.

One further point. Almost all the varieties have different cooking times. Respect them. The variation is down to the size of the grains, but it's crucial for the end result, which must be neither too sloppy nor too dry, with the grains neither too crunchy nor too soft. Practice makes perfect, so if you haven't done so already, get to your stoves and cook.

ROME

I HAVE HAD A LINGERING FANTASY THAT ONE DAY MY ITALIAN relations would appear as if from a puff of genealogical smoke. I just knew there was a nest of Rossellis somewhere, waiting to link up with their long-lost English cousins. There would be tears and laughter. They would all have perfect teeth, yachts and spoilt babies, and would immediately suggest that I, as the instigator of this communion, should stay in the family villa and use the helicopter whenever I wished. Plates of exquisite spaghetti would be brought to us as we shared our family memories with benign old men. Ah, memories!

I hadn't thought out quite how I would find them, but I was closing in. From the photograph in Turin, I had discovered the Mazzini museum in Pisa. And from the museum's librarian, Andrea Bocchi, I had learnt that there were Rossellis still alive and kicking and living in Rome.

Imagine the tension as my finger rested barely centimetres away from the doorbell of an imposing apartment block in Rome. On the name plaque was written: Dottore Aldo Rosselli. He was my distant cousin. Aldo's great-great-grandfather was my great-great-grandfather's brother. I am not sure what precisely that made us, but cousin seemed appropriate at the time. However, there was a difference. His father, Nello Rosselli, was a courageous anti-fascist and liberal socialist who had been murdered, along with his brother Carlo, in France in 1937 by the Fascist *cagoulards*. My father was called Brian. He was an aeronautical engineer, and died watching television.

I had made contact with Aldo a few weeks earlier, and we had spoken on the phone. I liked the way he called me *professore*. When I told him I really wasn't a professor at all, more like a fish merchant/writer manqué, he generously kept to the *professore* rather than the *piscatore*. 'In Italy,' he said, 'we always call writers *professore*. It doesn't matter at all if you aren't a real one. Nobody cares much.' So *professore* it was.

Aldo's father, Nello, had two older brothers. One, another Aldo, had been killed in the First World War. Both Nello and Carlo, the other brother, became deeply involved in the struggle against Fascism in Italy, and wrote, thought and fought against what they and their family had always struggled against: tyranny, prejudice and inequality. Carlo Rosselli was the founder of what might today be seen as akin to a Blairite social democratic movement, which he called Justice and Liberty. It was a little more than that – a brave attempt to create a radical socialism that learnt from the Russian Revolution on the one hand and from liberal socialism on the other. But Italy in the 1920s was entering one of its darkest and most illiberal phases, and the Fascists were profoundly wary of gallant liberal intellectuals.

And in the peculiar way of things, I had also discovered that Carlo's son John, who had been a real professor, had taught me a short course on Indian Literature at Sussex University. I was studying Anthropology, but this was a notoriously liberal university in those days where you could study anything, take endless amounts of herbal medicines and still get a degree. If only I had been a little more curious then about his name. Sadly, he has since died.

I buzzed.

I waited. I buzzed again. No answer. Just as I was preparing to pull out my trusty *telefonino* and call him, a distant robotic voice came through the speaker and said: 'Come up to the first floor, *professore.*'

Up I climbed, and was ushered into his very modest apartment. Aldo has worked in publishing. You can tell this by the fact that books have nearly pushed him out of the entire apartment, and only grudgingly allow him *lebensraum*. He spoke perfect English and, although slightly frail, he had a glint in his eye and a fine sense of the ridiculous. He liked the idea, as did most Italians, funnily enough, of looking at Mazzini through a plate of pasta (figuratively, you understand).

'You have no idea how boring most of the books written about the Risorgimento are,' he told me. I did actually. I had read quite a few. But luckily some real gems have been written about the Risorgimento in English. G. M. Trevelyan's account of Garibaldi and the Roman Republic is truly gripping, written at a time when there were still survivors alive to talk to. Garibaldi's life was so electric it would be difficult to write about him and make it boring, but it has been done elsewhere. Mazzini was different. He was more secretive, cerebral. Although both were stubborn, intensely patriotic, passionate men, it was really Mazzini who was the more devoted Republican, more consistent in his pursuit of this great idea. Garibaldi's main strength was his extraordinary ability to inspire, and to enthuse his followers, and it was truly fortunate that such a military genius should arrive on the scene just as Italy so badly needed one.

The Rosselli brothers had obviously grown up in an atmosphere that owed a lot to the Mazzinian dream of a republic, one without religious prejudice. Aldo, Carlo and Nello were the sons of Giuseppe 'Joe' Rosselli and Amelia Pincherle. Joe was a soft-hearted romantic musician, while his wife, Amelia, was a respected author and a strongly principled mother. It was Amelia's character that seems to have had most influence on the three children. The Pincherles, like the Rossellis, were part of the secular Jewish elite and had been involved in Manin's brave but ultimately unsuccessful attempt to establish a Venetian Republic in 1848. It, too, like the Roman Republic of 1849, foundered under military weakness and simple inexperience.

Joe was the son of Sabatino Rosselli, whose brother Michelangelo was my great-great-grandfather. His marriage to Amelia lasted nine years, so that much of the child-rearing was under her auspices; he seems to have retreated into his music when the marriage broke up, and he died ten years later, apparently a little bitter about life. Amelia sounds the stronger of the two. Her nephew was also a writer: Alberto Moravia, who was to base the character of Professor Quadro in his book *The Conformist* on Carlo Rosselli.

Aldo and I sat and talked and I looked at his domed forehead and thought that mine looked the same. We liked books. We had domed foreheads. Aldo even had a penchant for France. He called his sister, Silvia, who lived on the other side of the city, and arranged that I should meet her too. She was a retired psychoanalyst, with a piercing gaze, but was charm itself and looked spookily like my mother. By the end of the day, with no sign of helicopters, I trudged back to a particularly ghastly hotel and reflected upon my side of the family, who had been happily into banking, breaking stocks, counting money and living comfortably in Kensington, unaware, it seemed, of the raw courage of their Italian cousins.

* * *

I knew what had drawn me to Rome. The living Rossellis, of course. But there was also the peculiar story of the Roman Republic of 1849, the brief, inspirational period when Mazzini finally achieved real power and proved himself to be a gifted, generous administrator. All was to be wrecked by the French, who were to be as perfidious as the English ever were. They consigned the republic to history, hardly fitting for supposed Republican revolutionaries. And then there was the ghetto, shoehorned into a site between the Portico d'Ottavia and the river Tiber, chosen to be as miserable a location as possible. The ghetto is a curious part of Rome. Still separate in a way, and still definitely, almost defiantly, Jewish, it not only has its perplexing history but it has preserved relatively intact what is called *la cucina romana ebraica*, Jewish Roman cooking. The main drag of the ghetto is the Via del Portico d'Ottavia, which runs down from the portico originally built by Augustus to honour his sister Octavia. And along this street is an array of shops and *trattorie* that will make you salivate. So it hadn't been too arduous to shimmy down to Rome on another no-frills wonder.

Gorgeous and sexy though Rome is, I had learnt that Italian cities can give you a severe case of gastro-interestitis. They simply have too much to offer. And Rome, like a pandered supermodel, is a city tired of the hangdog love of the foreigner. So as I set out for the Roman ghetto, my heart thumpingly obvious on my sleeve, I joined the thousands of others who were simply gobsmacked by the city's sublime beauty.

Breezing into Rome's main station, Roma Termini, I noted the admirably Fellini-esque vision of a legless beggar chatting animatedly in his wheelchair on a smart mobile, and was then welcomed by a band of Albanian kids who attempted to treat me as a walking cash machine. Hurrying below to the metro, I bought my daily BIG, a *biglietto integrato giornaliero*, a ticket that allows you to travel all day long on trains and buses throughout the city. I marvelled that you could not only get onto the metro without having your nose thrust into a stranger's fetid armpit or being spiked by a dripping umbrella, but you could actually sit down, and in the rush hour too. Anyone who has travelled in London will understand my shock and delight. So, off to the Colosseum in wonderment, only to find a new band of villains: *faux* Roman soldiers, with helmets and swarthy pre-Gillette chins, fleecing tourists of vast amounts of money for the holiday snaps they had posed for. Marching on ghettowards, I passed the most magnificently hideous and ill-positioned building in Rome, possibly the world: the monument to King Vittorio Emmanuele II, the usurper of the Republican cause. Tucked inside it is another museum to the Risorgimento but one that barely mentions Mazzini or Garibaldi and is instead stuffed full of busts of pompous soldiers and generals; rather more of a paean to the royalists than anything else. Still, you get a mighty good view of Rome from the top.

If you head straight down to the Tiber from here you should get to the ghetto. I was still absorbing the idea of having a centilitre or two of Jewish blood in me. I know from my great-grandfather's birth certificate that not only was his father Michelangelo a Jew, but so was his mother, whose family name was Piperno. Which is not only about as famous a Jewish name as you can get in Rome, but is also the name of an equally famous Jewish restaurant in the ghetto, strongly recommended to me by Silvia Rosselli. It's odd, but my Kensington grandmother, the sender of soap and crystallized fruit, never once let slip any hint of Jewishness. History might have helped dissipate it, for, as my mother sagely reminded me, her mother and her uncles lived through the Second World War. It would be tragic if this was why the Jewish part of the family heritage had been swept under the carpet. But I suspect it was less conscious than that.

Although the Jewish community in Rome is Europe's oldest — Jews first arrived here in 161 BCE when envoys from Judas Maccabeus sought help from the empire in their fight against the Greco-Syrian alliance — it has had only the briefest moments of peace and tranquillity. A wave of exiles arrived after the Romans' brutal sacking of the Temple of Jerusalem in CE 70, as well as an even bigger group of Jewish slaves, captives from the battle, who were eventually absorbed into the Roman Jewish community.

In case you need reminding of the role that Rome played in the troubled history of Jerusalem, walk down to the Forum one day and take a lingering look at Titus' Arch. You cannot fail to see the sculpted images of a long line of Roman soldiers carrying away the Temple's treasures, the sheets of gold, the menorah: the soul and wealth of the Temple carted off by Emperor Vespasian's son, Titus. Titus himself was destined to become emperor for a brief two years from 79 to 81, succeeded by his brother Domitian, who never quite took to public life and was murdered by his enemies in 96.

At about that time a curious religious sect had appeared in Rome, who worshipped an even curiouser man, one who had claimed to be the Son of God. They called him Christus. Enter the Christians to the Roman scene. Initially, the Roman emperors did not look upon them too kindly, although some of Domitian's relatives allowed them to use the land that stretched out along the Via Appia. The Christians began to construct an immense network of underground burial chambers and places of worship called the Catacombs, the spiritual birthplace of European Christianity, where saints and relics were lovingly stored and Christians gathered to worship their god. Despite persecution, the popularity of Christianity grew and grew, but brutal intolerance proved to be an inauspicious parent to this nascent religion. Perhaps it was just man at his most manlike, but as the Christian era began and the Roman Empire collapsed, so the Christians too exercised the same barbaric practices that had once been used on them.

By the fourth century, the Jewish community in Rome was well established, about 40,000 strong, and relatively free. It was divided into separate communities, each with their own synagogues and schools, and at that time was mainly based in the Trastevere, the area of Rome set aside for foreigners and immigrants: *tras* or across the Tevere, the Tiber. With the demise of the Roman Empire, the Pope became the highest authority in Rome and the Jews had to put up with a constant succession of peculiar characters whose attitude towards them ranged from pragmatic tolerance to rabid hatred.

It was in 1492, while Columbus sailed off to do the dirty on the unsuspecting New World, that Ferdinand the Catholic announced the wholesale expulsion of Jews from Spain. Many Jews found their way to Rome and came upon a thriving though concerned community, wary of Christianity's increasing intolerance. Their lot was to change with the accession of Pope Paul IV.

Giovanni Caraffa was elected pope in 1555 and ruled with a rod of colossal bigotry until 1559, when he passed away. This miserable old man proudly boasted, 'I have never conferred a favour on a man,' and was therefore thought to be ideal papal material. His avowed wish was to strip Rome of its classical statuary, 'pagan works' as he called them, and he would have destroyed Michelangelo's 'Last Judgement' had he had his way, but in the end he succeeded only in stripping the Villa Giulia of some of its statues. His election did not bode well for the Jews of the Pontificate, and in 1555 he signed the infamous Papal Bull called *Cum nimis absurdum*, the gist of which was that it was 'absurd' that Jews should be considered the equals of Catholics. As a result of this, Rome's Jews were confined to the ghetto for the next three hundred years.

> It is absurd and inconvenient that the Jews, who through
> their own fault were condemned by God to eternal
> slavery, can . . . show such ingratitude towards Christians
> and affront them by asking for their mercy . . . have
> become so bold as to not only live amongst Christians but
> near their churches without any distinctive clothing.

* * *

Enclosed in their walled ghetto from dusk to dawn, the
Jews were deprived of anything that smacked of luxury,
and had to create, from the Pope's miserable shopping bag,
food that tested their inventiveness to the full. And this
essentially is the genius of Roman Jewish cooking. Of
course, given the restrictions of kosher the choice was even
harder, but if you look at the make-up of the Jews of the
Roman ghetto, you can get a clue as to where they were
likely to travel, foodwise.

At the time of the expulsion of the Jews from Spain in
1492, Sicily was under Spanish rule, so the Viceroy of
Sicily, following King Ferdinand's instructions, ordered all
Sicilian Jews to leave within the required three months.
They congregated at Messina, from where a soulful rabbi
wrote: 'We are leaving, and for ever, this land where we
were born, where our fathers were born, where our nation
has known to a lesser extent than elsewhere the pain of
exile.'

Wherever the Sicilian Jews were to go, they took with
them some of the culinary richness they had developed in
Sicily. The aubergine, known by the Sephardim as
berenjena, was previously little eaten by the Romans and
avoided almost entirely by Christians, who thought it to be
toxic – which is why, by the way, the Italians call it
melanzana, derived from the Latin *mala insana*, or apple of
insanity. The Sephardim had learnt about the aubergine
from the Arabs, who called it *albadingen*, which, like

berenjena, is derived from the Sanskrit *vatin gana* (the aubergine is believed to have come originally from India). Although it is an immensely adaptable vegetable, the Roman Jews mostly fried it, or, rather as they did with the courgette, marinated it and then fried it.

The *melanzana* has only relatively recently been adopted more widely in Italy. Even Pellegrino Artusi, who wrote his masterly *Science in Cooking and the Art of Eating Well* at the beginning of the nineteenth century, notes that they were practically impossible to find in the markets of Florence 'as they were considered Jewish food and abhorred'.

The courgette was often considered too valuable a vegetable to be used in the ghetto, so there evolved a tradition that is still very much alive of using the male flowers as a receptacle and baking them with cheese, or breadcrumbs and anchovies. The flowers might once have been considered inedible and thrown away.

Fiori di zucca ripieni

Stuffed courgette flowers; serves four.

16 courgette flowers
120g breadcrumbs from home-made or good quality white bread
4 anchovy fillets, chopped
large handful parsley, finely chopped
1 egg
salt and pepper
olive oil for frying

Pick the flowers in the morning before the heat has made them wilt. Clean them gently under water and dry with kitchen paper. In a bowl mix the breadcrumbs, anchovies, parsley and egg together and season. Fill the flowers with the stuffing and fry them in hot, but not smoking, olive oil until the filling begins to turn golden. Drain and serve.

I first tasted this wonderful dish at Piperno's, a venerable restaurant on the edge of the ghetto, built on the site of a castle that once belonged to the notorious Cenci family. A merry lot, by all accounts, who were infamous for the murder of one of their own: Francesco Cenci, who before his death in 1598 pursued the family traditions of violence and depravity with gusto. His many children and his second wife Lucrezia tired of his behaviour and took matters into their own hands by throwing him from a tower.

In 1860, Pacifico Piperno took over one of the old stables of the Cenci palace to open an *osteria* with a menu that was in all probability very much like the one you'll find today. Piperno's is comfortable. You could take your granny there with ease, and your granny might even like to take you. The waiters are utterly professional and deeply charming, and, when faced with my questions, willingly unearthed for me my very own brochure that tells the story of Piperno's in black and white.

The menu is full of the megastars of Roman Jewish cooking: courgette flowers, *carciofi alla giudea*, salt cod, and the curious-sounding Grandfather's Balls. After I had scrunched into the *fiori di zucca*, I ordered a generous chunk of fried *baccalà*, and wondered again at how infinitely variable salt cod can be. And that it just doesn't give that same balance of fishiness and pungency when chefs use salt cod that they make in their own kitchen by adding salt to cod. There is more to it than that. In Norway and Iceland the skills of salting have been handed down through the generations, and to use the real thing gives a far happier result. The key is that the fish are salted

in huge batches for a few months, then cleaned and salted
again. The ghetto's ancestors would no doubt be horrified
that *baccalà* has now become one of the most expensive
items on the menu, thanks of course to the global overfishing of cod. The best of all *baccalà* is still called, even
more irony here, San Giovanni, after the capital of
Newfoundland, St John's, now entirely devoid of cod after
the collapse of the Grand Banks fishery. The only fish considered permissible for the Jews to eat were either
preserved or what the Italians call *pesce azzurro*, 'blue fish',
meaning pelagic, shoaling fish, which were once caught in
huge numbers off the coast of Lazio. Both were cheap. So
they ate cod salted and dried – *baccalà* and *stoccafisso* – and
fresh or salted anchovies and sardines; in other words, fish
suitable for the very poorest of society.

When I asked what I could have to round off this festival
of frying, the waiter without a moment's hesitation said:
'You must try Grandfather's Balls.' Of course I agreed,
and waited for two healthily round balls of ricotta, studded
with chocolate, to be brought to the table. Fried, of
course. And struggling to bat away an image of my own
grandfather's testicles, I sliced them clean through and sent
them down my gullet to join the rest.

Of all the dishes you can eat in the ghetto, it is the
artichoke that has become its most iconic food, most
perfectly expressed in *carciofi alla giudea* (Jewish-style
artichokes). This is a disarmingly simple dish. Yes, it is on
one level little more than fried artichokes, but to eat they
are so divine they deserve a better name than that. If you
feel like cooking them yourself, take this advice. First,
choose the right artichoke. In Rome you will see the large,
rounder variety called Romanesco that are the best to use.
You should avoid gross, flabby artichokes and any that have
been shrink-wrapped and shipped around half of Europe.
As with everything, the fresher the choke, the better the
dish. A rather quaint familial hierarchy has grown up

around the artichoke: the larger ones are lovingly called *mammole*, best boiled and nibbled. But many prefer to use their children, the *figlioli* or smaller artichokes that grow further down the stem, or the even smaller ones still, the ones they call *nipoti*, grandchildren. To make *carciofi alla giudea*, chop off the outer edges of the artichoke before you fry them. But try doing this with a spiny Sardinian artichoke and you must prepare yourself for an uncomfortable time. Some markets in Italy cut them for you, lopping them before your eyes as you buy them, which saves you some of the hard work. It is likely that the artichoke was originally from Sicily, so the incoming Jews in the fifteenth century would have known just what to do with this glorious variation on the Mediterranean thistle.

Carciofi alla giudea

Keep the artichokes in acidulated water until you're ready to cook them lest they blacken, then drain them well and pat them dry. Grip the stem of an artichoke and smash the bulb straight down on your work surface repeatedly while keeping the stem upright, so the petals of the artichoke open out like a flower in bloom. Once they're all open salt them, pepper them, and fry them in hot oil sufficient for them to float. When the outsides are golden, wet your hand and flick a few drops of cold water over them; the oil will crackle and the leaves will become crunchy. After a few minutes drain them well and serve them hot.

Frying food made good sense. Ghetto dwellers didn't have the space for large complicated kitchens, and all frying called for was a pan and a flame – and, of course, copious amounts of olive oil, which believe it or not was once cheap. It was also one of the few permissible ways that

Jews could make a living: selling food on the streets, or running a *friggitoria* the Romans would travel into the ghetto to visit. Their other choices were hardly inspiring: selling old clothes, and lending money, which was forbidden to Christians because of the laws of usury. Fried foods could also be eaten cold on the Jewish Sabbath when there was a restriction on cooking. Hence the fondness for Sicilian *caponada*, a glorious mix of aubergines, peppers and tomatoes, cooked with sugar and vinegar and served cold, better by far when eaten the next day.

A further variation on the theme of frying is the Jewish Roman *fritto misto*. This is a world away from the Piedmont version, which uses the most esoteric bits of an animal that can be eaten. The Jews used a simple mix of vegetables, fried in a light batter in olive oil.

But not everything was fried. It didn't take long for the Roman Jews to create a masterly combination of *indivia* – the slightly bitter, distant relative of chicory, possibly better known to us in its French form, *scarole* – and fresh anchovies, creating the highly esteemed, quite delicious dish called *aliciotti con indivia*. It's one of those combinations that really, defiantly, works.

Aliciotti con indivia

Enough for six to eight people.

1kg fresh anchovies
1kg *scarole*, roughly chopped

Clean the anchovies. Fillet them by running your thumb along both sides of the spine and lifting off the fillets. Line the bottom of an ovenproof dish with *scarole*, cover with a layer of anchovies, and repeat in layers, finishing with the *scarole* on top. Bake in a moderate oven, 180–200°C, for 15 minutes or so, or until the water from the *scarole* has evaporated.

It was not until 1870, when the Papal States became part of the Kingdom of Italy, that the Jews were finally allowed to move freely within the newly united realm, which may help to explain why the Jews of Italy were generally supportive of the Italian monarchy, although many still hankered for a democratic republic: the Mazzinian dream. And few had forgotten the momentous events of 1849 when the Romans all too briefly rose up and established the ill-fated Roman Republic. All this was to change during the Second World War when the Italian royal family and the papacy proved to be utterly unworthy: they remained silent while the Jews from Rome's ghetto were forcibly removed during the Nazis' Final Solution.

When Pope Gregory XVI died in 1846, the Papal States were in a condition of semi-permanent revolt, particularly in the wild and distant corners of Romagna on the eastern coast. The world had been pressing the papacy to implement much-needed democratic reform, but Pope Gregory was not the man to do this – he was profoundly conservative. He fiddled and tinkered rather than offering radical change, so when the conclave settled down to choose his successor the world watched with real interest for that wisp of white smoke to emerge.

At the fourth attempt, on 16 June 1846, a liberal cardinal from Senegaglia, Giovanni Mastai-Ferretti, was elected and somewhat reluctantly accepted the papal tiara, taking the name Pius IX. 'My God,' he said. 'They want to make a Napoleon of me and I am just a poor country parson.' The conservatives cried foul. The Bishop of Milan, with clear instructions from the Austrians to veto any liberal reformist candidate, had arrived too late to vote and the liberals won the day.

The people of Rome and the Papal States were over-joyed. Garibaldi wrote him effusive congratulatory letters. Even Mazzini was enthusiastic. It seemed to be a propitious event, but no one really knew what reforms Pio Nono, as he was called, would introduce. Almost immediately he announced a general amnesty, and everyone began to believe that here at long last was a truly liberal reforming pope.

It proved to be an illusion. At first, wherever he went he was greeted with what at times verged on uncontrolled hysteria by crowds all over the Papal States. In April 1847 he decided to bite the papal bullet and establish a series of measures that would at last bring the people the chance of real democratic reform. Even Mazzini wrote that he would be prepared to accept the Pope as a life president for a united Italy if needs be.

But in 1848 the status quo in Europe was profoundly disturbed by the populace cheekily demanding far wider democratic rights, and in Italy revolts in Milan and Venice added to the general excited anticipation of the Republicans. While Pio Nono tried to establish a legitimate and effective government in the Papal States, he ran through three prime ministers before choosing the strict, authoritarian and much-despised figure of Count Pellegrino Rossi. On 15 November, despite warnings that something was afoot, Rossi proceeded up the steps of the Chamber of Deputies and in true classical tradition was stabbed to death by a gaggle of Republican sympathizers. The Pope's attempt at reform had been dealt a fatal blow. The Republicans' star was in the ascendant and the streets buzzed with Republican fervour.

The next day a large demonstration assembled in front of the Chamber and the Pope, under duress it has to be said, agreed to calling a constituent assembly and to the appointment of several ministers proposed by the crowd.

The Swiss Guard was disbanded, and a Republican Guard took its place. The Pope had effectively lost all control of events.

During the night of 24 November, Pio Nono escaped somewhat ignominiously from the back door of the Quirinale Palace disguised as a priest and went into exile in Gaeta. Rome was left to the Republicans. The winter was chaotic, but on 8 February 1849 the assembly proclaimed the Roman Republic. Mazzini was invited to Rome

Mazzini, Triumvir of the Roman Republic.

and offered full, honorary citizenship and was then elected as one of the ruling triumvirate, the first and last time that Italy's great Republican hero actually ruled.

Garibaldi came too, riding in from the city of Macerata in the Marche where he had eventually settled after being diverted from fomenting revolution in Sicily by the Livornesi. Mazzini's rule was said to have been thoughtful, generous and, even by some of his critics, remarkably successful. He took a small room in the Quirinale and set about ruling, armed with his morality and little else. But the Republic found itself with few friends. The Piemontese King Carlo Alberto believed he had a divine right to become king of a united Italy and rule over Rome. The Austrians were implacably opposed to the Republic, as was, understandably, the exiled Pope Pio Nono. The British had always been fairly tolerant in their attitude towards Mazzini, and although the Republic had its supporters among the overexcitable tea-drinking classes of the English bourgeoisie, the British government was a spectator rather than a key player.

But it was the attitude of the French that was most crucial. Louis Napoleon Bonaparte was elected to the French presidency on 10 December 1848 after many years of plotting and dreaming of a return to his fatherland. He had even served briefly, and rather strangely, as a special constable in London during the Chartist disturbances, but the French welcomed a Bonaparte once more to the upper echelons of power. He was in need of Catholic support and judged that upholding the Republic of Rome would not be particularly wise, especially since Pio Nono had already made successful appeals to the Austrians, the Spanish and the Neapolitans to send troops to Rome to crush the rebellion.

With French and Neapolitan troops massing not far from the city gates, Garibaldi once again proved himself to be an extraordinarily brilliant military commander, initially out-thinking and out-manoeuvring both the Neapolitans and the French while vastly outnumbered. The French retreated, surprised by his ability, and regrouped. There then followed an event that was to sour for ever the relationship between Mazzini and Garibaldi. The great general wanted to chase the French back to the very sea, to their base at Civitavecchia, but Mazzini, for political reasons, refused to allow him to do so. He seems to have had a lot of pent-up goodness in him for he even ordered that the captured French troops be wined and dined so that they would go back with tales very different from the stories of anarchic hell that were beginning to circulate in Europe's conservative press.

The French then decided to play a characteristic game of stick and carrot. The human carrot was Ferdinand de Lesseps, later to be famous for overseeing the building of the Suez Canal, and the stick the odious General Oudinot. On 31 May De Lesseps signed an agreement with the Triumvirs that called for the French to protect the Roman Republic from the Austrians and the Neapolitans, on condition that they were allowed to billet troops within the city. In reality the future was always pretty bleak for the largely friendless Republic, but this did at least offer the vague hope that something of its democratic nature might be salvaged. However, since no mention was made of the Pope, or what exactly was to become of the Roman Republic, the pact proved to be little more than a short-term sop. And in any case, perhaps sensing that the agreement wouldn't be entirely welcomed by his seniors, De Lesseps had thoughtfully added a clause that said it would be valid subject to ratification by the French parliament.

General Oudinot was less accommodating. The French government recalled De Lesseps and Oudinot called off the truce and declared war on the Roman Republic, stating clearly that, in order for French citizens to have time to leave the city, no attack would take place until Monday 4 June. That gave them three days. The French, however, were not true to their word. On the night of 3 June, they quietly infiltrated the Villa Pamfilj, then blew a hole in the outer walls to let in the troops, thus gaining an important vantage point. From there, the French moved towards the Villa Corsini, which also fell. Things looked bleaker still for the Republic. With the bulk of the Republican troops across the Tiber, it was some time before they were roused and longer still before they were able to retaliate. Garibaldi was sick and out of action, troubled by ancient wounds and rheumatism. However, when a messenger arrived with the news of the French attack, he gallantly leapt from his bed and rode over the river towards the scene of the battle.

The city also leapt into action. The church bells sounded the alarm, and the troops rushed through the streets to their assembly points. Garibaldi instinctively knew that the only way they could survive was to retake the Villa Corsini, not an easy task, but this fortified and well-protected palazzo held the key to supremacy over Rome. The battle was fierce. The villa was lost and won several times throughout the day, but always the Republicans fought with incredible bravery, led by the superhuman Garibaldi. Tactically, however, Garibaldi was for once found wanting. Reinforcements, Lombard *bersaglieri* who had been held in abeyance against their will, were finally ordered to join the fray but were cut to pieces and massacred. Garibaldi's inventiveness was sorely tried and, in an act that might have seemed to be one of sheer desperation, he asked twenty volunteers to try to retake the Villa Corsini on their own. They too were easy targets for the French. They also failed and only six returned alive.

A stalemate ensued, and Rome was laid to siege for all of June, pounded by French artillery. Oudinot decided that street fighting while Garibaldi was in command would not be wise. The denouement arrived on 30 June as the city below tried to celebrate St Peter and St Paul's day as it had always done, with a deal of carousing and candles lighting up the streets and churches. The assembly called Garibaldi to an urgent meeting and he rode swiftly through the streets, increasingly bitter and angry at the turn of events. As he entered the Capitol in his bloody red shirt, the delegates stood and applauded. His advice was urgently needed. There were three options proposed, but his position was clear. To continue fighting risked the complete destruction of the city under French fire. To capitulate would be unimaginable. His suggestion was this: that the fight should be carried into the countryside. '*Dovunque saremo, colà sarà Roma!*' Wherever we go, there will be Rome! So, the assembly declared: 'In the name of God and the People: the constituent assembly of Rome ceases from a defence that has become impossible and remains at its post.'

Garibaldi, now joined by his wife Anita and his closest supporters, hurriedly left Rome and crossed the Apennines, pursued and harassed by the Austrians but still with luck on his side. Mazzini purposefully stayed in Rome where the French left him to wander the streets. He eventually escaped to Marseilles by boat but he was never to hold power again.

The news of the fall of the Republic was greeted with delight by Pio Nono, still exiled in Gaeta. When he finally returned to the eternal city, he had left behind any pretence of being liberal and settled down to a long reign of more traditional conservatism. He had, however, definitively lost the respect of the Roman people.

GAETA TO NAPLES

WHY WAS IT THAT A SUCCESSION OF THE DISPOSSESSED, THE
ejected and the dejected in Italian history made their way,
voluntarily or not, to this particular corner of Italy? The
name Gaeta kept on appearing in books and stories but I
had no vision, no idea really, where on earth it was. I did
know about its olives, but that didn't help me geographically. So, to the maps, the guidebooks, the Gaeta dotcoms,
and I began to build a picture of a port with a particularly
dramatic past. Not long ago, Gaeta was a border town,
dividing the Papal States to the north and the Kingdom of
Naples, a.k.a. the Kingdom of the Two Sicilies, to the
south. Blessed with a very prominent promontory, Gaeta
has been a military and naval base for generations, and it
still is.

As you drive down into the bay, you can sense Naples
in the distance and just about see the top of Vesuvius. You
might even spy a few Americans chewing gum slightly
uneasily, driving around in alarmingly obvious cars, drifting in and out of the NATO base, huddling together
protectively. This is the military end of town, where
ancient crumbling streets and a cluster of spectacularly

beautiful towers and churches have been built around the port. Gaeta is the birthplace of the Italian navy and still bristles with keep-out signs, antennae and even the odd gun. Glance up above and you will see a massive, thick-walled castle, secure enough to keep an army of desperate aliens at bay for several lightyears. It also managed to keep out the Saracens, the Goths and their good friends the Visigoths, and the Lombards, but succumbed to the Normans in the eleventh century. It was strengthened by the Aragonese in the fifteenth century, which is why it's called the Aragonese Castle these days, but in reality it is infinitely more ancient than that.

For our story, there are no fewer than three crucial figures who became familiar with the narrow streets of Gaeta: Pope Pius IX, King Francesco II and Mazzini himself. Pope Pius IX was, as we have seen, forced to flee to Gaeta after the assassination of his prime minister, Rossi, in 1848. He railed and ranted from his new base in Gaeta, protected by King Ferdinand, and watched with relief as the Republic crumbled under attack from the French.

Ten years later illustrious citizen number two arrived in Gaeta, but this time it was an even more complex story. He was the tragic, pious young Bourbon, King Francesco II of the Two Sicilies, who happened to appear on the scene as some of the most extraordinary events of the Risorgimento were about to take place in his own back-yard, Sicily, and whose kingdom was to be consigned to the historical scrapheap. Francesco inherited the kingdom on the premature death of his father, King Ferdinand II, or *Re Bomba* as he was called after he had bombed his own citizens in Messina in 1848. He died broken and exhausted at the age of forty-nine, and on 22 May 1859 Francesco was crowned king and inherited a complex dilemma. Should he give in to liberal sentiments and allow an eruption of popular discontent in the rest of his kingdom, or should he follow the conservatives and strongly repress any liberalism, thereby risking revolution from another quarter? The following year the decision was wrested from him, for on 11 May 1860 Garibaldi and the *mille* landed at Marsala, Sicily, and miraculously managed to overcome a regular army of over twenty thousand. Exactly what happened is still debated to this day. The *mille*, the thousand, or more exactly the thousand and ninety, were a group of young men, many from the northern city of Bergamo, who had become passionately enthusiastic about the idea of a united Italy, and who agreed to sail with Garibaldi from Genoa all the way down to Sicily to stir up revolution. It was an astonishingly daring campaign, helped by a combination of good luck and sheer ineptitude on the part of the Neapolitan troops. Did the commander of a British naval boat moored in the harbour turn a blind eye to their presence? Why was the local military commander absent that day? Maybe it was the good old hand of God again, but whatever the truth, the island quickly fell and Garibaldi declared himself the dictator of Sicily.

Garibaldi clearly demonstrated that Francesco's kingdom was no longer immune to the siren call of liberty, and on the international stage the king had few supporters to turn to. His wife Maria Sofia, the daughter of the Duke of Bavaria, was only eighteen when she became queen, and although she was related to the Austrian royal family she was clearly in favour of granting a constitution, and in later life was even to become a radical leftist. Garibaldi seemed unstoppable. He outwitted the Bourbon army at Calatafimi, famously rallying his troops with the cry: '*Qui si fa l'Italia o si muore!*' Here we make Italy – or die! He crossed over to the mainland and proceeded north towards the kingdom's capital, Naples. The Austrians, the Bourbons' natural allies, were terminally weakened, and the king could only call upon Louis Napoleon of France to come to his defence. 'Too late,' he replied. Although the French attack on Rome had been justifiable on the grounds of defending Catholicism, defending the Kingdom of the Two Sicilies proved to be impossible.

Francesco eventually decided that the only option was to reinstate the 1848 Constitution, allow Sicily some autonomy and hope for the best. The denouement was close at hand. As Garibaldi's troops approached Naples, his officers sent some entirely false telegrams to the king's military headquarters, pretending to come from his own troops, dramatically overestimating the numbers Garibaldi had by many thousands. Strangely, no one seems to have questioned them. The king's troops at Salerno were ordered to take evasive action and move to the hills, and Francesco decided that he should leave Naples and conduct the war from a safer place: Gaeta.

Garibaldi's passage to Naples was thus made much easier. As the king steamed out of the harbour with his wife Maria Sofia, his gunship signalled for the fleet to follow. It stayed put, and his powerful minister of the interior, Don Liborio Romano, who had already made contact with Garibaldi, telegraphed him to proceed without delay. The city would offer no resistance.

Amid scenes of extraordinary joy, the Neapolitans swept Garibaldi up and guided his carriage down to the harbour under the very noses of the remaining royalist soldiers still garrisoned in Castel Carmine, who never fired a single shot. They were perhaps as mesmerized as everyone else. It must have been a fantastic moment: the crowd, the infamous *lazzaroni* of Naples, and Garibaldi, strange heroes to each other, all moving en masse around the jubilant city. Meanwhile, in the caffès of Turin, Cavour was plotting the future for *his* kingdom, hundreds of miles away.

Cavour had worked out how he and his king, Vittorio Emmanuele, rather than Garibaldi and his Republicans, could inherit the spoils of the broken Kingdom of Naples. He had managed to convince Louis Napoleon of France to

The King of Sardinia, Vittorio Emmanuele, ultimately became King of Italy, thanks to the manipulations of Cavour.

acquiesce in a scheme that allowed Garibaldi to win Naples while the Kingdom of Sardinia annexed Umbria and the Marche. *'Faîtes, mais faîtes vite,'* the emperor said to Cavour as he left for a convenient two-week cruise in the Mediterranean where he was out of contact with the world. Do it but do it quickly. It was perhaps Cavour's finest moment, an act that brilliantly managed to associate the Kingdom of Sardinia with all the heroics and genius of Garibaldi. Although by nature a Republican, Garibaldi had accepted that the King of Sardinia was best placed to enable the unification of Italy, which Cavour had never really believed in at all. But although Garibaldi had taken over Sicily in the king's name, both Vittorio Emmanuele and Cavour were increasingly aware that the whole process might become uncontrollable, and that a republic rather than a kingdom could be established, encouraged by Mazzini waiting in the wings. Cavour's skill here was crucial.

The King of Sardinia, Vittorio Emmanuele, had travelled down to join the fray, and in a tense meeting with Garibaldi at Teano after Naples had been conquered, he took Garibaldi's hand and told him, 'Your troops are tired; mine are fresh. It is my turn now.' And with this infamous handshake, the Sardinian army took control of events, finally capturing the besieged town of Capua. In a final and ugly insult to the great general, the king failed to turn up to a special ceremony where the Garibaldini were symbolically to hand over their swords to the Sardinians. Garibaldi was deeply insulted, and sailed off to brood in his island home, Caprera, at the northern tip of Sardinia.

With Francesco still stuck in Gaeta, the remains of the Bourbon troops were pushed back to join him, and then, to everyone's surprise, as the Piemontese navy steamed towards the port to bombard it, the French emperor ordered his fleet to stand in the way and prevent any action. The British complained, the French gave way, and a month-long siege of Gaeta started. The matter became increasingly tense, and Britain's response was seen to be crucial. It came in a telegram delivered by Lord John Russell to Ambassador Hudson in Turin, giving full support to the Piemontesi and the 'gratifying prospect of a people building up the edifice of their liberties, and consolidating the work of their independence'.

The meaning was clear. None of the big powers would intervene in the light of British support and Italy could take a further step towards unification. In 1861 King Francesco, Maria Sofia and their most faithful supporters eventually capitulated and were escorted out of Gaeta on a French naval vessel, *La Mouette*, to exile. However, there was still the small matter of Rome.

* * *

Enter once more the man in black, Giuseppe Mazzini. Banished from Rome by the duplicitous French in 1849, he continued to plot and foment revolution wherever he could, and like Garibaldi believed that Rome must become the capital of a united Italy. By 1870 Italy had been a kingdom for ten years but Rome remained under the control of the pope. This was the final piece in the complex puzzle of unification.

So far, the Neapolitans had lost out heavily. Naples was once the third biggest city in Europe, the wild and glorious capital of a kingdom whose subjects had developed a surprising fondness for their Bourbon monarchs, despite their many shortcomings. By 1870 there was already plenty of discontent and disappointment with the new king. Garibaldi and Mazzini continued their fundamental dispute, with the red-coated one still seeing some hope in using the Piemontese royal family as a focus for Italian independence, and Mazzini, sticking doggedly to his principles, continuing to push for the Republic.

In 1869 the French and the Prussians were on the point of war, which meant, Mazzini thought, that Rome might at long last be freed from the overwhelming French military presence, leaving it susceptible to a spot of rebellion. Mazzini moved from Switzerland into hiding in Genoa, where, on home ground once more, he managed to remain untroubled by the authorities. He was still a popular figure, a real hero to many, and even his detractors could not but admire his nobility of spirit and his perseverance. Even in exile he remained a passionate Republican, dedicated to the country he loved.

Mazzini was well aware that rebellions were beginning to appear in various parts of Italy beyond his control, and although he was getting too old and was too out of touch to lead the Republicans effectively, he realized that it was important not to lose contact with events completely. So he agreed to try to stir up a rebellion once more, this time in far-off but sympathetic Sicily. In 1848 and in 1860 the Sicilians had been at the forefront of revolt, which was understandably focused on getting rid of their own rulers, the Bourbon royal family in Naples. Although there had been much bad blood between the Sicilians and the Neapolitans, they were not overly pleased with their new lords and masters in Turin either. The Sicilians had played a vital role in the battle for unification, bravely supporting Garibaldi, but to be subsumed in a kingdom that proved even more ineffective and more remote than the Bourbons was galling, to say the least. Mazzini, tempted by the idea that an uprising in Palermo might be the last chance to ignite the bush fire of spontaneous revolution that he always assumed was the key to his radical republic, travelled through Tuscany, apparently incognito, made his way to Naples, again apparently unrecognized, and then took a steamer from Naples to Palermo. But by now his arrival was expected. He had been betrayed, and was arrested, for the first time in over forty years, before ever setting foot on Sicilian soil.

The Italian government hurriedly met and decided to imprison Mazzini in the fortress at Gaeta. Mazzini was surprised that neither Palermo nor Messina rose up in revolt, but then his judgement had always erred on the romantic side. Confined to the castle, Mazzini pined for his books and human company. He wrote almost soulfully of the beauty of the night sky, which reminded him of the last time he was in prison in Savona back in 1830. (He seems to have chosen his prisons well.) The authorities, by all accounts, treated him courteously.

Despite his confinement, Mazzini continued to influence Italian politics, in ways he probably never fully realized. The King of Italy, the former Sardinian king, Vittorio Emmanuele, was a loose cannon. He had been making irresponsible commitments of military assistance to the

French in their war against the Prussians and was forced by the government to retract them, which was just as well, for Louis Napoleon was soundly beaten and lost both the war and his empire.

After intense pressure from his government, King Vittorio Emmanuele was forced to agree to invade what remained of the Papal States. And so, with Mazzini in prison and Garibaldi under heavy guard in Caprera, Rome was finally conquered and became the capital city of Italy. But it was a kingdom, and not the republic that Mazzini had dreamed of.

Wednesday. Market day in Gaeta. The market flows along the narrow streets, filling up every nook and cranny, for old Gaeta has little space for covered markets and barely enough for the slightest piazza. A little way along sat an old lady, gossiping away with her daughter, and on her stand lay a fantastic, chaotic collection of bottles and jars that drew me, helpless, into her tender clutches. Bottles poked out of blue, flimsy plastic bags, the ones that cut your hand so fiercely when laden you expect your fingers to be sliced clean off and drop straight into the *salsiccia*.

She seemed my type of girl. Wise. Plucky. Late seventies. I always feel the need to sit down for hours and days and suck these people dry of all their wisdom and knowledge, emerging like an enlightened zealot, as one of *them*.

'*Buon giorno*. Look at this!' She beckoned me over. She could see I was seriously nosy, and pulled out a bag, with a magician's swoop, from beneath the stand. '*Olivi di Gaeta!*'

Gaeta olives. I knew they were famous. You often see them in the finest food shops of Italy. Recipes called for them. But what, I wanted to know, made an olive from Gaeta any different from any other? There is always a story, always a reason why this is better than that. Why this place makes their food tastier than elsewhere.

'Go on. *Provalo!*' Try one.

And the olive story went like this. The Gaetan olive is neither black nor green but a vinous purple, smallish and intensely flavoured. The key is in the cure. First, she told me, the real ones, the best, are always picked by hand and soaked in fresh water – spring water is best, of course. They are left luxuriating in their cool bath just as the winter begins in November. And then they are packed into barrels of brine, where they begin to take on their purple hue and a mild bitterness, which is why they are so good when used judiciously, the bitter going with the sweet, a fundamental and ancient combination that characterizes Gaetan cooking. With octopus in a salad, on pizzas (we are within easy reach of Naples here), in salads, *torte* and *tielle*. I bought a kilo.

'Look at this!' she said.

A jar of thick luscious home-made *passata*. Put it on the tab, baby!

'And do you like olive oil?'

Do I like olive oil? I could bathe in it. I could drown in it.

'Wait!' And off she scuttled, past a lady selling goat's cheese who was beginning to look at me with a sniffer dog's interest. And back she came with two plastic mineral-water bottles full of intense, urine-yellow liquid.

'Put it in a glass jar when you get home,' she told me. She never asked whether I wanted to buy it. I guess it was all too obvious I did. All from her farm, she told me. And even if she was a complete swindler and lived in a sordid apartment in Naples, I cared little, and bought them both. It was olive oil. Extra virgin.

'*Signore! Signore!* Do you like cheese?'

Another question that needed only a slight movement in response to crank up the smile, the charm and the chat.

'Taste this!' A delicate, virginally white goat's cheese. Which of course I did. And of course I bought some.

And a melon, wrapped neatly in string, another speciality of the area. And some tomatoes of studied imperfection, gnarled and anarchically shaped, the sort of tomato that would give any supermarket buyer apoplexy.

All markets have a momentum of their own. Some are dull and unfriendly, too busy to be properly sociable. Others are full of weird and wonderful stalls, of cheeses, wild mushrooms, fish and this and that, things to eat that taste so fine and become so real that were once but remote words found in a recipe book. Gaeta was just right: small, friendly and full of wise women prepared to teach me more, more!

Happily burdened, I remembered one of the reasons I was here in the first place. Let me explain. There is this word *tiella*, which means nothing more than *teglia* in dialect. Which in English is a baking dish. Nothing particularly alarming there, but it reminded me of Sète in the South of France where I used to go to buy tuna, fresh, huge bluefin to sell to the Japanese. This was always, without fail, one of the most trying, tense and challenging things I ever did. Tuna has to be exactly right on so many counts that the Japanese usually trust only themselves to buy it, sending buyers around the world to monitor the catch, the packing, the colour, the fat content, even the way the fish have been killed – everything has to be perfect for the fish to be deemed suitable for the highly prized sashimi market. Occasionally I was honoured and allowed to buy on their behalf. The honour didn't count for much, for if you slipped up they would refuse to take the fish, which turned the blood as cold as the dead tuna.

The fish arrived every year in March, and when they began to disappear again the people of Sète turned to tourism, and a little light sardine fishing. In the evening, after the fishing boats had landed and the tuna had been packed onto the vast dripping trucks plying the night routes to Paris and Barcelona, I would relax a little, make a call or two and walk along the canals of Sète, stopping off at the stalls that sold piles of oysters from nearby Bouzigue, iodine-rich edible sponges called *violets* that you can eat raw, their flesh as brilliantly yellow as scrambled eggs, and the odd sea urchin. But best of all was the little stall that sold *tielles*. They sat in piles, freshly made, a pie with a crenellated edge, full of octopus, olives, tomatoes and a touch of chilli. I never ever saw them anywhere in France but Sète. I grew so fond of them that I asked one of my suppliers to send me a box every week, which he did for a while, but since no one else I worked with liked octopus, and since they never tasted the same in London, I gave it up, and just dreamt occasionally of Sète and its *tielles*.

So I was intrigued to see that Gaeta has its own *tielle*. In fact, the *tiella gaetana* is famous. So where, I asked my wise old ladies, was the best place to find one? And what, anyway, was a *tiella*?

This started a conversation that span like a vortex around the market as more and more people passed by, chipped in their own words of wisdom and then drifted off again. Someone dared to suggest a nearby pizzeria.

'No, no,' said someone else. 'They don't know how to make a proper *tiella*. They're from Naples!'

The ignorance of distant strangers, I thought. Naples is only thirty kilometres away.

'I know,' said someone who had joined this happy Gaetan quest. 'Try the Chinappi. Go up the Corso Cavour. It's just off to the right.'

So I trudged up the road like a greedy bag lady with my olives, my cheese, my tomatoes and my bottles dangling from my limbs, and found the Forno Chinappi. I asked whether they had any *tiella*. It would have been a good idea to look around first, for there were piles of *tielle* here, and everyone in the queue was after one. And the very same everyone looked at me as if I had asked the dumbest question of all time. Smile through it, I thought. Smile through it.

A serious, professorial face looked at me. 'Yes, sir, we do have *tiella*. We have . . .' And he reeled off a list, and pointed out the piles of neat, freshly baked *tielle*, all with that crenellated edge, all covered, and almost all with a combination of sweet and bitter. *Scarole* and pine nuts. Octopus and olives. Courgettes and cheese. It seemed as plain as day to me that the Gaetan *tiella* was the *mamma* or even the *nonna* of the *tielle* I had once known in Sète, which fitted, for I knew that among the fishermen who worked there were families that had come from Campania generations ago. That's my theory anyway.

Tiella

As adaptable as pizza. Once you've mastered the principles, you can be as inventive as you like. You line a round baking tray with dough, fill it with a filling, cover with a second layer and bake it. The filling is often sweet–sour – octopus with pine nuts and raisins, or scarole *and baccalà, for example – and always contains olives, Gaetan for preference, olive oil, garlic, chilli and tomatoes. This recipe is adapted from* Sapori del Lazio, *by Carla Bardi (Idealibri 2000).*

FOR THE DOUGH

20g fresh yeast or 7g dried or use a piece of old bread
dough as starter
water
350g plain white flour, plus 20g type 00 flour
dash of olive oil
salt

Prepare the dough as for bread, kneading it in a machine or by hand until elastic. Let it rise for at least an hour then knock back and let it rise once more until it has doubled in volume. Knock back again then divide into two and roll into rounds. Use one circle to line a round baking tray (about 25cm). Add the filling (see below for an example) then cover with the remaining circle, linking the two with a series of crenellations around the edge.

FILLING FOR OCTOPUS *TIELLA*

400g fresh or frozen and thawed Mediterranean octopus
2 garlic cloves, chopped
4 tomatoes, skinned and chopped
1 chilli, chopped
150ml extra virgin olive oil, more if needed
1 tablespoon pine nuts
1 tablespoon sultanas
200g Gaeta or black olives
1 teaspoon capers

Heat the oven to 200°C. Chop the octopus into chunks a couple of centimetres thick. Over a moderate heat, fry the garlic, tomatoes and chilli in the olive oil for 5 minutes. Add the octopus, pine nuts, sultanas, olives and capers and cook for 5 minutes. Spread over the dough base, cover with the second circle of dough and bake for 30 minutes or until golden on top.

For culinary closure, you should know that over on the other side of the Italian coast in both the Abruzzo and Puglia a *tiella* has become something else again. Although the word still means dish, the Pugliese version has fish cooked with potatoes or potatoes layered with tomatoes and vegetables, then baked. As for me, I'm looking south, and off down the coast to the city of my dreams, Naples.

People's jaws clench when you say the word. Cabriolets automatically close their tops as they cruise past the city walls. Naples has an awesome reputation, and although I want to write 'It wasn't always so' and go on to relay tales of Neapolitan calm and organization, history seems to tell another story. The essence of Naples is the adrenalin rush you get as you enter the city, the crowds, the noise. I think I love Naples, but I don't know Naples. Maybe I like the idea of Naples more than the reality. Give me twenty years and I'll tell you. It is almost impossible to get to grips with anything but the most superficial layer of a city so deeply tiered, so forgive me if I confine myself to something I know I can handle. I set myself a gastronomic challenge. I wanted to eat without sitting down. Street food, that is. Pizza, of course. And yes, I know I could have stayed in England and found one in any village store, or even made one at home. But this was Naples. The home of the perfect pizza.

O HOW I love Naples, so frolic, and gay,
Its skies are so bright, so delightful its bay;
The folk as they chatter impatiently prance,
And seem as if seiz'd with St Vitus's dance.
E'en the poor Lazzaroni *are courtly and nice,*
As they quaff a cool cup of their snow flavour'd ice:
They bask in the sun, love their ease, and their jokes,
And tho' they pick pockets are good sort of folks.
Like Venus, the Ladies so charmingly smile,
Or as Eve, when she meant Caro Spo' to beguile;
How voluptuous the motions, bewitching the air,
Of the sweet Neopolitan languishing fair;
The breezes sulphureous, they panting inspire,
Like matches of brimstone, each spark gives them fire;
While a currency dear, they add to their charms,
By shifting each night to a new lover's arms.
E Molti Averne, *they tenderly say,*
Choose one *out of many, for amorous play;*
But this rigid maxim, discreetly they soften,

By Cangiar Spesso, *that's change very often:*
Hence Cupid, they say, is still painted with wings,
And Constancy's no where, as METESTAS sings.

John Courtney, 1738–1816

Even on a cursory visit Naples seems anarchic. As I stepped out of the station, I heard strange foreign tongues, neither Italian nor Neapolitan but something with a distinct eastern trill. Polish? Ukrainian? Both. Around the corner were minibuses and coaches arriving with exhausted travellers, not holidaymakers but workers, many off to look after the elderly relations of busy Euro Italians who would once themselves have kept granny fed and watered as she slipped into senility.

And then there are the Africans. You can buy the latest Senegalese videos with ease in Naples. Cool African men sell shades and hats at street stalls, but Italy has found a more sordid occupation for some of the women. I've seen their miserable faces, dolled up with nowhere to go, from the dusty north to the dusky south. The Italians, for so long the émigrés, now have to find ways to adjust to their immigrés. It is not easy. Like all the European countries, Italy is saddled with generations of ignorance and a paranoid fear of the stranger. The Italian birth rate is one of the lowest in Europe and the country needs its immigrants if it is to continue to grow and prosper. One day, maybe we will learn to be interested in difference, stimulated by it and not so fearful. Pigs might fly . . .

Naples is truly the home of the world's most sublime pizza. No endless combinations of sun-dried tomatoes and lamb's tongues here. No miserable commercial dough need touch your lips. A mere skip from the railway station is a pizzeria so popular that you can wait for hours outside only to discover that you should have taken a ticket. This is Da Michele, snuck in a little gastronomic triangle where you can, if not on a mission to test the strength of your legs, sit down and eat in a perfectly acceptable pizzeria just opposite. If you are in town on a Saturday night, hurry on down, bring as many people as you can and join the other few hundred waiting with you. It is an event to mill among this ordered and enthusiastic crowd, where no one appears to glower or be drunk and there is no sense of threat in the air.

Inside, Da Michele has an air of 1950s minimalism, paper tablecloths, marble tables and a constant throng, but get there early and you might almost detect a sense of calm. The menu is so simple it makes me want to cry. There are two pizzas: the Margherita and the Marinara. And a *calzone*. And that's it.

It is said that the Romans were fond of a proto-pizza they called *picea*, which was like a *pizza bianca*, baked dough with a few herbs and a dribble of olive oil on top. But pizza's popularity stems from the days when it was hawked in the streets of Naples, carried around on the pizza-seller's head in a metal stove called a *stufa*. The first customers of the day would be the sailors and fishermen arriving back in the early hours from a hard night's sailing or fishing. They preferred the simplest, purest and cheapest of all pizzas: garlic, tomatoes, oregano and olive oil, which became known as the Pizza Marinara.

Although pizza was always popular among the poor, it wasn't exclusively so. King Ferdinand II liked the pizza he ate at 'Ntuono Testa at Salita Santa Teresa so much that he had a pizza oven built in his own kitchens. You can just imagine the old king settling down to a pizza in front of the TV with a few beers. And in 1889, when Princess Margherita of Savoy tried and liked the pizza created for her by Pizzeria Brandi's Raffaele Esposito, the pizza was elevated to new heights of popularity and prestige. Hence Pizza Margherita, which we all know and maybe even love for when cooked well it is quite the best: tomatoes, mozzarella or *fior di latte* (mozzarella made with cow's milk, of which more anon), a few leaves of basil and some olive oil, a patriotic combination of red, white and green. When the princess asked what her pizza was called, Signor Esposito tactfully replied, 'Margherita, your highness.'

While you are munching on your pizza in Naples, you will no doubt feel elation at reaching the pearly pizza gates and relish your moment of grace. Your consumption might be brief, but the process of making the pizza is not, or should not be, and involves more than the few minutes the pizza fizzes and bubbles on the volcanically hot stone floor of the wood-burning oven, watched over by the *pizzaiola*. Pizza might be, alongside its greasy cousin the hamburger, at the very core of fast food, but there is more than a little art involved in making it.

There is in Naples real concern at the global bastard-ization of the pizza, their pizza, and a sense that they must preserve the purity of the *verace pizza napolitana*. Slow Food is there, of course, helping things along, fighting the fight against all the crap in the world that is called pizza, and it has helped set the rules that govern how and when a Real Neapolitan Pizza can be called a Real Neapolitan Pizza.

We start with dough. Slow dough. I am as guilty as the next amateur breadmaker of using easy packet yeast, among whose little granules are quickening agents and enhancers. Not what the purists call for at all. If slowly risen dough provides taste, the golden key to good food, the purest and tastiest of all is the one that rises using a chunk of yesterday's dough as a starter. This is how they make pizza at Da Michele, by the way. The process is cyclical and can be eternal, with every day's dough having its own character, changing infinitesimally with the weather, the flour and even the water. The flour itself might come from far away. The Italians are quite realistic in accepting that the best bread flour doesn't have to come from Italy, and many prefer the gluten-rich Manitoba flour from Canada. The tomatoes next. These should be San Marzano. Canned ones are perfectly suitable. As to whether any mozzarella used should be buffalo or not, I may diverge from the *purissimi* and say that bovine *fior di latte* seems quite acceptable, to me anyway. But one thing you really do need is a wood-burning oven, a *forno a legna*, for it is only this that can cook the pizza at a searingly high 500°C or so, and give a slightly smoky edge to the whole, delicious bubbling thing that sits before you.

The stars and the megastars of the pizza world, Da Michele, Brandi et al., are constantly busy. It must be exhausting working there. But I finally lost my pizza heart to a smaller, more manageable pizzeria along the Via dei Tribunali, a street that seemed to my English eyes to be exactly how Naples should be. Shops selling figures for the *presepi* at Christmas time. Bakers, butchers, fishmongers. There's the entrance to *Napoli sotterraneo*, where you can voyage deep into the ancient guts of Naples and take a tour in the underground cisterns and caves that were both used as churches and supplied the city with water channelled in from the hills. This I did one evening as the sun was setting. Then I stopped at a little pizzeria, the Pizzeria del Presidente I think it was called, and ordered my farewell Margherita. In less than three minutes it was handed over with a smile, and I ate it with an even bigger one. It was very very very good.

You cannot fail to notice that Neapolitans like hanging around outside, ogling, chatting – well, more accurately shouting at each other – gesticulating continually in a way that is pure *napulitano*. Walk through the older parts of the city and you'll begin to see why, with the houses packed so closely together, many stretching up five or six storeys. Life was much more amenable in the cooler air outside, especially during the hour of the *passeggiata* in the early evening. And then there is this tradition of the underclass, the infamous *lazzaroni*, many of whom lived on the streets and were the forefathers of today's street culture. Of course they had to eat, and in the late nineteenth century a whole variety of street food could be bought for under four soldi, the crucial limit to what was considered affordable.

So they ate bowls full of spaghetti covered with cheese and tomato sauce, craning their necks skyward and stuffing their mouths with the long strands. Some street-sellers specialized in soups, such as snail soup and *minestra maritata*, which would be poured over a thick slice of bread. Others specialized in fried foods, bits of pig, or fish fresh from the sea. Yet others sold *scapece* – fried courgette – and aubergine mixed with tomatoes, garlic and oil, served with cheese and a little vinegar. There were the coffee-sellers, the *granita*-sellers – just about everything that was needed could be bought for very little. Naples learnt to love the streetlife that is still so much a part of that magnificent, vibrant city.

COMACCHIO

IF WE HUMANS THINK SEX TO BE A COMPLICATED BUSINESS, pity the poor eel. Come hell or high water, this primeval teleost has an urge to reproduce of such persistence it puts the most hardened Lothario to shame. Eels slither over walls and through endless miles of swamp before undertaking a transoceanic super-swimathon that simply staggers the mind, all in the name of reproduction, the sacred act of eel jigginess. For European eels have retained an urge to reproduce in an obscure and distant corner of the world, the Sargasso Sea in the far-off Western Atlantic, a mysterious, becalmed patch of seaweed-rich ocean dreaded in ancient days by sailors but beloved of eels.

Our story takes us to the bleak north-east of Italy, to the biting cold fog of the Po delta and a *città* called Comacchio whose very foundations are steeped in the fish slime of the European eel, *Anguilla anguilla*. This is the Romagna, where squat Romagnoli speak their own, rather squat dialect. '*Va be'*,' they say to each other by way of greeting. Comacchio's roots are ancient. The settlement grew from little more than an earthy prehistoric mound in a vast freshwater lagoon into a city that modelled itself on its very unsupportive northern neighbour Venice, passing through an Etruscan moment on the way. Canals run through Comacchio's centre, and it has two fine sixteenth-century bell towers and a glorious three-pronged bridge, but otherwise very little of the magnificence you will see in La Serenissima. What marks Comacchio is the lagoon, an immense, mysterious aquatic plain they call the Valli, rich in fish and exquisite migratory birds. Exotic flamingos now pass by in increasing numbers, but, although it has a certain magic, surviving here was never easy. If the word 'lagoon' suggests Polynesian warmth and happiness to you, visit Comacchio in winter and your fantasies will for ever be dispelled. This is where cold meets misery in the name of the eel.

These days Comacchio's city walls are no longer surrounded by water as they once were. Where now you see endless lines of apples and pears and a land tilled and fertile stretching to the horizon, was once water. The fields are dotted with the odd tractor spewing insecticide, but little else. I've been to Comacchio three times, and thrice it rained, and thrice the wind blew with an icy thoroughness. The streets of Comacchio, dripped onto from every ancient gutter, were empty but for the odd car that splashed by, driven, you half expected, by a foul-breathed creature from the black lagoon. Open any bar door and fierce Romagnoli, in ankle-deep water, eels slithering around the tables, looked at you.

This part of the Romagna is famous for its *scarriolanti*, the canal-diggers, Romagnol radicals who were among the many to be systematically attacked and even murdered by the Fascists in the 1920s. Their skills were handed down through generations: many of their ancestors had been employed by the Venetians and the powerful Estense family of Ferrara, and Mussolini happily shipped them off to help drain the Pontine Marshes south of Rome and the infamous marshes on Sardinia from which sprang Mussolinia (of which more later).

The eel is a catadromous fish, which means that for most of its life it lives in fresh water. At about eight years old the eel begins to change colour from yellow to silver and eats prodigiously to fatten itself for the long journey to the Sargasso, where it will spawn and then die in a miasmic final moment of eel love. The annual migration, when fat silver eels turn seaward, begins just as the weather is at its very worst: from November on to the end of December, with a second flush in February.

The Comacchiesi, knowing a thing or two about eels, built a series of intricate, rather beautiful fish traps called *lavorieri* where the natural breaches occurred and sea water flowed inwards to the lagoon, warm and bubblingly full of oxygen. Some are still used to this day. The eels, sensing the salt water seeping through, tried to escape, destination Love, but were confronted by these arrow-shaped traps made of tightly bound reeds – the *grisol* that still grow around the lagoon. The *lavoriero* was a masterly creation and provided a remarkably ecologically sound method of fishing. Not only was it completely degradable – no piles of plastic nets and traps litter the historical mire at Comacchio – but each spring they were opened up to let through the elvers arriving from the distant Sargasso, driven by the incomprehensible force of instinct back to their parental lagoon. And in too came the mullet, the bass and the silverside to give the Comacchiesi a little more than just eel to eat and a chance for the lagoon to maintain its biodiversity.

The fish caught in the first section of the trap were funnelled into the mouth, the *bocca di ceno*, hauled out and dealt with, but the eel, tougher than the other species, would wriggle on further, jamming its slithery tail into the barrier and forcing itself through, still drawn by the salty

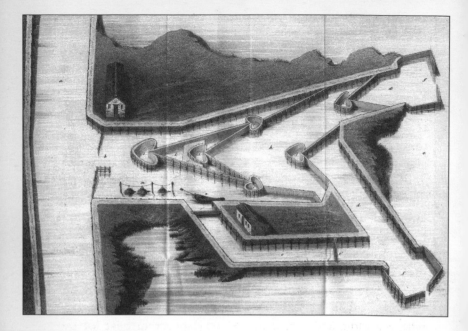

A fish trap or lavoriero, *through which the eight-year-old eels would try to escape into the open sea, heading for the Sargasso.*

tang that filtered through the mesh. The trap had a second, higher barrier to funnel the fish, now eels alone apart from the odd mutant Houdini from another species, into the *otela di testa*, the final Colditzian cell from which even eels could not escape. And so they awaited their fate, ready to be hauled out and placed into huge withy containers called *bolaghe* which floated just under the surface like icebergs, their small mouths on top and their round cavernous underbellies full of wriggling eels. Prime eel time coincides with the full moon, and work had to be carried out not just in the freezing cold but in silence so as not to scare away the eels that swam towards the traps.

An excellent way to think eel is to spend the morning at the Museo di Valli di Comacchio, which can draw in a thrumming mass of tourists in the summer, trying to find something slightly more interesting than posing on the *lidi* along the coast. If you have an hour to spare, you can take a boat trip and visit the traps and the *casoni*, the houses where the eel workers stayed during the fishing season. In termtime you are likely to be in the company of coachloads of Italian schoolkids and the occasional, rather tense teacher trying to keep them in control. These proto-preeners are quite diverting. You can see that they have already learnt to talk on mobile phones, flirt and develop a dress sense. I shied away from a trip that consisted entirely of schoolchildren and opted for the deeper stimulation of a group of Finnish birdwatchers, as morose and motley a group as I have ever seen, who rose excitedly only once when a flock of flamingos flew by. Eels never quite got them going.

The few *casoni* that have survived the rigours of time are bare-bricked and slightly spartan. Each had a wide fireplace with a griddle and a hearth, the only source of heat for the *famiglia*, a working team of twelve or so who worked and lived in the *casone* for the season. The hierarchy went something like this. At the head, with the biggest bed *and* his own room, was the boss, the *caporione*. Under him the *sotto caporione*, then the scribe, moving down to the odd *ragazzo* and, the lowest of the low, the *sotto ragazzi*, whose duties can barely be imagined. The scribe recorded the catch and in his spare moments wrote endless poems eulogizing eels. No one was allowed to leave the *casone* except on urgent business.

With both men and eels firmly under control, the administration, the eel-masters and rule-makers in Comacchio, would then decree their fate. The eels remained blissfully unaware that there were ideas for their final moments that involved something rather less enjoyable than the *petite mort* they were dreaming of, while the men and women were allocated jobs according to their skills. The choice wasn't that great. The first option was to sell the eels alive, and to make this easier the ever-resourceful Comacchiesi invented a rather impressive underwater boat or *marotta* that allowed water to flow over the eels to prevent them expiring in transit. Long lines of *marotte* would be towed northwards to feed the hungry citizens of Venice.

The Comacchiesi were rather keener on a second option, which gave the city a little more work and kept the community just out of absolute poverty. This was to make *anguilla marinata*, marinated eels, which to this day remain one of Comacchio's great specialities. This too was a highly controlled business. One man had the stimulating job of eel-executioner, grabbing his unwilling victims, placing them on a block and mercilessly severing eel from head with a machete the long day through. Tradition had it that the eels now be left alone until all twitching had well and truly ceased, for the locals said that no good would come of eating an eel that twitched. Most of the post-death work was done either back in Comacchio or in some of the larger *casoni* on the lagoon. One person would spend the season as an eel-spiker, endlessly bending chunks of the eel's body onto a long spit for roasting. As the spits, standing some two to three metres high, slowly rotated in front of the fire, the dripping eel fat was caught in a narrow tray at the bottom and used to fry the *acquadella*, the tiny silversides that once swam in huge numbers in the lagoon. When the eels had cooled a little they were packed tightly into wooden barrels, covered with a vinegary marinade, sealed and marked with coded letters on the side. Even this called for some skill, particularly when they were packed in olive oil, which once cost more than the eels.

Each worker received an allowance of eels to eat, the *ciberaria*, which used to feed the family when the eel season was over. But the administration discouraged the eating of anything but the scrawniest of eels or, on days of real

Preparing anguilla marinata: *one man would cut off the eel's head, another would bend its body onto a long spit, and a woman would turn the spit.*

extravagance, leftover heads. This fondness for eel bits and pieces has stayed in Comacchio's culinary consciousness and they still prefer to use heads in the *brodetto*, a 'little broth', and even make an eel-head risotto. More distinctive still is the eel salami that was once made by carefully skinning the fish, refilling the skin with odd leftover bits of eel and drying it to be stored and used through the year. Some elder Comacchiesi still hanker after eel innards stew, made from the carefully washed guts of the larger eels after draining them of any blood, which they believed to be toxic.

But even if the diet in the *casoni* was restricted, there were moments when the workers would settle down in front of the fire and cook what is their simplest and perhaps finest way of serving eel: *anguilla ai ferri*, wood-roasted, served piping hot with a good slice of polenta and a glass of Eliceo di Bosco wine. So when you see the stalls and restaurants around the lagoons serving *pesce ai ferri*, think back to those frozen souls who once spent their lives living and loving for *Anguilla anguilla*.

Comacchio was once attached to the Byzantine exarchate in Ravenna but lapsed, like Ravenna itself, into the arms of the Pontificate, almost despite itself and for the lack of any other takers. Romagnols had a reputation for independence of spirit, and never felt any real attachment to the Pontificate, preserving their distance, and their radicalism. When Napoleon came along in 1796 and started his brief rule over Italy, he recognized this and allowed the Comacchiesi to have more say in their affairs than they had ever enjoyed before. But when he was defeated and hurried off to breathe the sea air of Elba, and later when the ruling powers sat down and carved up Europe at the Congress of Vienna in 1815, Romagna slipped back under the control of a conservative and repressive papacy. The Comacchiesi had cherished their brief moment of relative liberty and were uneasy at the prospect of being subsumed into the Papal States once again. They decided to send a delegation to the Congress to offer some of their finest eels to Prince Metternich. Although the story has a touch of the apocryphal about it, I like the idea that this staid, stuffy Austrian was so moved by the gift of a barrel of eels that he agreed that the community of Comacchio could finally look after their own eels.

Eels are, of course, not unique to the lagoons of Comacchio. Wartime London was full of cheerful Cockneys eating jellied eels and laughing endlessly into their pie and liquor while bombs dropped around them. Earthy French Loirots and Burgundians cook their exquisite eel *matelotes*, but how lucky they are to have red wine to hand rather than jelly. The Dutch, of course, smoke theirs, incorrigible old hippies that they are. In Galicia, elvers are fried in chorizo fat, the pans sizzling enticingly on the riverbanks as the elvers swim upriver. After a mighty three-year ordeal across the ocean I can't help feeling that eels somehow deserve a better end than this.

In England we sometimes call elvers 'glass eels' and once they swam up the river Severn in such profusion in the late winter that they were fished from the river bank and cooked for breakfast, fried and encased in a thick omelette. Sadly, you are unlikely ever to see them, let alone eat them these days, for they have become so horribly expensive that most of the elvers that are caught are now used to restock the continent's eel farms, which have become the prime source of European eels.

You can hardly walk the streets of Comacchio without being seduced by eels in windows, beckoning voluptuously from their tins and jars: grilled eels, smoked eels, marinated eels, fat eels, eels long and short. The whole gamut of eel physiognomy is there. And as you would expect, eel is on menus everywhere. However, only one place in Comacchio was said to do the eel justice: a trattoria called Da Vasco e Giulia. Having 'da' in a restaurant's name is an excellent start in my view, so on yet another damp and windy night in Comacchio I donned my wetsuit and waded out into the dark. The city was deathly quiet. Signs creaked in the wind. The ancient bell tower heaved into action. Amber streetlights added to the sense of gloom, but on I pressed. The last time I had tried to eat here it was well and truly closed, but I am nothing if not persistent. Comacchio is a small place. In fact, to call it a city at all is a technicality; it is by our standards a town, and a small one at that. The 400 metres or so I trudged were nonetheless enough to get me thoroughly wet and pissed off, and I rounded the corner to see Da Vasco e Giulia looking less than welcoming. It didn't look particularly open either. In fact, it was once again firmly closed. You really do need to be on the case as far as closing days are concerned. There must be a sort of logic about them, but at the time it escaped me. However, I guessed that on the next day it just had to be open, and so, a glutton for punishment perhaps, off I went again, for this was the rounding off of my eel story, a continuation of the rounding off of me. And the sun shone as I walked through the door.

'*Buon giorno!*'

I felt that saying I wanted to try some eel was somewhat superfluous as there was little else on the menu, but I asked the owner what there was to eat that day.

'Well, there's . . .' and she smilingly reeled off the dramatis personae of the eel cast. Eel risotto. Eel *brodetto*. Marinated eel. Smoked eel. Grilled eel *ai ferri*. Even salted eel, served with a little rosemary. But what I really wanted was *anguilla con le verze*. Eel and cabbage, but it sounds better in Italian, and it was and is a Comacchiese speciality, an excellent, warming winter dish, best with a bottle of local wine from the sandy spit that runs between the lagoon and the sea: a red Fortana. I'll have the *anguilla con le verze*, please, if I may, oh mighty eel specialist that you are.

'*Anguilla con le verze?* Sorry. We're not doing that today. Why don't you try the *brodetto?*'

With a sullenness only an eel could have understood, I did. A *brodetto* after all is hardly a rarity, an eely broth here in Eelsville. However, I admire authenticity and I asked how this was made.

'In the old days it was made with seagull broth, but now we make it just with eels,' she told me. This had, I was assured, a pungency, a gamey fishiness that is almost impossible to reproduce, but if any spare seagull broth should ever come your way, send me a drop and I would make without hesitation the Comacchiese *brodetto*, a warming, luscious way to savour their great local speciality.

Brodetto alla comacchiese

Serves four. Good with slices of grilled polenta. This recipe is adapted from Comacchio a Tavola *by Luciano Boccaccini and Franco Luciani (Editoriale Olympia 1997).*

3 live eels about 150–200g each
1 onion, cut in slices 5mm thick
150ml olive oil
1 tablespoon white wine vinegar
salt and pepper

Ask your fishmonger to kill the eels and clean them. Cut into pieces 4–5cm long. In a wide pan, fry the onion in the oil until golden. Add the eels, vinegar, seasoning and enough water just to cover the fish. Cook until the fish is done: test by piercing with a fork to see if it is cooked through.

If seagull broth and slithering eels should fail to excite you, there is always the drama of 1850, for Comacchio also has its Risorgimento hat to wear. The story involves our red-shirted hero, Garibaldi, and his gallant and admirable wife, Anita. And if you were to find yourself driving around the lake one day, to get yourself in the mood you could stop by the town named after her.

When Garibaldi left Italy as an exile in 1835, he sailed off to South America, landed in Rio de Janeiro and ended up fighting for the besieged Republic of Uruguay against the Argentinians. He proved to be an inspirational leader and a superb tactician. It was here that the Garibaldi legend began to take shape, and it was here that the famous red shirts came into being when Garibaldi and his troops took possession of a load of shirts destined for the Argentinian abattoir workers, who sensibly preferred blood-red for their working clothes. And on top of all this, in 1839 he fell passionately in love with an equally valiant, fearsome young Brazilian woman called Anita, or more correctly Ana Maria de Jesus Ribeiro da Silva. She was eighteen. Garibaldi was thirty-two. The story is the stuff of Hollywood. They fell in love at first sight, and she, already married, left her drunken slob of a husband for 'José', the hunky captain from Italy. They fought battles together, herded cattle for hundreds of miles across the pampas, and then Garibaldi joined up with the Uruguayans fighting their own battle for independence. In 1847, with two children in tow, Garibaldi, well aware of the revolutionary rumblings in Europe, decided to leave and return to Italy, whence he, like Mazzini, had been banished by the Piemontese authorities. While Garibaldi followed the Republican breeze around Italy, Anita was supposed to stay with his disapproving mother in Nice, but when she heard of the extraordinary events in Rome she hurried to join him and left the children in his mother's care.

As the Republic collapsed under French firepower, Anita and the general fled Rome and began a long and arduous attempt to link up with the Venetian Republic. They marched for weeks, crossing the Apennines, doubling back to try to confuse anyone following them, and eventually managed to take a boat from Cesenatico on the east coast and land on the shore near Comacchio.

By this time Anita was seriously ill. She seemed to have contracted malaria, and became dangerously feverish on this dramatic boat journey. The eel fishermen of Comacchio, who had moved among its endless canals and islets for thousands of years, knew how to evade the Austrians, but those of them who had decided to help Garibaldi were unsure what to do with Anita. Eventually they took her to rest in a hut on the edge of the southern lake at Mandriole, and then on to a farmhouse nearby. 'Take care of the children,' she said, and died in Garibaldi's arms. It was a terrible blow. Garibaldi had to leave her and escape in order to save himself, for the Austrians were closing in. Anita Garibaldi was quickly buried, but in the night wild dogs dug up her corpse and devoured it.

For the next few days Garibaldi continued to evade the Austrians, helped by the gallant Romagnoli. One evening, as he hid in a safe house, he heard local *contadini* talk of the incredible story of Garibaldi's escape and how Anita had died and her body had been bespoiled by animals. Garibaldi could bear it no longer. He pushed open the door and stood before the alarmed *contadini*, tears streaming down his haggard face, but before he could say anything he was pulled back to safety behind the door and hurried away. The Austrians captured many of his colleagues. The great Ugo Bassi, the radical priest, was shot. Ciceruacchio, the wine dealer from the Trastevere who was one of the key instigators of the Roman Republic, was caught and shot with his two sons, one of whom, Luigi, was thought to have killed Rossi on the steps of the assembly. But with luck once more on his side, the general managed to escape, and lived to fight once more for the unification of his country, Italy.

PART TWO
ISLANDS

SARDINIA: I

ALGHERO IS PROUDLY, YOU COULD ALMOST SAY SMUGLY, Catalan. An exquisite, venerable walled city, it is full of houses that would fit happily in the back streets of Barcelona. Indeed, it was called Little Barcelona as long ago as the sixteenth century. It is a marvellous city, full of crumbling dead ends, just small enough to save you from becoming completely demented if you get lost and you trudge repeatedly through the narrow sidestreets. Alghero was once a great place for seaweed-gathering, too. The city's name evolved from Aleguerium to the more mellifluous *Alguer* in Catalan after the huge banks of *algue* that were once washed onto the rocky shores nearby. And in case you think I am deviating unnecessarily, Alghero isn't in Catalonia at all but hundreds of miles away on the north-west coast of Sardinia.

You might get the impression from the number of Catalan flags, the street names and the general enthusiasm for *Catalunya* that Alghero had just been conquered by hordes of Barcelonans on a rampage. But any rampaging happened over six hundred years ago, and yet Alghero has somehow managed to preserve its Catalan identity. Catalan is still spoken – in a very odd form, I am told – though Italian is more likely to be heard on the street. *Catalunya* is fervently supportive of this little linguistic enclave, for it all fits in very nicely with its own political agenda, which states quite simply that anyone who speaks Catalan is Catalan. Given the fact that the language was the target of sustained linguistic genocide under Franco, speaking Catalan is still a very sensitive, and very political, matter.

But in a sense it's all a bit of a historical sham. The reality was that Alghero had already begun to thrive as a mercantile seaport long before the Catalans and their allies the Aragonese came along. In 1354, the Aragonese seized Alghero from the Genovesi and their allies after a year-long siege. Aragon and Catalonia had long had designs on Sicily and Sardinia, and the King of Aragon, Pedro IV, a particularly devious monarch who liked nothing better than intrigue and plotting, handed newly won Alghero over to his allies the Catalans as a reward for their assistance in conquering the island. However, they were to be eternally troubled by this distant fiefdom. But then they didn't exactly foster a spirit of tolerance. Many of the native-born Algheresi were forced to leave the city and settled nearby in the hilltop town of Villanova.

Quite probably unknown to King Pedro, the indigenous Sardinians had developed a system of government that, unusually for the time, was almost democratic. The island had been divided up into four separate kingdoms, then called *mereie*, during its brief rule by the Byzantines in the fifth century, and the system had endured. Over time, the kingdoms became known as *giudicati*. Each *giudicato* had its own monarch, but they ruled in a remarkably liberal way. For example, they didn't actually own their kingdom, and were obliged to refer to an assembly of subjects, the *corona de logu*, on matters of importance. The *giudice* of Arborea was allied to the Dorias of Genoa and became the implacable enemy of the Catalans, causing them and King Pedro a good deal of trouble and strife. It was as a result of this dispute that the Aragonese seized Alghero from the Genovesi in 1354.

These days, as well as all the flags, the *placas* (squares) and the *carreras* (streets), the edible part of Catalan culture also lives on, reflecting a little of the city's complex past. And I, inquisitive and hungry as ever, was keen to step out into this curious living anachronism.

Catalan food is distinct even within Spain, so the idea of Catalan food within Sardinia was especially intriguing. In Alghero, there's a tendency to direct interested gastronomes towards spending enormous amounts of money on *aragosta alla catalana*. The rocky shores and islands that stretch from the north right down to Bosa are an excellent habitat for the local rock lobster *Palinurus elephas*, the said *aragosta*, which were for many years caught relatively harmoniously using lobster traps, *nasses*, made from the reeds that grow around the swampier parts of the coastal belt. But such has been the demand from the mega-wealthy tourists who come to the Costa Smeralda over on the east of the island, where billionaires munch *aragosta* for lunch without batting an eyelid, that the stocks are in danger of collapse.

Nevertheless, Alghero has decided to devote most of the month of May to promoting rock lobsters, a none-too-subtle touristic wheeze. Hopefully not too many people are aware that female lobsters are tastier than the males. And that you can mix the eggs with the lobster's liver to make a sublime form of red rock-lobster caviar. For without these egg-laying females the lobster population would have great difficulty in surviving.

Those with slimmer wallets may prefer to try *agliata*, which, we are told, is typically Catalan. Although the word 'typical' can be an indolent coverall, pulling in unfortunates off the streets in their search for authenticity where no such thing exists, Italian food really does express

itself in a way that most other European countries can only
dream about. Cooking is, after all, as fluid, as immutable
as painting. So *agliata* can be many things to many Italians,
although all versions share the use of garlic: *aglio*. To the
Piemontesi it is a sauce made from garlic, walnuts, lard and
breadcrumbs, which is often spread on bread or served with
tagliatelle. The Ligurians call it *aggiada* and add vinegar, and
might even use ground-up ship's biscuits – *galettes* – instead
of breadcrumbs, and you can't get much more Ligurian than
that. But by the time it gets down to Sardinia it has changed
again. Here it tends to be red for a start – tomatoes and garlic
form the base – but it is still used as a sauce, mostly for fish,
and is also served cold as a starter. The sea is inevitably much
more a part of the Alghero diet than the land.

One evening, desperately seeking Catalonia, I set off
into the setting sun looking for a restaurant called La
Nuvola, which I was told could be found just off the Capo
Caccia road. It seemed a happy sort of place, even if it was
happy in slightly dismal clothing. A lovely terrace, a few
tied-up, madly barking goats. And happy smiling people.
Looking forward to a laid-back, relaxing dinner *à un* on the
terrace, I was surprised to be bundled into an empty room
at the back. This apparently was the restaurant, stuffy,
enclosed and rather tacky. What a fool I had been to expect
to eat on the lovely terrace with its view down to the sea.

Empty but for a single German man, reading a book.
The scenario tempted me. Should I go and sit next to him,
and invade his psychological space? Well, of course, I
didn't. I'm English, after all, and well versed in the art of
avoiding eye contact. We have only fairly recently
managed to get into the idea of social kissing and hand-
shaking, and saying good morning. It made me wonder
whether we all have the same notion of private space anyway. I suspect not. Once, when I was eating a pile of fried
squid rings in Crete as the sun was setting and the
bouzouki were wailing, a German woman came up to me,

in a manner I thought to be utterly shameless, and asked whether she might sit next to me. And the awful thing was that I said no. Well, there were empty tables around! Italy made me a little less anal. There are busy *trattorie* in Italian cities in particular where you simply have to sit next to complete strangers or you won't get anything to eat at all. There the choice is far simpler. But before you cry miserable bastard, may I defend the practice of eating solo for a moment? Just think, no embarrassing children vomiting or throwing Barbies at each other. No need to try to interpret the true meaning behind your companion's every word and gesture. You can look as bored as you like and no one will care a jot. But this was my first ever evening in Catalan Sardinia and I was really looking forward to a lengthy menu browse, and being very relaxed about everything I simply sprawled and waited.

I think I waited about fifteen minutes – NB, restaurant owners, not generally a good idea with solitary middle-aged men keen on their food. I picked frantically at the bread – flat crispy *pane carasau* – and the fat luscious olives. I was keen to get my order in before closing. The waitress was so fabulously charming and so fabulously beautiful, however, that all was forgiven when my telepathic requests were duly answered and with a smile, and not a touch of why-is-this-stupid-Englishman-fidgeting-so, she took my order. I plumped for *agliata* of octopus, followed by pasta with a donkey sauce. Both things are hard to come by in Penge.

Polpo con l'agliata

Serves six.

1.2kg fresh or thawed frozen Mediterranean octopus
20g sun-dried tomatoes, finely chopped

2 cloves garlic, chopped
1 chilli, chopped
200ml olive oil
salt and pepper
200ml water
1 tablespoon white wine vinegar

If the octopus is fresh, boil it in salted water for 25 minutes. Cool, then chop into 2cm chunks. If frozen and thawed, just cut into chunks and heat through.

Make a *soffrito*: cook the dried tomatoes, garlic and chilli in the olive oil for 5 minutes over moderate heat. Season with salt (unless the tomatoes are from Italy and are already salted) and pepper. Add the water and cook for 10 minutes over a moderate heat. Add the vinegar, increase the heat and allow it to evaporate. Pour this over the octopus and serve warm.

The octopus is renowned for being a clever creature, technically a mollusc, but sadly its brilliance hasn't got it very far, for it is patently not yet up to fooling the world's fishermen into thinking that it no longer exists. And living fairly close to the rocky coast it provides the Mediterranean's fishing community with a particularly easy catch. If you do rush off to buy some octopus, grasp a tentacle and check that it has at least two rows of suckers. For these are far tastier and more tender, even if frozen, than the rather smaller North Atlantic octopi which have only one row of suckers. Alas the poor genius of the sea, for when the octopus is caught it can suffer a fairly un- dignified end. I remember coming across a fisherman in Sicily who twirled a small live octopus around his wrist, using it in the same way that Greeks twiddle their worry beads and priests their rosaries (and small boys their willies), talking and fiddling at the same time, while the octopus desperately tried to get back into the sea. He even let me have a twiddle. Cold and slimy, it slithered along my arm, its tentacles doing their best to get into my armpit. It's fine when you see an octopus gyrating on someone else's arm, but on my own it was far too un-controllable and Venusian a feeling, especially since I knew that an octopus can bite and that this one had every right to bite as freely as it liked.

The fisherman eyed me scathingly. Here I was doing the very thing that drives me up the wall, like the people who walk into a fish market and pucker their faces and say, 'Eughh – stinks. Errr – look at that.' I handed back the doomed octopus. He picked it up and appeared to kiss it, upon which the beast fell limply into the bottom of the boat. He had bitten it quickly through the nerves in the back of its head, still chatting away while he did so. A cold kiss of death.

For the cook though, there is the small but necessary matter of tenderizing the octopus. This involves somebody beating it endlessly against a rock; the Greeks are said to recommend doing this at least a hundred times. You can be fairly certain that while you sit and read with the cool Mediterranean lapping at your feet, somewhere close by a not-so-cool Mediterranean will be fiercely pummelling a dead octopus against a rocky shoreline, watched by a host of salivating locals, sipping wine, laughing and smoking coarse cigarettes. Your octopus will then be ready for cooking. Needless to say, this is seen as neither revolting nor brutal in the Mediterranean, but will no doubt anguish many in the cold and hypocritical north. Far better to munch on chicken nuggets, lovingly produced from chickens raised in conditions of pure happiness.

In an age when many like their food to be as bland and soft as possible to avoid any use of teeth, you could say that octopus isn't quite of the moment. You really do need teeth. When I was writing the *Fish* book way back in the last century, the one thing that the photographer – noble, dedicated and experienced as she was – had real difficulty with was the dish of stewed octopus that needed to be cooked for three hours or so. Her house began to stink, so she said, like a Greek fisherman's crotch and the smell lingered for days. *Tant pis.* This is wimpish talk, frankly. I am of the opinion that octopus is quite one of the most exquisite things to come from the sea, and the Sardinian Catalans have found a brilliant way to marry its marvellous sweetness with a touch of sourness. And, yes, with the rubberiness as well. *Ecco. L'agliata.*

The very best *agliata* I ate was further down the coast in Bosa, where the dogfish – look for either *gattucio* or *gattopardo*, estimable fish and oh-so-underrated in Britain where its name hardly promotes the idea of excellence – is a perfect foil. As is skate, by the way. Bosa is well worth a detour. Treat yourself one day to a lingering lunch in Alghero, and take the coast road down to Bosa as the sun is setting. This may be a long and winding road but it is intensely beautiful. So desperate was I to live here, on this wild and remote part of the island, that I drove it twice in three days, each time sighing endlessly, eating freshly picked cherries from the market in Alghero.

On my first trip down, I gave a lift to a soldier who was so beautiful with his voluptuous chocolate eyes that he made everything seem ridiculously lovely. Even the laybys seemed perfect. Bosa had changed in the fifteen years since I was there last, so much so that I didn't remember I had been there before until I saw the river, for Bosa is fairly unusual in parched Sardinia for having a river at all. On the far side, the Bosan equivalent of the Left Bank, I guess, is a thin row of dilapidated fish warehouses where once the rock lobster trade thrived. No more. A supermarket thrives instead but I did see someone weaving a reed fish trap (a *nassa*) in a riverside bar, made to a venerable design that can be seen, though in ever-diminishing numbers, all around the Mediterranean.

But, after the simplicity of the *agliata*, it was time to challenge another culinary taboo. It was time to eat some donkey. Eating donkey isn't, of course, a purely Sardinian thing. The logic is quite clear. Friendly beast of burden begins to falter. Family reflects and sends it off to be slaughtered, making old friend into a sublime selection of sausages. (Donkeys apparently don't make good prosciutto.) I can testify that in the right hands, donkey can also make a marvellously pungent sauce, which I happily ate at La Nuvola with a modest sprinkling of the island's finest pecorino, served over a plateful of Sardinia's favourite pasta, *malloredus*.

Months later, I began to look more deeply into the cooking and eating of this friendly beast of burden and scanned libraries, books and the web for donkey-cooking hints. I found out that a donkey *salamini sagra*, or sausage fest, is held every autumn at Castelferro in Piedmont, but sadly I missed it. All was not lost, however, for during the winter I found myself back in a city whose citizens are still unashamedly fond of eating donkey. This was the wealthy, northern, rather exquisite Lombard city of Mantova, Mantua in English.

Mantua has a long history, and is a classic example of an independent city whose success was bound up with the fortunes of its ruling family, in this case the Gonzagas, who reigned from 1328 to 1707 and built a city of fabulous wealth and beauty. These days its citizens seem to spend most of their time shopping for clothes, probably taking a day off from shopping in nearby Milan to do so.

And just as the Tuscans have retained their surprisingly simplistic one-pot dishes, so the Mantovani have kept their own particular culinary identity. Their salami are some of the best that can be found in Italy, and they have a fondness for a *torta* called *torta sbrisolona*, which to my eyes looked suspiciously like an English crumble, and pretty dry and charmless at that, but was doing a brisk trade when I was there. But if, as I did, you see *Stracotto d'asino* on a menu, hurry on in for this is essentially donkey stew, mostly served on mushy polenta, and not too dissimilar from a slightly stringy beef stew but with a definite asinine twang, a perfect dish for a languid lunch in Mantua on a foggy winter's weekend. It is the very opposite of fast food, requiring at least seven hours' slow cooking to tenderize the meat. You will, of course, have to jettison memories of any donkey you may have known and loved, and learn to relish a bit of cultural and culinary difference.

Stracotto d'asino

Donkey stew for four people. Adapted from Cucina Mantovana *by Cia Eramo (*Franco Muzzio Editore 2002*).*

600g donkey meat
5 tablespoons olive oil
50g butter
2 carrots, finely chopped
2 onions, finely chopped
2 sticks celery, finely chopped
4 or 5 ripe tomatoes
1 sprig rosemary
4 leaves fresh basil
1 bottle Lambrusco
salt and pepper

Cut the donkey into equal pieces, as you would beef for a stew. In a large flameproof terracotta dish, warm the oil and melt the butter. Add the pieces of donkey along with the onion, carrot and celery and brown on all sides: about 10 minutes. Add the tomatoes, rosemary, basil and wine to the donkey stew, adjust the seasoning, cover and cook in a slow oven for 7 to 8 hours, checking and stirring from time to time. Serve with mushy polenta (made with a little more water than usual so that it is looser in texture).

* * *

Back in Sardinia, there is a restaurant in Alghero that deals with eating *à la* Catalana in a very different way. Al Tuguri is run by a gentleman called Benito, not a name that inspires much warmth in me. It is the one serious Catalan restaurant that people suggest you visit, so I did, rather hurriedly, and was in awe of the fabulous talent that arranged anchovies in pretty patterns. But sadly it seems that all the attention has gone to its head. Benito is a media personality and has been elected the local representative of Catalan food, this despite his spending much of his working life in Switzerland and Germany. The restaurant takes itself far too seriously. Lighten up, guys! This is Alghero, the city of sea, sun and seaweed. The pretension isn't helped by calling the restaurant Tuguri, which means 'hovel' in dialect.

There was a certain mean-spiritedness in the air, particularly when I failed to order any wine. The couple who ran the place seemed familiar. Benito was undoubtedly smart in his chef's whites, but give me an ancient granny chef any day. These two were clearly bored with each other. Cold and tired. I imagined them bitching in the morning and well into the witching hour. I didn't stay too long. And they had tablecloths.

But there was one thing I did like and it was again billed as 'typically' Catalan. This was their *torta de menjar blanc*. If ever a dish reeked of medieval banquets and jousting, this is it. It is about as ancient a food as you can get, but whether even this is purely Catalan is doubtful; it could well be Spanish in origin. But no matter. It is perceived as Catalan and gives Alghero a dish that helps keep that old Catalan feeling alive and well, and is at least slightly more original than the fairly ubiquitous *crema catalana*. What we do know is that wherever *torta de menjar blanc* truly comes from it has spread around Europe over the centuries, appearing in Britain as blancmange, having reached us via the French, who also lay claim to being the originators of this estimable, at times exceedingly wobbly pudding. But was it always wobbly? Was it always a pudding even? This is its story.

That it is an ancient dish is easy to prove. Chaucer mentions it and notes that it is made with beast ('beste') – meat.

> *A cook they hadde with hem for the nones*
> *To boille the chiknes with the marybones,*
> *And poudre-marchant tart and galyngale.*
> *Wel koude he knowe a draughte of londoun ale.*
> *He koude rooste, and sethe, and broille, and frye,*
> *Maken mortreux, and wel bake a pye.*
> *But greet harm was it, as it thoughte me,*
> *That on his shyne a mormal hadde he.*
> *For blankmanger, that made he with the beste.*

The Cook's Portrait, from the General Prologue
of Chaucer's *Canterbury Tales* (1387)

It seems that the blancmange Chaucer knew had passed northwards relatively unsullied for it was made almost exactly how the Spanish or Catalan versions were made: with a combination of ground chicken or capon, almond milk (made from fresh almonds), sugar and rice flour. It was a dish for the rich rather than the poor. Rice was then ground and sold as a spice rather than a staple, and was more highly esteemed than humble wheat. *Blankmanger* would have been served at banquets, its whiteness giving it *carte blanche* for ready consumption in abbeys and monasteries, notable seats of gluttony and fine dining. Its name, *menjar blanc* or blancmange, simply meant 'white food'. As Christianity entered a more proscriptive stage and fasting was more strictly observed, particularly during Lent, the ground poultry was replaced by ground fish or simply omitted.

And it is in this latter form that Catalan *menjar blanc* still exists. Although the odd reference can be found to old ladies who to this day echo the medieval spirit and make their *menjar* with chicken stock, it is now almost always meatless. It can even be found in far-off Chile by the way, where its colour is still impeccably white, which comes from using reduced milk mixed with sugar and a little vanilla. This is truly a well-travelled dish.

Blawmanger. Tak the two del of rys, the thridde pert of almoundes; wash clene the rys in leuk water & turne & seth hem til thay breke & lat it kele, & tak the melk & do it to the rys & boyle hem togedere. & do therto whit gres & braun of hennes grounde smale, & stere it wel, & salte it & dresch it in disches. & frye almaundes in fresch gres til they be browne, & set hem in the dissches, & strawe theron sugre & serue it forth.

Utilis Coquinario, fourteenth-century English cookery book

Torta de menjar blanc

Serves six.

FOR THE PASTRY
750g type 00 flour
150g unsalted butter, softened
sugar

FOR THE FILLING
1 litre full-fat milk
20g *amido* – cooking starch (or use cornflour)

150g sugar
the zest of 2 organic oranges and 1 unwaxed lemon

Make the pastry in the usual way by mixing the flour with the butter and a spoonful of sugar, then adding enough water to combine into a dough. Divide in half and roll out into two sheets of under a millimetre thickness. Set aside.

For the filling, mix the starch with a little of the milk. Put the rest of the milk in a pan and heat gently, along with the orange and lemon zest and 5 spoonfuls of sugar, up to boiling point. Take off the heat and stir in the dissolved starch.

Heat the oven to 180°C and grease a round baking tray (25cm diameter should suffice). Place one sheet of pastry on the tray, pour in the filling and cover with the second layer. Artistic flurries using bits of leftover pastry are permitted. Bake in the hot oven for 25 minutes until golden brown on top.

SAN PIETRO

AT SEVEN O'CLOCK IN THE MORNING, CARLOFORTE ISN'T
exactly a hive of activity. The odd dog mooches around,
as does the odd writer looking for a story. But come the
early summer, a steady stream of scooters and cars drive
northwards out of Carloforte to the old tuna-canning
factory, the *stabilimento*. Every year from May to June it
leaps into life as the tuna traps, the *tonnara*, are set offshore.

Bluefin tuna have migrated close by for thousands of
years and despite everything, overfishing, pollution and the
weight of wisdom, they still do so, only to confront one
of Europe's last working tuna traps. Working, that is,
when the sea is calm, the sky crystal blue and the wind
little more than a limpid whisper. Otherwise there will be
no *mattanza*. No buzz of motors. Just a stillness in the air,
and a quiet electrical hum in the background.

I had cascaded down the road from the north of Sardinia
to its southernmost tip to visit the small island of San
Pietro. San Pietro and its capital Carloforte are somewhat
anachronistic, with roots part Ligurian, part African, but
with only the mildest tinge of Sardinian. I knew there was

only a vague chance of seeing the *mattanza*, but I liked the idea of this island that spoke an ancient Ligurian dialect, ate couscous and fished for tuna.

The Spanish word *mattanza* is still used for the seasonal cull that pits man against fish in a rather one-sided but spectacular battle. It has its fans, although few will be supporters of animal rights; more likely photographers looking for cultural gore and those who relish anything that is different and controversial. The bloody fest of tuna slaughter is a must for cultural anoraks like myself and a must-not for the effete, and the tuna, come to that. It has the same atavistic attraction as a bullfight, and inspires poets and artists and hypocritical judgement. But for Carloforte it is very much a part of how they live.

So here I was, not quite knowing what to expect. The thick iron gate set back from the road whirred into action. It too has its day when the *mattanza* is called, busily sliding and grating on its rollers, powered by a mysterious hand in the office. In spin the *tonnaroti*, all male, bleary-eyed, tough characters from Carloforte who chat and shout in their Genovese dialect. I slipped through with them.

'*Dica* . . . can I help you?' I was asked, a little fiercely, by a lady breathing through a cigarette.

'I'm with Luigi. I'm the writer. I think he told you about me.'

'Ah, the writer. Yes.'

'I'll wait outside for him if you want.'

And without waiting for anything as meaningful as an answer, I scurried out, fearful that I was going to be led away and interrogated by the tuna police, a rusty tuna tin pushed towards my face. No, no, I'm not from the WWF. Really!

And then Luigi arrived with a full team in tow. Luigi Pomata is a local chef, young, handsome and ambitious, who was finishing off his own cookbook and had just spent two days tweaking chives so his food would look perfect under camera. With him were his own media gang, the photographer, the real writer and the writer's special friend. Now with Luigi here it was all *ciao ciao* and hand-shakes, everyone much more amenable. It always helps to have a good local contact. We walked down to the quay and before me lay the solid, chunky boats that were to be towed out to the *tonnara*: the *vascelli* and the smaller, almost miserable *bastardi*. All were engineless. But one stood out. Solid, metal, it was like a barge built to take great weight. This was the *mosciare*, whose deep flat bottom would be filled with the astonished, gaping faces of the tuna when the *mattanza* was over. And the astonished, gaping faces of two writers.

We chugged off into the lolloping swell and arrived to find everything in place. The divers had been dispatched underwater to check that the tuna were there, swimming in the doomily explicit *camera di morte*, the chamber of death, the final section of the tuna trap, the only part where the net covers the sea floor so that any fish inside cannot escape when the net is slowly pulled in. You see very little of the *tonnara* on the surface, just a line of bright orange buoys following the net's T-shaped path. As rigid as the trap itself, however, is the way the *tonnara* is organized. On one side are the *gente di mare*, the people of the sea. The *gente di terra* stay on shore. And at the head of the *gente di mare* is the *raïs*, the chief, a man with experience, tough and well respected, whose name comes from the Arabic for 'leader'. This is not some weird political gesture but a legacy from the tenth century when the *tonnara* first arrived in Italy, brought in along with the lemons by the Arabs who ruled Sicily before the Normans booted them out. This *raïs* was much younger than I had expected. Another Luigi, he was a dead ringer for Bruce Willis, which made the whole morning even more tense, for you just knew that something, some violent eruption, a drama or an explosion of temper, would happen. It had to. Bruce was here. And there had to be blood. Somewhere in the enticing blue below lay the victims, still unaware that what was going on had real significance for them. Or maybe they did know. Gum was chewed. Cigarettes glowed. Tension flexed in the air.

The principle of the *tonnara* is quite simple. Nets are placed in the path of the migratory tuna, pushing the fish into a series of walled chambers from which they cannot escape. When there are enough fish in the last, the *camera di morte*, you haul the nets in and take the fish from the water. If this sounds easy, it isn't. It requires a concerted hour or two of sweaty male heaving. Tuna are large, muscular beasts that can weigh up to 300 kilograms. Not long ago you could catch fish that were even bigger, up to 400 or 500 kilos each. That is a lot of tuna. And getting them into the *mosciare* is the job of the *tonnaroti*, a band of tough local characters who wouldn't be seen dead eating quiche, armed with sharp gaffs, muscles and a few gantries and winches that can haul the tuna up before they slide down into the hull.

But things have changed radically over the past few years. Where once the fish were taken to the local cannery, the economics of the business has meant that canned European bluefin tuna can no longer compete with the cheaper species caught in warmer waters by powerful industrial fishing fleets. The industrial boats are lightly manned and shoot massive longlines behind them, often hundreds of kilometres long.

Luckily, bluefin tuna have one very particular and rather wealthy customer: the sashimi eater, mainly but not exclusively Japanese, but the only people prepared to pay the price for good-quality bluefin. This market has been the saviour of the few remaining *tonnara* in Europe. Favignana in Sicily is now said to be owned by the Japanese. Bonagia too. Nowadays all the best fish from Carloforte are sent straight to Tokyo, so the *mattanza*'s

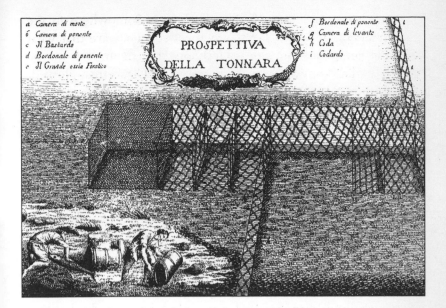

The T-shaped tonnara, *with the fine-meshed*
camera di morte *on the left.*

success entirely depends on what the Japanese market is
prepared to pay. To reflect this new reality, the hierarchy
now includes a small team of itinerant Japanese tuna
buyers who follow the bluefin as they migrate around
the Mediterranean. They travel light. An electric
thermometer, a sampler to test the colour of the meat and
a very sharp knife are all they need. Except maybe for a
bottle or two of soy sauce.

Towards the end of May, the tuna that swim off
Carloforte are in perfect condition. Fat and agitated, keen
to shoot their loads of sperm and eggs in a fishy orgy just
as their ancestors have always done. At this stage they are
called *tonno di corsa* and are picky about their food. If you
have a hormonal teenager *di corsa* at home you'll fully
understand. But as soon as the spawning has been completed they become scrawny, flabby fish, *tonno di andata*,

which no Japanese would touch with a chopstick. When post-loadshooting fish are caught, they often land up in second-grade sashimi markets, masquerading as the best. But the ruse seldom works. Beware the fool who tries to supply the prime sashimi markets with them. It's a dangerous game. I've tried it.

I had been trying to see the *mattanza* for ages. Ten years earlier, in the midst of making a crappy TV series that mostly involved the crew knobbing each other, not on camera I hasten to add, we had spent three days in Sicily waiting endlessly for the *tonno* to arrive. Three days of waiting was about as much as the budget stretched to, so we went off to film an old lady making marzipan flowers instead, but it somehow lacked that touch of Hemingway. So I was slightly incredulous that I had, after all these years, managed to wangle my way into this, the notoriously secretive Carloforte *mattanza*. And I sat in the *mosciare* and reflected, watching as the men in the boat opposite, still fifty metres away, prepared to haul in the net and bring the fish to the surface.

Suddenly the *tonnaroti* hurrahed and whirled into action, breaking into the musing and the gentle relaxing of the spectators in the *mosciare*. Lined up on the edge of their boat, the men began to draw the net slowly in from the water, closing in on the fish below. I hoped for some plaintive chanting but there was none. Just a lot of sweat and fevered panting and the eternally anxious *raïs* watching with the eyes of a hawk on speed. More shouting. A giant swordfish leapt from the water and thrashed its sword rather irresponsibly. Bruce – Luigi the *raïs* – raced into action. He danced across the edge of the nets, shouted and drew in a net to block its way. Someone grabbed it by the tail and threw the flailing fish into the bottom of the boat. Meanwhile, there was another problem. In the far corner a breach in the net had allowed a couple of tuna to escape. Luigi leapt, and with his years of experience in the ways of Hollywood he knew just what to do. A young lad had attached a hook to the net and started to haul it up. Luigi exploded. His head almost burst with anger, and he sent him off to the other side in disgrace. Still the nets drew in, the gap between the boats narrowing further while the *mosciare* remained stock-still.

Outside the net, a happy shoal of anchovies swam by, sneering at the tuna, which were powerless to gobble them up and probably had their mind on other things, such as their imminent destruction. The water inside had begun to seethe as the tuna sliced through it in panic. Their gloriously deep bright-blue backs shone briefly, like phantom fish dipping in and out of the water's surface. We were getting nearer the denouement. Another boat had arrived, stuffed to the gunwales with bags of ice and carrying the monarch, Signor Greco, the owner of the *tonnara*, an old and respected man, incongruously dressed in suit and tie. Everyone on the *mosciare* made way and wished him good morning. He lit a cigarette and watched the spectacle imperially in the corner. His son, scuba-ed up, was the prince; Luigi, the *raïs*, the prime minister. And then another character stepped into the *mosciare*: Ozawa, the man with the sharpened dagger, dressed in waterproof clothes from head to foot. Ambassador plenipotentiary. The executioner.

Soon the time came when the net was so tight, so close to the surface, that the sea erupted into a continual inverted tropical rainstorm. And still the net drew in. Unannounced, the first tuna had been gaffed and the water began to redden, slowly, at blotting-paper speed. With the sea still frothing and bubbling, a tiny stream of blood trickled down the fish's armoured head and into its wide, astonished eyes. The pace quickened. More and more tuna were hauled out of the water. The two lines of boats had almost closed in as the net had been pulled right up from the bottom of the sea. Ozawa, standing in the hold of the *mosciare*, quickly thrust his dagger into each and every tuna's flanks and slid the blade sharply under their gills, cutting their throats. Killing them sharply.

He lined the fish head to tail on one side of the hold, some still thrashing in their final death throes, flipping their tails with monstrous speed, spraying us all with a livid bloody spume. The Japanese insist that everything be done their way now. And it is. I didn't see a single fish being gaffed in its side, which ruins the flesh for sashimi. All had been gently lowered into the icy blood-red slurry that would keep them cool and keep the colour of their flesh at the correct degree of redness. The one thing that no one could know until the fish had been taken back to the *stabilimento* was just how fat they would be. This can be resolved only by feeling a small piece of flesh cut from behind the tail or from deep down behind the side fins. It made me anxious just thinking about it, for I used to deal in tuna, and used to check the colour and the fat content and hope that it would be good enough for the Japanese clients I had in London. It usually wasn't.

I tried to keep track of the amount of fish that had been caught and guessed it to be around 1500 kilograms. Not a bad haul. Not one fish had been dropped and bruised. *Bello lavoro!*

While the last few fish were being pulled up from the net, the atmosphere relaxed. Bruce called for a cigarette, smiled and knew that he had avoided disaster. Signor Greco departed, looking content. Ozawa's brow unfurrowed. Silence reigned once more. Soon the *mosciare* piled full of dead tuna was towed back to the factory, where the fish, shaded from the sun and covered in ice, would be checked and packed and cosseted in their death as they never were when alive. In two days they would be far away from home, in Tsukiji fish market in Tokyo, blissfully unaware of their honourable fate.

The *mattanza* may sound barbaric. But it didn't seem so to me. It is horribly beautiful. Visceral. Remember that it isn't the *tonnara* that have swept the seas of tuna. They haven't sucked the bluefin stocks to virtual extinction. Fishing boats have become impossibly powerful, dragging their long, baited lines hundreds of kilometres behind them. Purse-seiners surround shoals of fish and drag them from the sea, guided by satellites and machines of faultless efficiency. We have yet to learn how to fish at sustainable levels. So even though the *tonnara* have survived for so long, they will remain in obscure corners of Europe only as long as the Japanese will pay good money, and as long as the fish are still to be found. Fishing is a bloody business, but the size and beauty of tuna give the *mattanza* a special aura. I for one was in awe of the scene before me, watching man and animal slug it out, the whole of the island coming together to keep the *tonnara* going. For those brief few months when the tuna are running it gives Carloforte a profound sense of community, something to do other than feed louche tourists with pasta and *gelati*. So if you ever come this way in the early summer as the spawning fish pass by, be prepared to eat, sleep and dream tuna.

It doesn't take a genius to see that a tuna bears little resemblance to a pig. But long before pigs became over-bred, fast-growing super-beasts, they were an immensely valuable food resource, an animal whose every little morsel had a use, from the snout right down to the tail. And one whose slaughter was the time for everyone to gather round and stuff innards, cook blood, cut hams and generally make merry. And so with the tuna in Carloforte. In the old days the canning factories buzzed with activity during the tuna season, and although it wasn't quite as homey an occasion as killing a solitary pig on a farm, families decamped to the *stabilimento* as the tuna gathered in the nets. These days, a little canning still goes on, but most families are more interested in milking the rich tourists who flock here throughout the summer. Carloforte is an immensely charming place, busily remote and highly attractive. And look out for Carloforte tuna. It is darker and denser than warm-water tuna and delicious, too – the best I have tasted.

Before canning had been invented, tuna was packed into wooden barrels. This might appear more ecologically sound and attractive, but the barrels didn't survive as long as cans so the producer was always up against dodgy dealers exploiting the fragility of the product. As soon as canning came along, tuna became an easily exportable commodity.

The islanders have developed very particular ways with tuna, their marine pig. Even if the bulk of the meat went to the canneries, that left a whole load of other bits and pieces that had their uses too. My first night on the island, as I unwound in the Hotel Paola, I asked for a plate of tuna for dinner. Out it came with piles and chunks of dark salty meat and lighter bits of this and that, some I recognized, others I didn't.

'Did you enjoy it?' Paola's mother, who ran the front of house, asked me.

'*Fantastico.*' I love that word, and kept on saying it about everything, even the bills I was running up. 'I particularly liked this,' I said, pointing to a delicate pale morsel on my plate. 'Is this the *ventresca* – the stomach? It seems so tender.'

'Ah no, signore. They are the testicles.'

'Ah.'

The next day I called on two of Carloforte's foremost tuna experts, Niccolò and Luigi Pomata, father and son, to guide me through the complexities of tuna bits and pieces. It was Luigi who had arranged the *mattanza* trip for me. The Pomatas also happen to run the town's best restaurant, one of the very few with tablecloths that I would unhesitatingly recommend.

I asked Luigi, 'How did people keep the tuna before canning came along?'

'Pa!' Luigi shouted at Niccolò, who had dozed off in the corner. 'Can you tell us about the tuna!' He sprang to life. Chefs have a unique ability to doze and spring like this. It comes with the job.

'How much will you pay me to tell you?' Niccolò laughed. 'We're not called Genovesi for nothing!' Now Niccolò really does know his tuna. He has a fierce passion for the fish, which I share, so I listened with fascination as he talked me through how they used the tuna on the island. He began to draw me an outline of a tuna. Although it looked like a distressed goldfish, I got the sense of it.

'We'll start here.' He pointed at the innards. 'There are the eggs, which we salt and dry to make *bottarga*. You can eat it grated over pasta, or just as it is with a bit of lemon.'

Bottarga is well known in Sardinia. Further up the west coast is a dusty little fishing port called Cabras, where the brackish lake that stretches out towards the sea is rich in grey mullet, whose roe is also pressed and salted. Indeed most people, though not in Carloforte, would suggest that mullet roe is far superior to tuna, and I would have to agree. It is infinitely subtler, and good Cabras *bottarga* has a beautiful golden colour to it.

'And with the male fish we eat their *figatelli* as well.'

'Ah,' I said, 'the testicles. I ate them last night.'

'They're not really testicles, you know. We also call them *lattumi*, like *latte di tonno*, if you see what I mean.'

In English we often call the sperm-carrying part of the fish the milt. It sounds odd — a little like milk to my ears. Milts, particularly herring milts which are fried or devilled, have their own devotees. Excellent they are too. Tuna milts can weigh a thwacking 10 kilograms, so Niccolò advises that you cook them for at least an hour and a quarter and then serve them marinated or fried. But somehow I liked the idea of 10-kilogram testicles.

'And then there's the stomach, *u belu* we call it. And the *gurezi*, the oesophagus. Both of them we salt and eat with potatoes. And the heart. That's really good too. We eat that a lot here. Salted tuna heart.'

U belu
Salted tuna stomach Tabarka style

Leave the stomach to soak in water overnight. Wash it well and cook in boiling water for an hour or so. Prepare a soffrito with 250ml olive oil, 1kg chopped onions, 500g chopped tomato, parsley, a touch of fresh chilli and 250ml white wine. Cook for 30 minutes and then add 1.5kg potatoes cut into even pieces, 200g olives and the stomach cut into strips. Cook until the potatoes are done. Serve with a Sardinian red wine: vino rosso dello Spalmatore for choice.

But the *pièce de résistance* is the fillet, again salted and dried, a perfectly sensible way to preserve your food in a salty dry place. This is called *mosciame*. Once upon a time, before we got all sensitive and caring, dolphin were also caught in the traps along with tuna and their fillets too were dried, and made, I was told, excellent *mosciame*. *Mosciame* has a vague resemblance to a salty prosciutto, and is best nibbled in the sun with a glass of cool Vermentino. It even makes a mean sandwich, mixed with rocket and a tomato or two, but its strong taste can pall after a while, and you may find it a little monotonous. But the weirdest thing of all has to be what they call in dialect *fugassa*, Genovese for *focaccia*, but this has little to do with flour and yeast, and seems to be a now-forgotten type of tuna blood pudding. Sadly, I never actually found any to try.

Another island activity that has slipped into the mists of history is the making of salt, but all is not lost for the salt pans just outside the town are an ideal location for flamingos and a host of other twittering migrants. Only I never came across a recipe for salted flamingo . . .

Tuna heads were about the only thing that wasn't salted and dried. They were ground up and added as fertilizer to the island's soil. You still find the odd tuna bone in the fields. The roots of Carloforte's food are crystal clear. Tuna in various forms was used as a staple, and boiled with potatoes or cooked with a tomato *soffrito*. The wind, the heat and the salt dried the fish, and this is what has long been eaten, and is what people expect to eat, on this odd little island.

Luigi Pomata has become a bit of a TV star, and is, I am told, a regular on the Italian version of *Ready Steady Cook*. I was particularly impressed when he told me he had come second in the recent World Couscous Championships held in Sicily, muttering darkly that the Palestinian delegation had won only because of politics. It might strike you as a little odd that he had entered at all, couscous and Sardinia perhaps not being natural companions, so now comes the time to tell the story of couscous in this little corner of the world. You need to look at San Pietro's particularly tangled history. You will already have noticed the odd reference to Genovese dialect. It might have struck you as a little peculiar. We're in Sardinia. You're sharp.

Drift back to the sixteenth century, when Genoa made its daring but brilliant switch of allegiance to the Spanish monarchy from the French. Much of this was as a result of the shrewd manoeuvrings of Genoa's Doge Andrea Doria, the selfsame spindly aristocrat we came across earlier in the book. As a consequence of Doria's Mediterranean machinations, Genovese merchants and traders, not to say the Dorias themselves, stood to gain from any of Spain's military adventures, be they in the new world or the old. It was said that Genoa's Casa di San Giorgio bankrolled the militaristic dreams of the Spanish Empire. So when the Spanish king used Doria's fleet to invade the coast of Tunisia, the Genovesi were quick to find ways to exploit their newfound good fortune.

The town of Pegli on the Costa Levante, east of Genoa, was the fiefdom of the powerful Lomellini family, who decided to send a number of the town's expert citizens to work the rich banks of coral found off the Tunisian coast. The Lomellini had already cornered the important coral market based in Genoa but had quickly exhausted local stocks and were keen to destroy coral banks elsewhere. It was a lucrative business requiring little capital, and just a few experienced divers. Eventually they chose a well-protected peninsula called Tabarka. In 1544 the Lomellini received exclusive rights to market any fish or coral that was harvested there, and sent ten families to settle permanently.

All went well for many years and the community thrived, but with a change of regime after the Ottoman invasion of Tunisia, together with increased French interest in the area, the future began to look rather bleak and the Tabarkini started to think of moving on. By the beginning of the eighteenth century, the population had reached two thousand, far too many for the little peninsula. Newlyweds were threatened with expulsion. Many began to leave any-way, crossing the sea to Liguria, but Carlo Emmanuele III, nominally King of Sardinia and one of the few members of the House of Savoy to take any real interest in the place, learning of the problems the Tabarkini were having, allowed them to settle on the then uninhabited island of San Pietro, off the south-western tip of Sardinia. The first Tabarkini arrived in January 1738, followed by a second wave in June, who, together with another group who travelled from Liguria to settle on the island, formed the core of the population, which hasn't been massively diluted to this day.

If the settlers thought they had opted for the easy life, they were to be sorely disappointed. Three years later Tunisian pirates invaded the island and carried off nine hundred of its citizens. For fifteen years many languished in slavery before being released when the King of Sardinia once again intervened on their behalf. In honour of King Carlo Emmanuele, the Tabarkini called the capital of their island Carloforte. It has a peculiarly un-Sardinian feel about it. Sardinia was, and in a way still is, a pastoral society whose cultural soul is high up in the mountains, so the Tabarkini and the Sardinians never really mixed, and each preserved their own linguistic peculiarities. One Carlofortese told me they still thought of themselves as Ligurians living in Sardinia, rather than Sardinians. Others were more tactful.

Not everyone left Tabarka in the eighteenth century. Apart from those who moved to Carloforte, there is another weird offshoot in Alicante, Spain, still called Nueva Tabarka, and yet another on Sant'Antioco, the larger island opposite San Pietro. This lot mingled with a group of Piemontesi, so the town of Calasetta, right opposite Carloforte, has more of an air of Turin about it – with its rigid grid streetplan – while Carloforte has a definite touch of Genoa, with narrow *carugi* in abundance.

However, matters back in Tabarka improved significantly when a local woman married the bey of Tunisia's brother in the nineteenth century. Their son, Ahmed, eventually succeeded to the throne (if that's what beys have). Educated in Paris and somewhat keener on western ways than his forefathers, Ahmed allowed the Tabarkini to thrive once more, and even let them advise on the construction of Tunisia's first railway system.

But wherever people go they tend to bring along their cultural baggage, so the Tabarkini from Tunisia have not only retained a fondness for couscous, or *cashca* as they call it, but have retained and enhanced a deep love of tuna that few can rival.

SARDINIA: II

THIS IS A STORY ABOUT MAGGOTS, BANDITS AND SHEEP. WE'RE high up in the wild mountains of central Sardinia, the *barbagia*, where mean-eyed, gun-toting sheep wait on every corner. Take the road, the 'new' road they call it, from Dorgali in the middle of the eastern coast, in the province of Nuoro. As you drive up into the mountains you'll get a distinct sense that you are veering off the beaten track. Actually you are already off the beaten track, but follow this road, stick to it firmly through thick and thin, and drive on through the holm oaks, until eventually you'll see Orgosolo, mountain-perched and slightly forbidding.

I had been to Orgosolo once before, about fifteen years ago, drawn, I think, by the stories of *banditismo*. Just about every swarthy Sard I passed seemed to be hanging around looking for a rich foreigner to kidnap, but, percipiently, they left me well alone. Anyway, I can remember feeling distinctly unwelcome, and even though it was *ferragosto*, 15 August, which turned out to be the biggest feast day of the year, and despite bumping into a religious procession, Orgosolo didn't exactly shout out, 'Come back soon!' But here I was again, in spring this time. And the locals looked like they hadn't moved from the doorways and bars along the high street for at least fifteen years.

What had changed, though, was the huge bustle of tourists, who longed not to be kidnapped – this had by now become slightly *passé* – but to see the town's *murales*. In 1969, a group of Milanese anarchists decided to daub one of the town's walls with a highly political mural of a not very statuesque Liberty, looking rather like a cross-dressed Uncle Sam holding a pair of scales, with a silhouetted figure and a car in one hand and a shepherd with a few desultory sheep in the other. The outline of Italy is to her side, also looking a bit girthy, but where Sardinia should be there is just a poignant little '?'.

During the 1960s, Italy, like the rest of Europe, was seething with discontent. Rebels were chucking flowers at each other, Americans were being radical – remember those distant days? – and the world's rulers, be they democrats or dictators, were quaking in their boots. And here in little Orgosolo they decided that wall-daubing was quite an attractive notion. It was a bit of a delayed decision, actually, and it wasn't until 1975, to celebrate the thirtieth anniversary of Liberation and the 'fall' of Fascism, that local schoolmaster Francesco del Casino, a Sienese by birth, began to paint the town not only red but blue, white, green, purple and black, and even indigo, cobalt and lilac, and so gave birth to the Orgosolo *murales*. Hence the tourists.

The murals are beautiful. Intriguing, often deeply political, at times Picassoesque, with a hint of Miró and a touch of the great Mexican mural painter Diego Rivera. The town now has well over a hundred dotted around its walls and buildings. In time Del Casino was joined by a homegrown painter, Pasquale Buesca, whose work is more naïve, earthier. Walls have become paintings for all to see. It's truly fab.

But enough of this culture. I was on the trail of a maggot.

A very particular maggot with a fondness for cheese. The maggot, in fact, of the fly we all know and love as *Piophila casei*. This fly, like so many of its relations, is a deeply un-attractive insect. If you happen to die in some remote part of the northern hemisphere far away from friends, family and funeral parlours, the cheese fly, sometimes almost cheerily called the cheese skipper, might well lay its eggs in any little crack or fissure it can find in you, attracted by the process of liquefying fat. The eggs become maggots and you can imagine the rest. If you have any forensic entomologists around for dinner, let them tell you more.

So it may surprise you to learn that this fly has con-tributed handsomely to the gastronomy of Sardinia. Possibly relieved to discover a less controversial crack, *Piophila casei* will also lay its eggs in any cheese it comes across, and in Sardinia, with its surfeit of udders – the sheep population is over five million – there is at times a surfeit of sheep's cheese or pecorino. Particularly in the days when the *caseificio*, the cheese factory, shut down in the summer. In the old days, when such things as factories were beyond the imagination, cheese would be made on the mountains by the shepherd, sold or eaten by his family, and that was that. It was very simple. Milk, unpasteurized of course, was heated over a wood fire to 38 degrees, a little rennet was added, scraped from a dead sheep's stomach, and the milk would slowly coagulate. Pressed into shape, salted and left to mature in the mountain air, the cheese gradually evolved into the pecorino you can still buy called *fiore sardo*. Originally the whey was poured into wooden moulds (*pischedde*) made from local chestnut with a flower carved into the base (hence *fiore*). These days stainless steel is used, but the name remains. A quick and subtle nibble should reveal that it has also retained an ele-ment of smokiness. Once the cheese was hung in the smoky *pinnedu* before being sold, but now it is lightly smoked en masse to satisfy customer demand.

Pecorino sardo is held in high esteem by pecorino-lovers the world over. The Ligurians still use it for preference to make pesto, thanks to a trade established long ago by the old *giudicato* of Arborea with their Genovese allies. *Pecorino sardo* is also found as far afield as the USA, where demand has been constant thanks to the homesick tastebuds of Italian émigrés.

Now don't think that I'm going to say there are still shepherds in Sardinia who spend the whole winter in the mountains milking sheep and making pecorino. There aren't. These days most of the cheese is made in modern, anodyne factories that have to conform to EU hygiene regulations. But pecorino is still essentially an artisanal cheese, and the Sardinians, being generally quite positive Europeans, have embraced the Italian system of DOP, *Denominazione di Origine Protetta*. Linguistically, English can't really handle the word 'denomination' very well. It smacks of priests, nuns and domination. So *Denominazione di Origine Protetta* loses a little in translation to Denomination of Protected Origin. However, for the cheese-maker it offers a natty little label and the justification to demand more money for a better product, but one that in all probability costs more to produce anyway. Importantly, the DOP helps protect the market from being supplied with pretenders, with bowdlerized pecorino.

Sardinian pecorino can be utterly gorgeous. Although some will prefer the Tuscan and others *pecorino romano* – much of which, by the way, is made in Sardinia – I worship at the door of the Sardinian version. Try to find a slightly old, say nine-month cheese, from a small producer, and nibble.

The end result of a pecorino that has been chewed and regurgitated by cheese worms, however, might sound a little unappetizing. It certainly proved tricky to track down. Many denied making the cheese at all let alone eating it or liking it, but Maria Teresa, my very able

Orgosolan contact, had found a family who were proud to say that they ate it and loved it, and were happy to initiate me into the pleasures of what they called *casu marzu*.

The head of the family, Francesco Augusto Sinis, was seriously old. He had the pallor of a doll, skin that was paper thin and eyes that had lost their lashes but not their sparkle. Born in 1899, that made him a hundred and two at the time of the interview, and he loved to talk. He talked and talked, and even laughed and walked. If that makes him sound even more like a doll, that seems to be how you get treated when you're over a hundred, and although I'm not too sure whether I got everything he was saying, I caught most of it, and have it on tape. Francesco had spent all his life in Orgosolo, save for once, the only time he had ever left the island, when he went to fight the Austrians. He had been orphaned when he was seven, so he had never been to school, and spoke Sardinian, and only a little Italian.

Francesco had spent many of his many years watching the flocks and making and eating cheese. In the winter he would live up in the mountains, under cover in a chunky Sardinian tepee called a *pinnetu*. A fire could be lit inside to protect the shepherds from the elements, while underneath the wooden top were shelves and nooks for hanging sheep carcasses and maturing cheese. There was a certain knack to building a *pinnetu*. A strong, round, stone base echoes the Sardinian *nuraghe*, the mysterious stone towers that can be found all over the island and were built by the Sardinians three and a half thousand years ago. The *pinnetu* traditionally has a juniper roof, which if well made would allow the smoke from the fire inside to escape from the top while keeping most of the warmth inside. Here the pecorino would sit and slowly mature and take on its hint of smokiness. Most of the *pinnetu* have now crumbled away and the shepherds tend to stagger back home after a heavy day's milking rather than leave for months at a time, but that was how life was once led.

Get yourself up into the hills behind Orgosolo, go and eat in a restaurant called Ai Monti del Gennargentu and you can still see a *pinnetu* in action. And if you want they can even arrange a barbecue where you can eat sheep, and sheep's cheese in all its many forms, and sing Sardinian sheep songs, and generally be ovine for a whole evening. Men were and are the ones who look after the animals, and even if sheep seem to dominate, the odd pig and cow also roam among the pastures on the hills, making conversation a little less monotonous for the *pastori*.

The diet of the Sardinian mountain villages still reflects this overwhelming reliance on the sheep. '*Latte!*' Francesco said when I asked him what he liked to eat. 'Milk!' He smiled.

'Come on, you can't just eat milk!'

'Why not? I like it.'

'Yes, but isn't there anything else you'd like to taste for your perfect meal?'

Francesco thought. His daughter said something in Sardinian.

'Yes, *casu marzu*,' said Francesco.

I turned to Maria. I hadn't come across the Sardinian name before. 'What's that?'

'It's that cheese you were talking about. The one with worms in.'

'Ah! The rotten pecorino!'

'No, it's not rotten. It's not bad food. It's good food.' And Francesco told me about how in the early summer you would eat the cheese spread on a little bread with the worms wriggling lightly in it. Later on in the season, the maggots turn into flies and the cheese is maggot-free, which, thankfully, was how I ate it. What happens is this. The maggots slowly chomp through the cheese, transforming it from something hard and tangy to a mush of worm poo and regurgitated cheese. Yum.

By the way, in Sardinian, *casu* means cheese. *Marzu* means rotten. So it's not entirely wrong to call it rotten cheese.

Francesco's daughter got up, went to the kitchen and brought back a glass, almost surreptitiously. 'This is *casu marzu*.'

Here it was. This bizarre cheese is quite difficult for anyone but a Sard to eat, especially those of us brought up on the idea that food must be pure, germ-free and worm-free. But I had eaten rotten shark in Iceland and this was not going to defeat me. *Casu marzu* is surprisingly soft, quite pungent, a little *piccante*, with a taste not far from the tanginess of Stilton, less creamy, but good. In fact, it was really good. And as we talked, I dipped and nibbled my way through most, but not all, of the jar they had, for apparently it wasn't very easy to get *casu marzu* any more and I didn't want to cat them out of house and worm. These days the cheese-making season goes on much longer to keep customers happy, so there is less left over, and anyway the EU rules that this product doesn't conform to regulations. It's different. It has been around for hundreds of years so it is bound to be dangerous.

The Sardinian *barbagia* is an excellent place to be a sheep. Free to range over the mountains, mollycoddled by shepherds, they thrive, and their cheese in any form is among the best in Italy. Sheep have an endearingly convenient cycle and they like to holiday around August time. So just as the sheep's lactation is calming down, the cheese factory shuts and everyone gets ready for the *ferragosto*. This was a time for courting, Francesco told me, when 'foreigners' would come and join in the *festa*, travelling in from neighbouring villages. Getting around was all down to the horse, and the people of the

Gennargentu still have a reputation for being expert horse-riders. Lean and wild, their horses seem eternally pent-up and overexcitable. The Pony Club has yet to make any real impact over here.

I was brought up in a part of England where the horse played a very different role. Thousands of pounds were spent in the deep Sussex countryside on pushing little Charlie and Camilla onto their vile ponies, and mummies and daddies would spend hours and hours, and small fortunes, making sure their darlings went to all the right occasions – starting at the Pony Club, of course – until the day when they left for university to become drug addicts or city alumni. Possibly both. It is a world away from Sardinia.

I have been riding twice in the last fifteen years. Once in Hungary I was made to gallop around on an unruly horse in traditional Hungarian riding gear and was then plied with *palinka* until I became monstrously drunk, all in the name of a TV programme. The other time was in Sardinia, on my first visit those fifteen years ago, probably not too long before the Hungarian incident. I remember it well.

Sardinian: 'Have any of you ridden before?'

Me: 'Yes, a little.' Remember, I was a Sussex boy.

'OK, you can take this one.'

Me: 'Well, I haven't ridden for quite a long time!' as I saw a slavering, quivering beast being led towards me.

'It's OK, he's friendly. Don't worry. But don't go in the middle or he will bite the horse in front and kick the one behind. Keep him in front, so he can only kick. Take him around a little bit. Get used to him.'

God knows if this horse had a name. I suspect it was Benito. We set off, going way up into the mountains with me in front. The horse pulled like a train and ran as close to the edge of the vertiginous path as he possibly could while keeping a sharp and vicious eye on the horse behind in case it got within a hundred metres or so. In the end I pleaded exhaustion, let the whole group pass by and opted for the rear-end position, which was no easier, and my steed did indeed bite the poor horse in front with real venom, the sort of thing David Attenborough might have recorded on the plains of Mongolia where wild horses are allowed to do what they like best: run wild. Here they had been trained to attack tourists.

So, given that I had prior knowledge that Sardinian horses are, how can we put it, a little exuberant, I was gripped by the prospect of seeing the bi-annual Orgosolo horse race. In the morning a lot of mad galloping had already gone on up in the hills, but I had missed this and, rather admirably I thought, spent the morning chatting about maggoty cheese. But in the afternoon, when every-one had come down from the hills, the Orgosoli began to move slowly down towards the church and the road that ran alongside it on the edge of town, as straight as a horse's fetlock. The idea was quite simple. It was to gallop as fast as possible from one end to the other right down the middle of the road. This you could do in one of several ways. There was the solo scramble. Or the multiple scramble. The non solo gallops were judged on the elegance with which they rode, arms locked together with-out breaking line. It was magic. In a way it was also utterly pointless, but thrilling nevertheless. Maria, my contact, treated me like a ten-year-old, clucking at me and making sure that I, as a dumb foreigner, didn't feel the need to hurl myself like a suffragette under the pounding hooves.

I was told that I was unlikely to meet a *carabiniere* at one of these horse races for they knew full well that this sort of thing is in contravention of just about every European Safety Directive ever created by the boys and girls from Brussels. And even though they are notoriously pedantic (as well as often plain stupid), some of the island's law enforcers think that the people of Orgosolo are nothing more than a bunch of wild, lawless bandits who are not to be crossed. Perhaps one sad day we will see the kerbstones clothed in approved foam rubber, the riders wearing helmets and harnesses, and white-coated veterinary inspectors sitting the horses on couches to analyse their feelings, but as yet, as with so much around these parts, the races are still defiantly Sardinian.

Both the *ferragosto* and the earlier spring festival I was at are ancient fests, with much drinking and eating and inevitably a dose of religion. But what gives them their special flavour is the *gara poetica*, or, as Maria called it, the Poetical Competition. Sadly, this isn't a matter of poets speedily writing round bends and chicanes, nor of poets walking along a fashionable catwalk. It's an atavistic verbal joust between *tenores* (yes, tenors) well versed in this ancient form of vocal ping-pong, who sing an elaborate story with no accompaniment other than a chorus. The sound, when I eventually heard it, reminded me of the anguished Bulgarian women who came to fame in the 1980s with their *Mystère des Voix Bulgares*.

At each poetical competition there is a theme, and the tenors take on a role that represents different versions or interpretations of this theme. So one of the tenors might play a lawyer and the other a doctor, and they enter into a lengthy – and I mean lengthy; these competitions can go on for hours – singing discussion based on the chosen theme. In another village, not far from Orgosolo, a French musicologist once dutifully recorded the words. Here the discussion was between art and nature. And the subject? Why, making cheese.

So imagine this. Sitting on a stage, two tenors begin to sing in Sardinian, inventing the lines as they go along. After each chunk has been sung, the chorus steps in, in the same gurgling Sardinian vocal style, and prepares the next tenor for his little ditty. And so on, into the night. This is what the musicologist recorded:

Piredda *(Art):*
Oh, esteemed colleague, calm yourself
Now listen to my answer
All kinds of sheep, I take them and shear them closely
I curdle the milk in the milk cart
And when it is curdled, I make cheese
You can see that I use it like an expert
But you are unable to do so

(Chorus)

Budroni *(Nature):*
So, in your opinion, I'm of little worth
And you say as much to everyone
But you do not put yourself out to make an effort
For it is I who puts you to sleep
And to make cheese you need curds
This you cannot deny
Why then do you brag and swagger?
For without me you would be unable to curdle it

from Bernard Lortat-Jacob, *Sardinian Chronicles*, translated by Teresa
Lavender Fagan (Chicago Studies in Ethnomusicology, Chicago UP
1995)

Cynics might feel that it loses a little of the drama in translation. As for the competition I saw, I became so hot and
bothered when I learnt that I had arrived in Orgosolo on
the only other day in the year, apart from 15 August,
when there was to be a *gara poetica* in town that I
completely forgot to note what on earth they were singing
about. And Orgosolo has even built a natty little
amphitheatre where you can sit and listen to these moaning poets as the sun sets. The audience was, I should say,
hardly rapt. Kids ran around, ate their *gelati* and fought as
only kids can do at inappropriate occasions. The poets
burbled on, the crowd grew and shrank, and Maria kissed

a thousand people – small-town life involves a lot of kissing – and attempted to let me know what the story was about. In the end I thought it better just to listen to the deep, earthy sound. It was Sardinian, utterly un-Italian. This island has by its own isolation kept a genuine otherness, and I doff my shepherd's hat to this.

Francesco had told me earlier that day that one year the theme was the story of a famous bandit from Sassari, Giovanni Tolo, who had been accused of robbing some coalminers. Tolo, however, was a good *bandito*. He knew full well who the guilty ones were and followed them up into the hills. The guilty *banditi*, presumably saying 'It's a fair cop, guv,' asked him whether they couldn't perhaps share the money. One of the tenors took the role of a lawyer, and the other a shepherd. The lawyer would bemoan all this illegal activity and the shepherd would defend it, and so the competition began. And so it would end. Hours later, in the dark warmth of the Sardinian night, the audience, taking for granted that it is quite a normal thing to listen to chanting poets, would gradually filter away, back home.

Romans, Aragonese, Bourbons, Savoyards, Piemontesi, French and even Austrians have all passed through Sardinia and tried to impose their ways on it but have given very little in return. The relatively democratic period of the *giudicati* in the fifteenth century was remote and brief, and exploitation and distant authority were the usual order of things. In response, the island's culture, particularly here in the heart of pastoral Sardinia, became one of profound resentment of central authority in any form. Closely linked to this is the sensitive issue of *banditismo*. Orgosolo has a reputation for fierceness, and the 1970s saw a few particularly brutal incidents of kidnapping and extortion. There is, as ever, a film. Made in 1963, *The Bandits of Orgosolo* quite clearly equates the two, and nosy writers like me are drawn to the place and to the mild adrenalin rush of danger.

But talking about *banditismo* is difficult. Francesco Sinis was happily telling me his thoughts when his daughter, surveying things from her seat in the corner, suggested that we talk about something a little more positive, which I could hardly refuse to do. I think the problem is this. First, they say that many of the more brutal acts weren't carried out by Orgosoli at all but by outsiders. Secondly, shepherds by the nature of their work live solitary, private lives, and since they freely wander the hills they were often tarred with the brush of *banditismo* by the *carabinieri* whose job it was to try to control things. But now, to some, *banditismo* is a sign of a distant, primitive past, one that the Sardinian young, who are more closely integrated into the rest of Italy than any other generation has been, have in a sense moved beyond.

But to many, bandits were and are heroes. Robin Hood-like figures who really did rob the rich to give to the poor. In a culture that has been utterly ignored, and one with little natural wealth, the state of things changed very little over the centuries – until, that is, the EU began to play the role of an uncharacteristically generous colonial master. These mountains can just as easily seem remote and inhospitable as peaceful and serene. It depends on you rather than them. Birdwatchers will find it calm and paradisical. Sheep-lovers, just paradisical. Nosy writers, intriguing. *Carabinieri* keen on promotion see endless bandits dressed as shepherds. The tendency to reticence and secretiveness is also part of the Sardinians' ambivalence towards the outside world, though not to progress, for few look upon the old days as golden days.

When I was there, I never heard anyone mention the murder of the local priest, Father Graziano Muntoni, shot dead in 1998 as he was about to celebrate Holy Mass, the first time a priest has ever been killed in Sardinia.

The work of outsiders, I was later told. Back in the 1970s, the son of a rich mainlander was kidnapped in the hills around Orgosolo, held to ransom and had his ear cut off and sent to his parents as a signal that further brutality was to be expected. Although *banditismo* might have an honourable place in the culture of Sardinian mountain life, it's difficult to justify such acts.

Without meaning to be sexist – i.e. I am just about to be – Sardinian women struck me as the wearers of the trousers, strong, very together, almost terrifyingly so, and immensely competent. They don't hang about in bars. They don't ride horses as fast as possible up the high street. They don't drive around town making as much noise as possible on nasty little mopeds. They don't kidnap people, as far as I know. No, that is very much a men thing. The women tend to keep things going.

Women make bread, for instance. And with their men away for such long periods, Sardinians have perfected the art of making a bread that keeps for months, is light and easily transportable, and can be made into a food that is so foolproof even men can make it. The bread is called *pane carasau* in Sardinian, although you may come across it as *carta di musica*, an Italian phrase that plays on the bread's paper-thinness. In Orgosolo, *pane carasau* is often made at home in a wood-burning oven, and baked every couple of months because it keeps for ever. The key is to cook the bread twice. Rolled very thinly with a long thin rolling pin, the bread is placed in the oven for a few minutes, taken out, then while still blisteringly hot cut sharply across the middle. The dough should have ballooned like pitta bread. It is stacked, allowed to cool, then cooked once more. When done, the bread is crisp and dry. *Pane carasau* are quite large, about 30–40cm across, and to make them more portable for the hungry shepherds, the women would often fold them in half after the first bake, before stacking and cooling them.

Making *pane carasau* in the family is still quite an event. Most families will cook at least 5 and sometimes 15 kilograms of dough at a time, firing up the oven, checking it, then rolling and baking the bread. Roles are clearly defined and everyone cooperates to bake the bread speedily while the oven is hot enough.

I defy anyone to go to Sardinia without coming across *pane carasau*. The bread has its roots firmly in the pastoral tradition of the mountains of central Sardinia – as has a dish that is so utterly simple, so utterly delicious, that it would make a three-star chef wince with pain as he spins sugar over his choux pastry swans. It is called *pane fratau*. And this is how you make it:

Pane fratau

Soak enough pane carasau *(carta di musica bread) in unsalted water for thirty seconds. Place on a hot dish – the bread will be soft. Cover with a good tomato sauce, grated pecorino and an egg. Bake in a hot oven for 5 minutes. Serve.*

To find this town welcoming when once it had seemed threatening made me wonder whether it ever was actually threatening at all. Have we got Orgosolo all wrong? I could observe and report back, but the more I knew the less I felt I understood. To me, it seemed that Orgosolo *had* changed.

The night before I left, my ears singing with the warbling poets and eyes seared by the flash of horses sprinting by, I was invited to dinner by Maria, and found myself for once being interrogated. In the corner sat Maria's father, relaxing after a long day's shepherding, watching Formula 1 on the telly. He was the strong, silent type. And while Maria rushed about doing familial things I met her mother, who was preparing the dinner, while her granny, struck by Alzheimer's, drifted in and out like a lost ship looking for an imaginary harbour. We ate *ministru* — which is either a thick soup or a thin bowl of pasta — fine pasta with a rich, sour, cheesy sauce that could have been made, but wasn't in this case, from the delectable *casu marzu*. When Maria's mother, after performing the job of hostess so ably, finally sat down, without any further ado she asked me this: 'So what have you noticed different about Orgosolo this time?'

What had I noticed? What *had* I noticed? That the town had become more European. That it seemed an easier place, with young people who looked like they do everywhere else. That the murals were even more startling, and that it was a shame that people came and left and never spent any time here other than looking at the murals and sending a postcard from the town of the Sardinian bandits. Europe has conquered where the King of Sardinia never could.

Ministru

For four people, use 400g home-made linguine *or* capelli d'angelo *cooked* al dente. *Keep a little of the cooking water back. Grate fresh young pecorino into a separate pan. Add the pasta and the remaining water, and stir until the cheese has melted and the* ministru *has a thick consistency. Serve.*

MUSSOLINI'S REVENGE

YOU MIGHT, LIKE ME, BE A LITTLE BEMUSED BY THE IDEA OF Italy ever being a Fascist nation. The country is after all supposed to be full of charming handsome people with an almost frivolous attitude to government, who spend their time flirting, eating *gelati* and riding Vespas when allowed out by their overwhelmingly protective mammas. But have we all been duped by this ridiculous stereotype? Is there lurking beneath the surface in the Italian psyche a nasticr side, an *Italia brutta*? The answer is yes. There is. There always has been. But then even the Swiss have had their nastier moments.

Fascism was born in an Italy that had been united for barely fifty years, a country ruled by a spurious monarchy, many of whose population felt distinctly cheated by the whole process of unification. The south had lost its capital city, Naples, and its kingdom, and gained a king for whom they felt little sympathy. It seemed that nowhere was truly elated by the results of unification, and the discontent nationwide became fertile ground for radical departures from conventional forms of organization.

As the First World War began the government and the

opposition supported a policy of neutrality but Mussolini, by then editor of the paper he founded and which became his voice, *Il Popolo d'Italia*, was belligerent. He wanted, as did the king, to join the fray for what he thought would be the greater good of Italy, and fight the Germans and the Austrians. Popular pressure for action was fuelled by Mussolini, and the government declared war in May 1915. King Vittorio Emmanuele signed a declaration without consulting his deputies, further evidence if it was needed that this constitutional monarchy was far from being a democratic one.

At the end of the First World War Italy had lost over 400,000 lives, and had little to show for it, despite promises made by the British and the French. By the 1920s things had degenerated to such an extent that many welcomed the prospect of strong government, and Benito Mussolini proved to be the supreme opportunist. Born in 1883 in the Romagnan town of Forlimpopoli not far from Bologna, he was originally a socialist. A fiery, thuggish journalist, who by a combination of circumstance and skill brilliantly wangled the job of dictator, a situation vacant if ever there was one. His true contribution to Italian history is still being debated. It soon became abundantly clear that his natural style was one of authoritarianism and a fierce nationalism that tolerated no opposition or criticism. The moment of his taking power was a classic piece of mass drama, stage-managed by himself, a theatrical deception. He claimed that he trekked and suffered along with thousands of other ardent Fascists on what was called the March on Rome, but the truth is different. He actually arrived in Rome by train. Under Fascism, intellectuals, liberals and writers were hounded from the country into exile or, as in the case of the Rosselli brothers, murdered.

Even in 1943, shortly before his ignominious end – he was caught by the *partigiani*, shot and strung from a lamp-post in Milan alongside his mistress Clara Petacci — he continued to flirt with the idea that he was in reality a socialist. Lenin agreed. He was, Lenin earlier wrote, one of the purest of all socialists. Perhaps you could argue that had Mazzini's republic ever been established, had the monarchy been ditched, Italy might have avoided this Fascist interlude altogether. No one can be too sure.

Above all, Mussolini wanted Italy to be a strong, virile and of course a Fascist nation, and when he came to power in 1923 he did everything he could to get the country out of its fairly hopeless condition. By the end of his rule over twenty years later he had helped Italy to poverty, defeat, civil war and utter chaos. Not a bad achievement for a man who could have remained a second-rate journalist had things happened differently. Even if his dictatorship was one of 'soft cheese', as some senior officials were said to call it, it was a very total form of totalitarianism.

Il Duce never quite mastered the art of delegation. In theory, every important decision had to be approved by him, which of course resulted in a huge backlog in the decisions-pending tray. And to add to this, so did every unimportant decision as well. And since he brooked no independent thought, he appointed a string of thoroughly evil henchmen to carry out the writ of his law. Dictators have tended to assume that not even a rat's fart will escape their attention, but there is a very obvious problem with this type of government. It doesn't work.

Given his heavy workload, it was hardly surprising that Mussolini didn't like to dawdle. Meals, he said, should take no more than three minutes, with a maximum of ten minutes per day. Nor will you be surprised to learn that for most of his life Mussolini suffered from acute digestive problems. Three litres of milk per day, masses of fruit and no alcohol or tobacco became his preferred regime, and he must have become very familiar with the country's network of *gabinetti*. He was a vegetarian, like his good buddy

Hitler, but his overfondness for milk and fruit might explain why he suffered acute digestive disturbances for so many years. It was long thought that he had ulcers but this proved impossible to verify on his death since his body had been so badly beaten up. He never liked to be seen to eat and would retire for his nightly milk unless a state banquet called, which he would attend only if absolutely necessary. No manly slabs of meat or writhing crustacea for him. Just gallons and gallons of milk. Hardly the thing, you might think, for an ardent fighter, but Mussolini was a man of some contradictions. *'Ho mangiato sempre in bianco'* – I've always eaten plain (white) food – he said in 1943, shortly before his death.

It wasn't until the last few months of his life, after the Germans had rescued him from imposed confinement in the Italian Alps, that he was introduced to a doctor who seemed to understand his condition. German doctor Georg Zachariae was to spend eighteen months looking after the dictator during the awful Republic of Salo (established in 1944 by the Nazis as a puppet regime with Mussolini at its head). Mussolini had lost twenty kilos in the space of three weeks, causing his German guardians some concern. Zachariae's solution was simple. He took Mussolini off his milk diet and after two weeks he was said to have recovered fully. His Fascist cheeks were flushed once more. More recently it has been suggested that he was suffering from Irritable Bowel Syndrome, brought on by his excessive consumption of milk.

Some of Mussolini's supporters thought that, just as Fascism called for a theoretical overhaul of the method of government, they could be equally radical when it came to the arts, to eating even. This theme had already been developed by Filippo Tommaso Marinetti and the Futurists. In 1909 Marinetti had published the Futurist Manifesto, which set out to establish a movement that would embrace modernism and, by implication, reject all that was fossilized and moribund in the Kingdom of Italy. It wasn't too far off the ideas that the Fascists put forward later on, and the two movements were always close. However, Marinetti was more of a cherry-picker than Mussolini, less of a politician. In the beginning it was art and literature that kept the Futurists busy. Their manifesto glorified the urban, the mechanical. They loved speed and 'beautiful ideas' and scorned women. They railed against romanticism and religious mystery.

In 1932, Marinetti published the bizarre tract *La cucina futurista* (*The Futurist Cookbook*), which moved the focus well and truly into the realm of eating. And it was pasta that the Futurists lambasted. While the Mayor of Naples had famously praised *vermicelli al pomodoro* as the food of angels, Marinetti called for the abolition of *pastasciutta* altogether:

> We call for the abolition of pastasciutta, an absurd Italian gastronomic religion. It may be that a diet of cod, roast beef and steamed pudding is beneficial to the English, cold cuts and cheese to the Dutch and sauerkraut, smoked [salt] pork and sausage to the Germans, but pasta is not beneficial to the Italians. For example, it is completely hostile to the vivacious spirit and passionate, generous, intuitive soul of the Neapolitans. If these people have been heroic fighters, inspired artists, awe-inspiring orators, shrewd lawyers, tenacious farmers it was in spite of their voluminous daily plate of pasta. When they eat it they develop that typical ironic and sentimental scepticism which can often cut short their enthusiasm.
>
> A highly intelligent Neapolitan, Professor Signorelli, writes: 'In contrast to bread and rice, pasta is a food which is swallowed, not masticated. Such starchy food should mainly be digested in the mouth by the saliva but in this case the task of transformation is carried out by the pancreas and the liver. This leads to an interrupted

equilibrium in these organs. From such disturbances derive lassitude, pessimism, nostalgic inactivity and neutralism.'

AN INVITATION TO CHEMISTRY

Pastasciutta, 40% less nutritious than meat, fish or pulses, ties today's Italians with its tangled threads to Penelope's slow looms and to somnolent old sailing ships in search of wind. Why let its massive heaviness interfere with the immense network of short long waves which Italian genius has thrown across oceans and continents? Why let it block the path of those landscapes of colour form sound which circumnavigate the world thanks to radio and television? The defenders of pasta are shackled by its ball and chain like convicted lifers or carry its ruins in their stomachs like archaeologists. And remember too that the abolition of pasta will free Italy from expensive foreign grain and promote the Italian rice industry.

The Futurist Cookbook by Filippo Tommaso Marinetti, edited and with an introduction by Leslie Chamberlain; translated by Suzanne Brill (Bedford Arts 1989)

Mussolini for his own political reasons was also antagonistic towards poor old pasta, for its consumption called for massive imports of hard wheat from abroad, primarily the US and Canada, a reliance that Mussolini could ill afford given his pact with Nazi Germany. So he came up with a plan to develop rural Fascism, where small model towns could be built from scratch to show the recalcitrant sceptics (especially the city-dwellers, who'd proved themselves far too inclined towards independent thought) the way forward. Rural development could also encourage the country to feed itself, part of this thing the Fascists had about virility, self-sufficiency and nationalism. Both Fascists and Futurists encouraged the use of rice, home-grown and more readily available, as an alternative to pasta, served in suitably bizarre ways.

In 1931 there opened the world's one and only Futurist restaurant in Turin, the Taverna Futurista del Santopalato. The menu was provocative – *antipasto intuitivo* (intuitive antipasto), *carneplastico* (model meat), *mammelle italiane al sole* (Italian breasts in the sun), *Pollofiat* (chicken Fiat) – and involved radical mixtures, such as nougat and mortadella, coffee and salami. The diners were encouraged to feel different textures with their hands while eating, and the room was to be sprayed with scents to stimulate the brain. We all had to wait until *nouvelle cuisine* before such radicalism would be seen again.

In 1925 Mussolini began what was to be called the Battle for Wheat. The full might of the propaganda machine whirled into action, and photos of Il Duce, shirtless, barrel-chested and hairy, showed him joining in the harvest in Littoria and Sabaudia, where functionaries recorded with mathematical precision the number of quintals he gathered. Imported wheat was to be taxed, but above all Italy must become self-sufficient. What this required was land, and how better to supply it than by reclaiming great swathes of swamp in order to show the world the Fascists' industry and competence. Some of these schemes had been started under the previous government but Mussolini carried them through and in doing so fundamentally altered the nature of much of the Italian coast. But the battle was not to be as simple as he thought. The land taken out of fruit and vegetable production to grow wheat caused serious economic problems. The authorities found themselves battling with a grave tomato shortage, not a good thing in Italy. The wheat yields were poor and the real cost was in the end far higher than that of the imported wheat anyway.

In the south, vast tracts of land were converted to wheat production on huge estates or *latifundia*, but production languished here too. One of the legacies of land reclamation is a string of peculiar, almost art deco-style towns dotted around the country, some loved and successful, others dismal and pointless. I was particularly attracted by the latter.

Mussolini's biggest and most successful reclamation project was near Rome in the Pontine Marshes, but Sardinia, with extensive marshy swamps that had given the island little but a nasty case of endemic malaria, was also deemed suitable. Not that *bonificazione* (reclamation) was to benefit the Sardinians very much. Fascist thinking was that the local population was moronic and incapable, so they shipped in hundreds of families from mainland Italy, mostly from the Veneto, experts in land reclamation.

Not far from Sardinia's gorgeous Catalan city of Alghero you can still see one of these dismal places, a small town called Fertilia. These days it is neither surrounded by fields of waving corn nor full of happy Fascist maidens with chaff in their hair, but it was an entirely Fascist creation, built to thrive off reclaimed land, a mini-paradise that went rather wrong. Fertilia is built in that particular Fascist style, a curious hybrid of St Trinian's and a Tyrolean mental asylum. The streets have a dead regularity about them, their names a heavy Fascist twang: Via del Fiume, Via d'Istria. At the centre of the town lies the church – Mussolini decided that the Catholic hierarchy had its uses after all – and the Casa del Fascio, the party headquarters. The old school still stands, and the perfectly straight high street runs down to the bay, passing dull square buildings, the odd bar, the very odd shop, and odder still a restaurant that almost actively repels any customers by looking so utterly gloomy. And in the background, twinkling away on the other side of the bay, lies Alghero.

Elderly and very un-Sardinian-looking locals still shuffle around. The park benches are rusted through. There is a monument to the fallen of Istria, which has a touch of the virile realism that Fascism so lovingly created. By the time

I had finished my walk around downtown Fertilia – allow five minutes max – I felt the urge neither to strut nor to shout but to leave, which I did rather hastily, passing the bloated corpse of an albino Alsatian. I couldn't quite work out the symbolism there.

At my hotel in Alghero, I asked about Fertilia and why on earth it was there. And it seemed that it wasn't alone. It had Fascist friends not far away.

'You should go to Mussolinia. That's even weirder!' the hotel receptionist told me. 'And there's Carbonia, too, but maybe that's too industrial, and it's right down in the south. Actually, they don't call it Mussolinia any more. It's Arborea these days. Take the road south from Oristano and it's not far from there. You can't miss it.'

So I did. And you can't.

As defiantly on the beaten track as Fertilia is off it, Mussolinia (OK, Arborea) straddles the main road and is bombarded by an endless stream of big trucks, big buses and big tractors. Which would have delighted the Fascist planners, who so desperately wanted everything to be huge, sprouting and virile. And, yes, although officially Mussolinia no longer exists, there's no point beating about the bush: the place exudes Fascism from its every pore. The story isn't too dissimilar from that of delightful Fertilia. This time the swamps were far more extensive and the lucky people chosen to work here – again, very few Sardinians – were mostly from Istria and the Veneto. Here was another golden opportunity to create a mini-Fascist adventure. But what sort of life was it? Pretty dire, by all accounts. Indeed so dire that within a few years many of the early settlers were pining for the Veneto, troubled by the malaria and the difficulty of living in this desolate part of the world. Arborea isn't beautiful. It's weird.

Renaming it Arborea was a clever wheeze if ever there was one. One of the few female heroes of Sardinian

Mussolini at the foundation of the new town of Carbonia,
18 December 1938.

history is Eleanor of Arborea, who was among the first to
have created a set of written laws and acted as a particularly wise *giudice* in the fourteenth century when the
Pisans were briefly the dominant power in this part of the
island. The Pisans built a few Tuscan-style churches and a
hefty wall around Cagliari but disappeared sharpish, chased
out by their eternal foe, the Genovesi, who effectively

lifted the lid of the historical dustbin and tipped the Pisans in for good.

When I arrived in Arborea it was early days in my bid to get to the heart of Italy, and I sidled up to a trio of Italian youth, trying to be as young and hip as possible, as only a middle-aged Englishman can do.

'So, this is Mussolinia,' I said.

'No. It's Arborea.'

'Someone in Alghero told me this used to be called Mussolinia.'

'Well, they would up there.'

'So. What's it like living here?' I expected them to pour out words of infinite wisdom and drag me off to meet their grandmothers, busily kneading dough under old photos of Il Duce.

'Sorry. We're from Cagliari.'

Mussolinia— stop it! Arborea doesn't have many hotels or restaurants. It has one of each, or did. Maybe it's sprouted a few more since then. One of the guidebooks I had was effervescent about the place. 'More redolent of Venice than southern Sardinia,' it said, which has to be one of the more preposterous misrepresentations I have ever read. The church was said to be a 'joyous pastiche of neo-Gothic style'. And so on. I could hardly wait to see all this, as I sat on my bed the night before, getting enormously excited about such architectural purity.

If you can sift the spectre of jackboots and bombastic blackshirtery from the architecture, some of it is striking. I love 1930s buildings. I lived in a bright and solid mansion block off Clapham Common for a few years and loved it. So I gawped somewhat ambivalently at the old Party Headquarters. And at a tumbledown villa that bore the name of the town's architect. And I thought that, hey, yes, I could handle a night in the shadow of Mussolini. I stepped into the hotel the boys from Cagliari had pointed out to me earlier and asked whether they had a room available.

'A room? For one person?' I was eyed by a rather severe doppelgänger of Mrs Danvers.

'Yes. Just me. If that would be all right.'

'I will see,' she said, shuffling off to the office. It was crazy really. There was this hum of people in the dining room and a good strong smell of pasta, steam and cheese, but I couldn't help thinking that if I poked my head around the corner the room would fall silent.

'Yes, we do have a room for one night. Would you like to see it?' she asked, smiling a little falsely and jangling a huge bunch of clunky keys.

'Yes, I should like that very much. Thank you.' Oh God, yes, I should love to stay in this place. But please don't rush at me in the middle of the night and smother me with a chloroform rag.

Up a gloomy wooden staircase, through a set of neat, immaculate rooms, spartan, like a school sanatorium, and into my room. A tiny bed. Militaristically tiny, with neatly folded, perfectly white blankets, a decanter full of warm, lightly bubbling water, no bathroom, no shower, not even a waffle towel.

'Yes. Thank you, that's fine. I'll come back later if I may and register,' I said, knowing that if needs be I could leg it.

Slipping off to the library for a little research, I found it empty but for the books and one bespectacled man reading intensely. Nothing too strange there, this was a library after all. Row upon row of telephone directories, from Aosta to Gallipoli. Shelves stuffed with Italian classics, encyclopaedias, dictionaries, all very mundane, but there was more. Tucked away in a little anteroom was the history section where I found some books that dared to mention the town by name, Mussolinia.

There were books with merry photos of the Duce's visit in 1935. The Italian king looked pompous and overdressed as usual. Buildings did indeed sprout. Some of these I liked, too. The old Casa del Fascio with its modern interpretation of the San Cristoforo Tower at Oristano, and the Casa del Balilla, both designed by Giovanni Ceas, are luminous, beautiful buildings. The houses designed for the immigrants from the Veneto had room enough for seven children, and the immigrants were even allowed to keep a share of what they managed to produce, unlike Fertilia where all produce was sold by the authorities. The idea was to create a veritable agricultural paradise, with fruit and wheat growing healthily from the alluvial soil. Sardinian agriculture was always based on sheep, but here things could, indeed would, be different. Cows and fodder crops were introduced, and novelties like cow's milk and butter spawned a whole new style of farming for the area.

And despite all the adversity, the malaria, the poverty, Arborea has managed, unlike Fertilia, to succeed. These days they produce food on an industrial scale. *Fior di latte*, mascarpone, ricotta, all emerge from Arborea's thriving factories to be delivered right across the island.

Time wore on, and although comforted by the endless swish of trucks speeding by I thought I ought to leave and get chatty with Signora Danvers again. The library was awesomely silent. The bespectacled man had gone. The door was closed. The door was actually a little more than closed. It was locked. Double-locked. And I was on the wrong side, stuck in a library in Mussolinia.

Thinking this to be a mere administrative ploy to keep the afternoon rush at bay, I turned the corner looking for another way out. There was no exit. Nothing but a television that didn't work and windows barred and tightly closed. Into romantic fiction. More barred windows. Psychology, architecture and politics. Shut. There could be worse places to be shut in. In a lift with a flatulent bank manager. In a deep-freeze. But my panic increased when I noticed there was nowhere to perform those vital post-prandial functions that coffee brings on. Should I stay by the door and gesticulate to passers-by? I tried, but there were no passers-by.

Where should I sleep? And what about my reservation in the hotel? I had already been away for three hours. I rushed through the library once more, increasingly agitated, and decided that there was only one hope: the bolted and chained door right at the very back. I had to bombard it, shove it as hard as I could. I hurled myself at the door, once, twice, and then, oh joy, it sprang open and I spilled out onto the pavement, right in front of the local police station.

Thank God there were no alarms, no howling Alsatians or jackbooted guards. Just the endless traffic and the soulless empty Fascist square before me. Was this the hand of Il Duce directing fate from some 1930s *palazzo* in the sky? Maybe. I had had more than enough and got into my car, which shouted electronic warnings at me that I was dangerously low on petrol.

I filled it up in Arborea (I promise I will never call you Mussolinia again, honest) and the good lady who ran the station plied me with scratch cards that offered free telephones, chocolates or a billion lire. I took the receipt and saw her name printed on the top. Fanny Colosso, Arborea. I set off back to Alghero.

ISCHIA

BEFORE I GOT THERE, AND WE'RE TALKING QUITE A FEW YEARS back in case you think I am completely fossilized, I had convinced myself that Kentucky had dusty streets, bars with swing doors, and cowboys chewing tobacco. The bars would be creaky, smelly and full of people who glared and spat when you walked in. A bit like a Welsh pub. But, alas, Louisville turned out to be just one of a thousand virtually identical American cities, full of police cars that went *whoop whoop whoop* all through the night and servers who commanded you to enjoy. Swing doors were not to be found anywhere. So I hurried on to Washington DC where I sold some terrible ice cream to American teenagers, many of whom probably went on to major in gun abuse and slaughter. This was the story of what would now be called my gapyear (important to run the two words together), which in those days was a more leisurely year off (very much separate words).

I am rather partial to global fantasies. After all, millions seem to think that London is perpetually shrouded in fog. That the French are all rude. So I am not entirely unique. But my dominant fantasy, my geographical Holy Grail, is to find an island, preferably Mediterranean, that is perfectly formed, scented, and full of fish, sea, warmth and colour. Many years later, I had noticed the island of Ischia, conveniently sitting off the Neapolitan coast, and began to think that I should check it out. It was triply enticing. It was an island for one. Enticement number two was that Anthony Minghella's fab film of Patricia Highsmith's even fabber book *The Talented Mr Ripley* had been shot there. It was this film that had reminded me that the sea, Italy, a gorgeous boat, a tasty body or two and a strong undercurrent of evil were particularly attractive. It had been a long and relentlessly wet winter in London. And enticement number three? They ate rabbits.

Rabbits are not easy for the British to admit openly to eating, let alone liking, from a gastronomic point of view, that is. Fluffy tails and whiffly noses generally preclude that sort of thing. Eating them is, well, not what you should really do to a rabbit. Maybe shoot them, yes. But raise them to be killed like a lamb to slaughter – no way. For us, rabbitophagy is a moral issue. The Cartesian French are not bothered by this at all, and raise rabbits by the million for food without a qualm. And the Italians, who are inspired ekers, are well aware that this quick-growing, easily reared animal is a fabulous source of protein and not to be sniffed at. Especially not on an island like Ischia, where the slopes are relentlessly steep and there simply isn't room, or the climate, for large cows, oozing udders and lush pastures. So the rabbit is a very practical solution to the protein problem. Even more so when, as was once the case, the men of the island went off to sea, or America, and were far too busy to rear animals.

Ischia is small and densely populated. It is definitely Mediterranean and in parts exquisitely beautiful, but it has a downside. It can get busy. Horribly so, and the season is elongated by one of its main attractions: volcanic mud. If you like the idea of seeing corpulent people with mud

The exquisitely beautiful island of Ischia, with
Mount Epomea brooding over it.

plastered over their faces, or of sitting in volcanically hot
springs with a load of ancient, arthritic Italians, then this is
the place for you. But if you like lolling lazily in the sea,
beware.

Long ago, the floating body of the dead siren
Parthenope landed nearby at Naples, where she was duly
honoured with a tomb, as you would expect. And which
is why, by the way, Neapolitans often refer to themselves
as Parthenopians. Indeed, even well before the mournful
influence of the Camorra, quite a bit of body-floating went
on. The body of an ex-patriarch of Constantinople, St
Costanzo, was washed up on nearby Capri, where he was
appointed the island's patron saint. Aeneas' pilot Palinurus,
whom I must say I associate with a genus of crawfish, was
also washed up, again very dead, on a nearby promontory
that still bears his name. And on Ischia itself, the body of
St Restituta floated all the way from Africa to land on the

beach of Lacco Ameno, where both a spring and a church exist in her name to this day.

But Ischia is perhaps more famous for being the mythological island of Typhoeus, a rebellious giant who irritated Jupiter into condemning him to perpetual enchainment underneath Mount Epomea, the highest mountain on the island. And it is his discontented rumblings that are said to be behind the island's intense and at times violent eruptions. On the one hand, you've got the everyday volcanic eruption, which fuels and heats the springs to which people flock from far and wide to sip at and sit in. But on the other hand, there is always the possibility of something utterly malevolent taking place, as happened on 28 July 1883 at Casamicciola.

At about 9.30 in the evening, the town was beginning to settle down for the night. The caffès were full of people. *Gelati* were flowing. In the square the locals were watching the Neapolitan actor Petito do his famous Pulcinella thing. In one of the town's smarter hotels, an Englishman was starting to play Chopin's Funeral March, which so annoyed an Italian guest that he walked out of the room, saying: 'I shall go into the garden. This English *signor* wants to bury us all.' And *whoom*! Within a matter of seconds an earthquake had completely razed the town, killing over 5,000 people, which for an island with a population of 26,000 was truly catastrophic. The hospital with its twenty-six patients was razed. As was the jail, and all the town's hotels. Russian nobles, Indian aristocrats, convicts, children, even the local bishop perished. So don't expect to see any buildings of remarkable beauty in Casamicciola today. And don't be surprised at a slight tension in the air if you hear a rumble or two.

You can get to Ischia quite easily. Fly to Naples and go straight to the port, where you will see a selection of heaving and rather disreputable ferries lined up, many of them a *Lauro* this or a *Lauro* that, which may remind you of those distant days when a band of Palestinian freedom-fighters furthered their cause significantly by tipping a disabled old American man into the sea. The infamous cruise ship, the *Achille Lauro*, wasn't there at the time I passed by, but I had been well briefed by a voluble Neapolitan taxi driver who, in the space of a forty-minute drive, managed to tell me how brilliant Napoli were at football, all about his family, how the Camorra still existed – this said in suitably hushed tones – how beautiful Sant'Angelo d'Ischia was, and how delicious was the rabbit, particularly the *coniglio alla cacciatore*. And how I must take the *aliscafo*, the hydrofoil, *rapido*, or I'd miss the last one.

This island thing of mine is not unusual, I know. It is shared by about fifty million other people. Sadly, just about every Mediterranean island has become heavily addicted to tourism. Which is, of course, the problem, and the paradox. Many of us would love to zip back in time to the 1950s or even the 1960s and check out post-pubescent Italian civilization in a *cinquecento*. We would love to see weird processions and sobbing widows, eat fabulously cheap food and get gloriously happy on a bottle of red wine. But here on Ischia, prepare to be disappointed. Ischia has become Teutonic. Not entirely so or even uniquely so, but a little oddly (especially since nearby Capri is so heavily anglicized). But the Germans, I was told, love Ischia, not only for the usual heat and sun but for the volcanic springs. The English, apparently, don't do hot mud.

A shameless selection of signs encouraged us all to take *Frühstück*, *Kaffee* and *Kuchen*, and *Wiener Schnitzel*; it all became a little, let's say, thought-provoking. Is this the way things have to be? Will we ever see teashops in Arundel proclaiming *carta turistica*, or *prima colazione qui*? I suspect not. And what about the German thing? It's tricky. Moan too loudly and you are a killjoy verging on the racist. But German culture does not fit in easily here. It is an interesting process we are witnessing, whose outcome is far from certain. Can Ischia keep its Ischia-ness? What is Ischia-ness anyway?

Historically, of course, the German influence is far from mysterious. The recent history of Fascism and Nazism will quite possibly, and quite rightly, never be forgotten by either Italians or Germans. But *Weinstuben* in Ischia are, to say the least, disheartening. The Ischians are being remarkably pragmatic, for this is the way that the island is, and will be for some time to come. Long gone are the days of swarthy fishermen, powerful priests and crucifixes. We are in the post-Christian, mad-consumer era.

Let's get back to the rabbits. I was at first a little bashful about my rabbit lust, but throwing caution to the wind I soon came out to the charming hotel manager. Forio, where I had chosen to stay, sounded remote. This was me fantasizing again. It wasn't. But at least the hotel manager was happy to rabbit on about rabbit. He even knew London quite well, and to make matters easier for me with my struggling Italian spoke fluent English.

'Yes. It's true. We love rabbit on the island. I don't know why. We always used to eat it on Sunday, sitting around the table. But we don't really have time for this sort of life any more. I mean, look at the hotel now!'

It was heaving. The guests, mainly rather wizened, creaky Italians, seemed to consider it quite OK to do things they would never ever do in a downtown Milan hotel, and they walked through the reception in ill-fitting white towelling robes, revealing stick-like chalk-white legs quite shamelessly. Equally shameless was their tendency to hang their massive and surprisingly inelegant knickers – inelegant for an Italian that is – outside their rooms to dry, so the hotel looked a little like a Neapolitan side street.

'Where should I go to eat a really good *coniglio all' ischitana*?' I asked.

'Ah, that's easy. The Sole Nascente at Ciglio. I'll ring up and book for you. I know the lady who runs the place. Sit down. Have a coffee and tell me about London. My son's working there at the moment.'

And we talked about London. About how good the food had become and how much his son loved being there. 'The island gets very boring, you know. Especially if you're young.'

He called but got no reply. Then one of his barmen, who lived in Ciglio, called his mother — and yes, he did live with her but he was a modest twenty-five or so — who knew the woman who ran the restaurant. The restaurant was closed but since it was getting near Easter the mother told her son that she would go and chivvy the owner up and try to talk her into a rabbit-cooking session.

'You know what you should try,' the manager said, as if conspiring with me, '*bucatini al sugo di coniglio*. Now that's what we like on Ischia. Then maybe have *coniglio alla cacciatore*. Or *all'ischitana*. Ah, *bucatini*.' A misty-eyed moment flashed across his busy brow. 'The thing about *bucatini* is the — how do you say it in English?' He sucked his breath and licked his lips.

'Slurping.'

'Ah yes, slurping. You see, *bucatini* have this hole right through the middle and when you eat you slurp the pasta and the sauce at the same time, and believe me the signora makes an excellent *sugo*. Quite delicious.'

This began to sound like a Japanese noodle bar, where the slurping can be quite deafening.

The phone rang. Contact had been made. I was off to a rabbit feast of possibly epic proportions.

Embarrassingly early I sauntered into the restaurant, almost expecting welcoming banners, stuffed rabbits and staff with fluffy white tails. I had ample time during my saunter to take in the view, which was truly exquisite. Below me was the port of Sant'Angelo where only yesterday I had tried to ease a little culture from the restaurant owner, but he had been keener to look at the vast, shimmering white, unfeasibly expensive motor boats in the yachting magazine I was wading through with my early morning cappuccino.

The Sole Nascente is unprepossessing, square and functional, but what more can you expect in a zone where the *terremoti* can be so terrifying? The door opened and the place was empty but for a woman who was slowly stroking the floor with a straw broom, whom I assumed to be the cleaner – how urban can one be? To my further embarrassment, she was actually the owner, and laughed heartily when I asked whether I could speak with the *signora* who runs the place. So, after committing a faux pas as only a foreigner can with any degree of shamelessness, I asked whether it was true that there was a rabbit waiting for me, quivering above the pot.

While I tried to disarm her with compliments, she disarmed me with a smile, sat me down and told me to wait. The rabbit would take time. And was I Swiss? Well, no, English.

'*Inglese!* We don't get many down here,' she said.

Time passed and I flipped through a little more historical stuff on Mazzini and wished he were here, being judgemental and reflective. He never mentioned Ischia, but he would almost certainly have seen the island when sailing to Gaeta from Sicily. When my *bucatini* finally arrived, they almost buzzed with the scent of oregano and wine and garlic. The plate gently steamed in the warm air. Divine food. Eaten, nay, slurped, with gusto. I drank red wine, eased myself lower in the chair and waited for my *coniglio all'ischitana*. Which was as holy and perfect as the *bucatini*. How much more enjoyable was this than the awful fussiness of my other rabbit meal on Ischia.

Coniglio all'ischitana

Serves four.

1 domesticated rabbit (not a wild one) of about 1.5kg,
cleaned and ready to use
20ml olive oil
2 cloves garlic
1 chilli
100ml red wine
500g plum tomatoes, chopped
4 leaves fresh basil
1 sprig fresh thyme
1 sprig fresh marjoram
1 sprig fresh rosemary
salt and pepper

Wash the rabbit, pat it dry and cut it into large chunks.
Brown the rabbit chunks in a flameproof terracotta dish
(or saucepan) in the oil with the garlic and chilli. Add the
wine and bring to the boil. Add the tomatoes, herbs and
seasoning and cook for 30 minutes over a moderate heat.
Adjust the seasoning and serve.

Rabbit meal number two was in the guidebooks' favourite
restaurant, a serious, tableclothy sort of place, obviously
proud of its three forks. By the way, I should add that this,
as were most of my journeys, was a visit very much off-
season, when the weather was being deeply radical. As I
drove my *seicento* from Forio to the port of Ischia – as
great a distance as is possible on the island – rain of such
intensity came down that the road seamlessly became a
torrent, while the sky erupted into a mesmerizing display of
pink-shaded lightning and a local firework display bravely
celebrated some obscure saint or other or the imminent
arrival of another messiah. So when I walked into this

seriously smart restaurant, it, like the Sole Nascente, was totally and bleakly empty. The people geared themselves into action and played the game of cloche-lifting and obsequiousness excellently, but this was so farcical and pointless I was dying to leave almost as soon as I entered. The rabbit was too fussy. And so was the client. Maybe there are people who like all this flim-flammery, but I loathe it. And it was here in Ischia that I finally learnt that food guides are a dubious pleasure. They invade your thought processes and hijack your investigative instincts. You might think they do the legwork for you, but I'm not entirely convinced they are necessary in Italy. After all, if you travel thousands of miles to get here, why all of a sudden relinquish your powers of reason to someone else? By now everyone must know only too well what any restaurant in the *Guide Michelin* will provide: variations on a French theme, tablecloths and high bills, and serious lavatories. In Italy, this school of cooking, urban and wealthy, is doing well, but only where the urban rich hang out. As they do in Ischia, for a time at least, in the summer. These are the restaurants with hordes in the kitchen and signatures on the chef's whites. Sommeliers and no sense of fun.

Sadder still are the wonderful old *trattorie* that have been discovered and have supped with the devil. American food writers, in particular, have immense influence and, much like Mr Parker's wine recommendations, any trattoria lauded by a writer who carries weight is then overwhelmed by awestruck food travellers, who by their very presence can ruin the restaurant. The ultimate paradox. Success almost always brings failure. I found one particularly famous trattoria in Ravello to be as difficult to enjoy as any in Italy, where the food is mediocre and the staff smug. There. Let's have a bit of artistic struggle and obscurity.

If there's one question you should master in Italian it is this: '*Dove posso mangiare bene qui?*' Where can I eat well here? It is worth its weight in *tartufi bianchi*. Even if you get it wrong or mispronounce it, the sense will be there. *You* are asking. *You* are seeking something out. So the next thing should be this: 'Who do I ask?' Ah, good point. Because you will get a thousand answers from a thousand people. And here I cite the good old hotel staff. They often, though not always, know the area. They probably like to eat, and are quite busy and not particularly rich so they won't want ruched curtains and *jus*. Beware, though, of cosy relationships with particular restaurants that might leave you seriously disappointed.

Then there are taxi drivers. Trickier this, for I have had a few duff recommendations and a few real crackers. But look at the guy. (Sorry, they are almost all guys in Italy.) Is he stick-thin with needle marks in his arms? If so, his judgement may be erroneous. Ask yourself whether he looks like he enjoys his food. Tourist officials can also be a great source of information, and they often seem to be out to lunch. Then there are complete and utter strangers, but preferably those who at least look as if they like to eat. And if more than one person suggests the same place, you could be in luck.

There is also an art to menu-reading. If you're in Ischia, for example, and they are serving Sicilian *pasta alla norma* or Emilian *agnolotti*, this isn't exactly local food for local people. Avoid such places. What the food guides are good at, particularly Slow Food's *Osterie d'Italia*, is drawing your attention to what the local dishes are, which in Italy can change rapidly from town to town.

And then there is, fittingly, gut reaction. A positive buzz, happy people, locals, and anywhere with a smiling old woman or two. There. That's my guide to eating well in Italy. *Buon appetito*.

Earlier in the day of my Sole Nascente lunch, I had decided to take a cruise around all the possible rabbit locations I had noted so far. All those relatively close to Forio at least. So with a freshly delivered copy of the day's European *Independent*, I set off into the stormy morning air. The taxi wasn't a taxi at all but one of those things you see all over Italy that I only recently realized were called Ape ('ah-pay'), which comes from the Italian for bee, rather than Ape ('ayp'). You know the sort of thing. Three wheels, noisy and, of course, the worker to the sharper Vespa, the wasp. The driver was slightly fazed by my weird request but no doubt used to people doing peculiar things on the island, so off we set.

He was not the prettiest man in town. Sixtyish, over-weight, sweaty and slightly on the surly side. He oozed neither charm nor interest. But what finally tipped the scales of my appreciation was his taximeter. It leapt up, clicking with the speed of an atomic clock, and with a currency like the lire it was alarming to say the least. As we were squeezing through the lanes, and as I began to see why the Ape was rather a good means of getting around, we passed a little shop with a sign that shouted out stop: *Coniglio*. I leapt out of the taxi, handed the driver a thick wad of banknotes and wished him Godspeed.

I was quickly relieved of a few pieces of my rabbit cultural baggage, for one old lady told me that wild rabbit was infinitely preferable to domesticated bunny but difficult to find these days. As for the rabbits they sold in the supermarkets, they might be cheap but they were not good to eat. And did I know that on the next island, Procida, rabbits still leapt and whiffled as they once did on Ischia? And for the very good reason that a reserve has been created to protect the little island's wildlife.

'What I would do if I could get my hands on those rabbits,' she said.

Another old lady chipped in. 'Well, when I was young we used to keep rabbits in a *fossa* and they were the best

I've ever tasted. I've heard they are trying to get them going again. *Coniglio da fossa*.'

These were, it turned out, a breed unique to the island, small-eared mini-rabbits with particularly attractive mottled grey fur, kept and fed in what the locals call a *fossa*, 'ditch' in English but more like an enclosed burrow.

'Now if you ever get to taste one of them, they are the best. Especially with *bucatini*.' They are nothing if not consistent on Ischia.

SICILY

I THROW THIS QUESTION INTO THE RING. WHAT CONNECTION is there between Admiral Lord Horatio Nelson, the famous, one-eyed, one-armed British naval hero, and a bowl of pistachio ice cream? The answer is, of course, Mount Etna. Confused? Bemused? Read on. And may your illusions be shattered. One: I am going to suggest that Nelson was a cad and a bounder. Two: perhaps even more astonishing, I am going to try to convince you that pistachio ice cream is a more interesting proposition than the lurid, bitter sludge you might be used to. Let's start with Nelson.*

After having trounced the French at the Battle of Aboukir Bay in 1798, Nelson sailed off to Naples to get his ships repaired and became deeply embroiled in the country's desperate politics. This is where he famously met Emma Hamilton, who as the wife of the long-standing British ambassador Sir William Hamilton had forged a close relationship with the Neapolitan king, Ferdinand, and,

* For a fuller, more closely reasoned argument read Terry Coleman's *Nelson* (Bloomsbury 2001).

more particularly, with the queen, Maria Carolina, sister of the recently beheaded Marie Antoinette of France. Nelson was to do his own forging later on. The relationship between the British and the Kingdom of Naples was close, for even if the king was considered by many to be a fool, his kingdom was an important regional ally and provided a means for the British to counterbalance the growing influence of French Republicanism. The Neapolitan First Minister was even English, an effective, inscrutable man called Sir John Acton, who at the time had the confidence of Queen Maria Carolina and worked closely with William Hamilton.

Italy at the beginning of the nineteenth century was divided into its various kingdoms and duchies and was greatly affected by the revolutionary fervour coming out of France. Soon Emilia, Tuscany, Liguria and Piedmont had fallen to Napoleon, who then took over the Papal States to the north of the Kingdom of Naples. A plot was hatched, with the connivance of Nelson, for King Ferdinand to invade Rome in an effort to stop the inevitable French invasion of the Kingdom of Naples, in the process liberating Italy from the Napoleonic scourge. This was fine in principle but for the fact that the army raised by King Ferdinand was singularly inept and unreliable. Over 30,000 occasionally shoeless troops marched on Rome and entered the great city on 29 November 1798, where the king ensconced himself in the Farnese Palace. But by 5 December they were on the move again, booted out by the superior French forces, and the king returned from whence he came.

Naples, however, was becoming a nervous, agitated city and the king and queen were distinctly uncertain of their future. Mindful perhaps of the unpleasant end of Marie Antoinette in post-revolutionary France a few years earlier, they prepared to depart the city under Nelson's protection and flee to Sicily.

The great mass of the Neapolitan underclass, the fiercely loyal, royalist *lazzaroni*, always an important element in the city's history, were not at all happy at the prospect of losing their king and queen and barricaded the palace to stop them leaving. But subtler tactics prevailed. The royal duo were hurried out through secret passages when it was thought they were entertaining a Turkish noble, and set off for Palermo in Nelson's ship the *Vanguard*, loaded to the gunwales with over two million pounds' worth of royal treasure. With the king and queen gone, anarchy reigned in Naples. King Ferdinand, meanwhile, was said to be greatly looking forward to a good day's hunting in the hills behind Palermo in this, the southern part of his kingdom.

Certain sectors of the population, mainly the educated middle classes, increasingly desired reform. They found it impossible to thrive under a king who loved hunting more than ruling. With the revolutionary wind from the north blowing at the kingdom's portals, and the king temporarily off the scene, a brief Republican period began: the Parthenopean Republic, established on 29 January 1799. These liberal ideas were anathema to the king, the queen, Nelson and the British. A long campaign to reinstate the king began. Republican blood was to be spilled. When the Austrians declared war against the French in 1799, the French, the Republic's protectors, were obliged to move troops northwards, leaving the Parthenopeans vulnerable to attack. The king, still based in Palermo, sent Cardinal Fabrizio Ruffo up from Calabria, at first with no troops at all. Ruffo, a curious character who wasn't really a cardinal and who was loathed by Nelson, amassed an army along the way, the infamous *Sanfedisti* whose apparent adherence to the Christian faith concealed their counter-revolutionary, reactionary intentions. They marched from Pizzo in Calabria up to Naples, and with the encouragement of the king, the British and their allies the Russians, proceeded to root out any Republicans they came across, replacing their symbolic Trees of Liberty with funeral crosses.

With Nelson in Sicily protecting the royal couple, a Captain Foote was made commander of the British Fleet poised outside Naples surveying the developments in the city. It was he who eventually agreed to a truce between the Republicans, now abandoned by their French protectors, and the loyal Neapolitan Monarchists. Our one-eyed hero, who sailed back from Sicily after the fall of the Republic, was far from happy with these arrangements. Despite his professed love of duty, discipline and honour, he refused to accept the agreement, which had been negotiated in good faith, to allow any remaining French troops and Republican sympathizers to escape scot-free and sail off to France. And so Nelson, fully supported by the powerful and sympathetic queen, attempted to renegotiate. This was too much for Foote, who subsequently spent years trying to preserve his own reputation and sully Nelson's – and justifiably so, for the end result was that the Republicans were not allowed to go free and many were shot or hanged. In 1999, on the bicentenary of the Parthenopean Republic, a number of Italian historians revived these accusations of Nelson's bad faith and deceit, and one even branded him a war criminal.

Black mark number two involved the trial of Neapolitan naval officer Commander Caracciolo. He and Nelson did not see eye to eye. When Caracciolo was not asked to accompany the king and queen on their flight to Sicily, he seems to have weighed up his position and decided to join the ranks of the Republicans, which boosted their morale considerably. However, he was eventually captured and handed over, pale, haggard and looking far older than his forty-seven years, to the Monarchists. Nelson learnt of this and took the law into his own hands. He arranged a hasty court martial of the unfortunate Caracciolo, who was hanged without the customary twenty-four hours allowed for the

To the Monarchists of Naples in 1799, Lord Nelson was a hero.
In this picture he is still shown without his eyepatch, although he lost
his right eye before it was painted.

victim to prepare to meet his doom. The body was thrown
into the sea, 'with three double-headed shot, weighing two
hundred and fifty pounds, tied to its legs'. A few weeks
later a panicky fisherman stopped off at Nelson's ship,
moored in the Bay of Naples, and said that he had seen
Caracciolo walking towards the shore, his head clearly
visible above the waves. Nelson took off to investigate and
he too saw the body, which had somehow managed to float

defiantly to the surface. Caracciolo's corpse was pulled from the water and given a Christian burial on shore.

However we might criticize Nelson two hundred years on, King Ferdinand's appreciation of the man was boundless. To the Monarchists, Nelson was a hero. He had been asked by the king to treat the uprising as he would have done an Irish rebellion, and that was precisely what he did, egged on, no doubt, by the fascinating figure of Emma Hamilton, who was said to have become as familiar with Queen Maria Carolina as she was later to become with Nelson. When the king and queen finally stepped onto the shore at Naples – for many weeks they had stayed safely on Nelson's ship the *Foudroyant* – Nelson was invited onshore and fêted at a number of wildly extravagant parties in the capital. Honour upon honour was bestowed on him, and as a very special favour King Ferdinand bequeathed to him and his heirs in perpetuity the Duchy of Bronte, which lay in a valley to the east of Mount Etna in Sicily.

I am not entirely sure whether King Ferdinand had a morbid sense of humour, but Bronte was, according to Greek myth, a son of the Cyclops, who lived in the turbulent innards of Mount Etna making fire for Zeus. So what better honour to give the one-eyed Nelson but a duchy at the foot of Mount Etna?

Charging up the dusty road from Catania in my mighty *seicento*, I set off into the mountain's upper storeys, passing through the town of Nicolosi, which had its own brush with eternity in the last major eruption in 2002. Tongues of lava stopped within spitting distance of the town, but further up the mountain burnt-out shells and charred walls of houses told a less fortunate story. In an attempt to keep out the lava the locals have built a network of some of the ugliest fences modern man has designed, not just around the town but far up into the hills. They are everywhere.

Perhaps the local fencing contractor was in league with the priest. Maybe they thought that the lava would obediently flow into the neighbour's patch or simply stop altogether, or maybe there is a far more mundane reason that I couldn't find.

Neither the eternal presence of the volcano nor the monthly bills from the fencing contractor have dissuaded intrepid humans from exploiting the great fertility of Etna's volcanic soil, and the peculiar combination of sun, soil and plant sex has created a microworld of the most ridiculously tasty fruits. I was so struck by the intense cherriness of the cherries and – even more so – by the apricotness of the apricots being hawked by the side of the road that I called home to say that I had just discovered apricot perfection in the foothills of Mount Etna. For some reason, there was an awed silence at the other end of the phone. I guess I do get rather overexcited about these things. Anyway, I held on to my apricots through thick and thin, and when I later took a train from Catania they were the talk of the ticket office. Never have apricots caused such a stir, and I am determined that I shall live to eat them again.

Anyway, to the pistachios. These plants are not indigenous to the island (neither are apricots, Ed.). They were introduced into Sicily by the Arabs, who in turn learnt about pistachio production from the Persians. That's the story anyway. The town of Bronte has emerged as the pistachio capital of Italy and produces a mighty one per cent of the world's pistachios. But all is not well. The pistachio is a difficult crop that takes a lot of man hours, and just as points mean prizes, man hours mean money. I had an inkling of this pistachio unease for I had heard that Slow Food had begun to draw the world's attention to the problem. I approached the estimable organization for information, but their response was, well, tardy.

So I was pistachio-blind here. I wound through Bronte's confusing backstreets, hoping to see stalls laden with pistachios. I saw nothing, and so exited onto the road that led to Nelson's Castle and followed it through to its bitter Nelsonian end. The *castello* was built around an eleventh-century abbey, whose own origins as a spiritual site are Byzantine.

Nelson never once set foot in Bronte, but he was given complete freedom by King Ferdinand to nominate whoever he wished to inherit the Duchy or, as it was so delightfully called on one of the notices there, the Ducky, and he passed it on to his awful, venal clergyman brother William, his father and his sister, before it found a sort of Nelsonian permanence with the descendants of his niece Charlotte, who married another of our naval heroes, Admiral Hood. In fact, Bronte became a bit of an embarrassment to Nelson, particularly when his behaviour at Naples became more widely known and his infatuation with Emma Hamilton gave the press much material for ribald comment. Why, the *Morning Herald* blasted, 'His lordship . . . very properly considers that a brave Englishman can derive no very great degree of credit from an Italian name.' Better still was Cruikshank's cutting cartoon at the time that showed Lady Hamilton, Sir William Hamilton and Nelson discoursing about smoking. Lady Hamilton says: 'Pho, the old man's pipe is always out, but yours burns with full vigour!' Nelson replies: 'Yes, yes, I'll give you such a smoke I'll pour a whole broadside into you!' The pipe is rather long and has a distinct look of the phallus about it.

The *castello* was acquired by the commune in the 1980s but retains a distinctly British feel. When I visited, I was alone but for a group of children singing hymns in one of the back rooms. Odd, that, I thought. You have to be guided through the castle, and dutifully learn, on entering a room with a bed, that it is a bedroom, and that a room with a bath is a bathroom. The Italians have a curious fondness for accompanied visits. I couldn't have seen Garibaldi's home in Caprera without one, but the most excruciating was the tour around the castle at Urbino, the one and only time I have been to Italy *en famille*. Since neither of my kids speaks any Italian other than pasta, they found it a little challenging until we broke free and played hide and seek and lost Sophie in the renaissance fog. It's a pity they have to go to school. They would have loved Etna, pistachio ice cream and the endless quest for perfect pasta. They would have loved pizza in Naples and truffle-hunting in Piedmont, though the *mattanza* in Carloforte might have been a little too much for my daughter, a confirmed vegetablearian, according to one of her schoolfriends. Bashing tuna on the head, however, would have been very much my son's idea of fun. But Nelson's Castle would have tried their limited patience. Even I was getting a little restless. I found solace looking out at Etna from the window, and glancing along the bookcase to see what the descendants of Lord Bridport (himself a descendant of Charlotte) read at night. Pony Club handbooks seemed popular, alongside the unsurprising books about battles, wars and H. Nelson.

When the tour was all over, I thanked the guide, and God, told him where Bridport was and asked, almost as an aside, whether he knew anything about pistachios.

Zino Sanfilippo's eyes brightened, and he pointed his thumbs into his chest in the 'do I know!' gesture familiar to us all. He grabbed me by the arm and showed me a depressed-looking plant in the corner. Meet the pistachio. Meet also a plant called terebinth, *scornabecco* in dialect, a relative of the pistachio that is even better at thrusting its tough little roots into the volcanic *sciare*, the lava surface. The terebinth is grafted onto the pistachio to induce fruiting, though to make matters complex the pistachio fruits only every two years: odd, rather than even, years in Sicily.

You might have thought, as I did, that growing pistachios was a simple horticultural matter, running along the lines of plant, wait, spray with masses of toxins, pick and sell, but it isn't. You need, for the usual reasons, male and female plants, although one male is said to be enough for every two hundred or so females. When you walk through the *lochi*, the plantations, it is difficult to put one foot in front of the other on the harsh volcanic surface, though the plants appear to thrive. Any mechanization is therefore out of the question. Come harvest-time it is another hand job, and the nuts are picked and then dried in the sun for a few days. From this you can see that the pistachio needs an inordinate amount of attention, and even if it does thrive on the volcanic soil, it costs a lot to produce, which is the heart of the problem. For although Italian production is small – the big producers are Iran and Turkey – there are fears that it is becoming too expensive to continue. If the future is to be bright, it must be with a fairly devoted niche market. A variety is produced here, called simply the Bronte Red, that is the pistachio apogee, exported around the world, loved and cosseted, but to most of us entirely unknown. The Bronte Red, though it sounds like a rare breed of hen, is the possible salvation of Sicilian pistachio production. There are times when these culinary obscurities seem almost tragic in their isolation. But these pistachios have a beautiful intensity to their colour, a voluptuous red on the outside and a remarkable, almost tasteful, green to the nut. And if this sounds like a little too much in praise of a pistachio, just wait until you eat a real *gelato al pistacchio*. Just you wait.

Gelato al pistacchio

You will need an ice-cream maker for this.

1 litre whole milk
800ml single cream
300g sugar
4 tablespoons cornflour
150g finely ground pistachios or pistachio paste, preferably
from Bronte
pistachios from Bronte, toasted, to serve

Heat 750ml of the milk to 85°C. Mix the remaining milk with the cream, sugar and cornflour into a smooth paste, and add this to the heated milk. Mix until smooth, then add the ground pistachios or pistachio paste. Return to the heat, bring to the boil, then take off the heat. Allow to cool to room temperature. Refrigerate, and put into ice-cream machine when cold. Serve with toasted pistachios.

Flowing on from how do your pistachios grow was the logical next step, eating them. I wanted to know if there were any peculiarities in the Bronte culinary heritage. Zino went to the phone and made a call.

'Go and talk to my friend Nunzio in Bronte.'

So it was adieu Nelsonian embarrassment, and *buona sera* Bronte.

Nunzio Sampieri is a young, immensely enthusiastic hotelier who runs a two-star *albergo* called Il Parco dell'Etna. There aren't too many places to stay around here, so I would suggest anyone with more than a passing interest in either Etna or pistachios wends his or her way to Bronte, and makes sure to eat Nunzio's pistachio ice cream, for it is ravishing.

Earlier on I had made the huge mistake of stopping for lunch just above Nicolosi. A restaurant with a spectacular view chose for unknown reasons to hustle everyone indoors to eat in a room full of plastic plants with a waiter who looked suicidal and music so loud you couldn't hear yourself think. The irritated exclamation – 'I can't hear myself think!' – echoed down to me over a distance of many years and I realized that it was my turn to be middle-aged. I love music and I like it loud, or so I thought, but Sade at twenty decibels above safe limits on a tranquil Mount Etna is unbecoming. My journal reads: 'Dreary leaden maccheroni. Was offered Parmesan or ricotta. Said was it old or young. The answer was in English: "Typical Sicilian cheese."'

So, it was extremely pleasant to talk with Nunzio. And my hunch was right. The Brontesi do have funny ways with pistachios. There is even a book with two hundred pistachio recipes, but Nunzio's repertoire was a little more typical.

Penne al pistacchio

Serves four.

400g penne
30g unsalted butter
1 onion, finely chopped
2 cloves garlic, finely chopped
50g pancetta, diced
1 tablespoon reduced meat stock
50g finely chopped pistachios or pistachio paste
100ml brandy
200ml single cream
salt and pepper

Cook the penne in the usual way. Melt the butter in a

frying pan and fry the onion and garlic in it for 5 minutes. Add the pancetta and meat stock and cook for another 5 minutes. Add pistachios or pistachio paste and the brandy, and flame. Add the cream, check the seasoning and serve hot.

To see if I could crib any more ideas I asked Nunzio whether I could have a quick look at his menu.

'My menu!' he scoffed. 'I haven't got one. I'll tell you why.'

For a moment, I could almost have been in London. When we all started getting serious about food back in the 1980s, every chef worth his *sale e pepe* loved to tell anyone who'd listen how he went to the markets every day and bought only the very best. I once worked out that, given that chefs usually leave the restaurant at midnight at the earliest and the fish market starts at five, and that they had to wind down, wash (sometimes) and watch TV, they were close to serious sleep deprivation. It was all complete rubbish, of course, and we – I was a supplier once, you see – knew it, but bless their little cotton toques they loved the attention. The difference was that Nunzio actually did it, but he had only to walk a few hundred metres and he was right in the middle of the land of perfect fruit and perfect pistachios. And ricotta, and cheese. He is doing what all those city chefs dream about, and most importantly he knows how to handle the produce. Cities draw in peculiar ingredients from far and wide but Italians stick closely to their roots. On some days *contadini* would arrive at the market with bundles of wild asparagus or *porcini* from the hills. There was even talk of *tartufi* to be found on Etna. And so Nunzio would buy whatever was best each day and create his menu from that.

Just then his daughter arrived, as sweet and pretty as the *gelato* I was eating. As was his wife, and his attention wandered. I thanked him, and drove off to spend the night being bitten to death by mosquitoes in Syracuse.

There could hardly be a more perfectly fitting place to eat pistachio ice cream than under the gaze of Mount Etna. Until nasty old refrigeration came along and ruined it for ever, there was a thriving trade in the ice of Mount Etna, collected in natural amphitheatres called *tacche della neve*. During the winter, snow was rolled down the hills in gigantic snowballs and piled in grottoes in layers with felt between them to stop the mass becoming one giant block of ice. Etna's snow was traded far and wide, all over Italy and as far as Malta. It was this ice that allowed Sicilians to develop their long-standing passion for *gelati* and *granite*, which although elemental and simple are quite possibly the finest things you could eat on a hot, a very hot, Sicilian summer's day.

The next day I was blissfully reminded of this. I was staying on the south-eastern end of Sicily, in Syracuse (Siracusa), one of the most staggeringly gorgeous cities I visited in Italy. If you ever go there, head for the Ortigia, the ancient *centro storico* of the city, and sit in one of the many caffès that line the Piazza del Duomo. The city was founded by the Greeks long ago in the eighth century BCE and its population once reached a staggering 500,000 before the Romans sacked the place in 212 BCE. Archimedes was born in Syracuse, and an ancient traveller might well have bumped into him running naked through the streets shouting 'Eureka!', for it all happened here. Post-Hellenic Syracuse suffered under constant attack from varied invaders, and a massive earthquake destroyed much of the city in 1693. Most of Syracuse, like Noto nearby, was rebuilt in the particular style called Sicilian baroque, creating a city of marvellous architectural purity. Some of the churches and grand *palazzi* fell into disrepair but have recently begun to be renovated. In my opinion, the most absolutely perfect place on the planet to have breakfast is in the Piazza del Duomo. And to eat? Ice cream, of course.

The Sicilians have developed a profound weakness for eating ice cream, not from a miserable old cone but stuffed inside a fresh brioche. It might sound a little odd, but it is, well, let me just say that my keyboard is dribbling with drool.

Further inland is the glorious architectural gem, the baroque city of Noto. The same earthquake that struck Syracuse in 1693 caused even more damage to Noto up in the hills, so much so that it was decided to move the whole city lock, stock and *barile* to another site slightly further down. If you get to Noto, you'll notice the *città alta* (upper) and the *città bassa*, for it was decided that there should be an administrative core away from where the hoi polloi lived up above. And the core is truly gorgeous, with a unique baroque purity and a fantastic, slightly tumbledown air. Another earthquake caused considerable damage to Noto in the 1990s.

I went there to worship at the altar of the *gelato*. I had heard that there was a caffè there, the Caffè Sicilia, that made the most exquisite ice cream, but sadly it was closed. So I went elsewhere. Sitting down at another caffè, I spied a luscious purple granita being brought to the next table and, feeling like a culinary David Attenborough, I asked what it was. I had stumbled across something that was, I thought, an endangered species: a *granita del gelso*, a mulberry *granita*. Mulberry is a fruit of the greatest fragility. When picked it lasts for little more than a few hours before turning into a vinous mush, but it is a most sublime, and sublimely refreshing, delicacy. It looks like a stretched blackberry, soft and indelibly purple. Its white relative was once used to feed silkworms, and you may even see a few for sale in the local markets. You can happily sip lemon *granita* all over the island, and elsewhere in Italy too, and it has become perhaps a little too popular. People are becoming lazy, cutting culinary corners and making it a little second-rate at times, oversugared or overfrosted. But the mulberry, for its rarity, deserves close attention, even if some people insist on adding a dollop of cream to it.

Granita also harks back to those days when ice was a commodity, rolled down the mountain slopes and stored in subterranean icehouses. Once hawkers would sell it from containers strapped to their backs, preserving the *granita* in ice made with two parts salt to one of ice, which kept it nicely slushy. These days, while we have machines in the UK that churn and disgorge blue raspberry slushes made with industrial extracts, the Sicilians still, thank God, take their *granite* very seriously indeed.

LIPARI

IF THE IDEA OF MEDITERRANEAN PEACE AND QUIET SEEMS AS
attractive to you as it does to me, you can understand why
I liked the notion of going to the Aeolian island of Lipari.
But ultimately it was Carlo Rosselli's ghost that brought
me here. Lipari was once a place where stick-thin
intellectuals, confined by Mussolini, chewed over the
thorny problem of what to do about Fascism. On the
mainland, Carlo Levi, confined to the deep south of
Basilicata, wrote the magnum opus of the confined
intellectual, *Christ Stopped at Eboli,* and drew some human
comfort from the bemused and distant inhabitants of
Lucania. On Lipari the Fascists unwittingly created a
hornet's nest of dissent by consigning a number of the
country's liberal intellectuals to a life of isolation where
they could do little else but sip coffee and plot. Mussolini
must have assumed that dissent would be harmless so far
from the machinations of Rome and under the watchful
eye of his minions, but he was mistaken. It was to Lipari
that Carlo Rosselli, the great anti-Fascist hero and my very
distant cousin, was sent, along with many illustrious
colleagues, such as Emilio Lussu, the Sardinian radical, and

Sandro Pertini, who was eventually to become the country's wise old president.

Rosselli arrived in December 1927 and became a model prisoner while simultaneously plotting his escape. His family were allowed to join him, and his English wife, Marion, wrote later that the time they spent there was 'like a second honeymoon'. One of the *confinati*, Gioacchino Dolci, was released and set about putting a plan into action, buying a speedboat in Tunisia with Rosselli's money and arranging for it to be piloted to Lipari where it would wait offshore to pick up Rosselli and take him to freedom. The bid was extremely daring and well planned. No one had ever escaped from the island under the Fascists' noses. It took three attempts for the plan to work, but on 27 July 1929 Rosselli was free once again. The boat took him first to Tunisia and then on to France.

The Fascists were furious and arrested his wife, who was released only after pressure from the British. His brother Nello, the father of Aldo whom I had met in Rome, was confined to Ustica, a barren island sixty kilometres north of Palermo. Both Carlo and Nello then became even more dedicated to the cause of liberal socialism, setting up the political movement they called Justice and Liberty in 1929. It was not entirely successful, and was called by some elitist, while others referred to it as a 'Jewish party'. But it brought together several important figures who were to play a significant part in post-war Italian politics.

When the Republican regime in Spain was toppled Carlo helped form an Italian brigade and went to fight for the Republicans in the Civil War. In 1936, after Mussolini had supplied the Spanish with still further military assistance, Carlo coined the slogan 'Today Spain, tomorrow Italy' to serve as a rallying cry for the liberal cause. By now he had also begun to think of a way to assassinate Mussolini. His heroics were to bring the brothers to an untimely and horribly brutal end.

Nello was eventually allowed to leave Ustica after five years' confinement, but the plan to eliminate the Rossellis had probably already been decided upon. On 9 June 1937, the brothers were driving along a country road just outside Bagnoles-de-l'Orne in Normandy when they stopped to help a car that had apparently broken down. They were set upon by Fascist *cagoulards* who had been lying in wait for them, and murdered. Carlo died immediately, while Nello, who was repeatedly stabbed, resisted as best he could but died soon after. Carlo's wife, Marion, had left that day to prepare for their son John's tenth birthday party, and never saw her husband again. Their funeral in Paris attracted over a hundred thousand sympathizers, who filed mournfully behind the procession as it made its way to the Père Lachaise cemetery, where the Rosselli brothers were laid to rest.

My side of the Rossellis had settled down to a mundane life of banking and anonymity, Londoners almost all, and I wondered why we knew so little of these Italian heroes. It will remain a mystery. My grandmother's generation is dead, and my mother's seems to have been as ignorant as I was. What was extraordinary was that I had unknowingly spent months sitting by the very man who could have saved me twenty-odd years of desultory wondering: Carlo's son, Professor John Rosselli, had taught me, rather incongruously perhaps, a short course on Indian philosophy. This was at Sussex University in the 1970s, a nest of bourgeois discontent where radicals cut their teeth by occupying the chancellor's office every now and again. Sussex's famous sit-ins. The words now seem as dated as *Emergency Ward 10*. We were from the post-radical generation: cynical then and now. We were the ones who opted for the herbal route instead of becoming Mr or Ms Angry.

Both Mussolini and the long-haired radicals of the 1960s are now long gone: one was shot and strung up from a

Milanese lamp-post, the others had haircuts and bought Volvos. I'm not too sure you can say that about Fascism in Italy. Has it gone, or is it still lurking somewhere in Italian society?

Jettisoning a car, half my luggage and a pair of shoes that made my feet smell, I set off for the Aeolian Islands. Two trains took me from Catania to Milazzo in four hours, a journey I could have driven in less than two. But at least I had an opportunity to relive my Inter-Rail years. I'd even got a backpack, all the better to turn myself into a human donkey. I probably looked like a perverted scoutmaster, though I dearly hope I didn't. I remembered it all so well. The heat. The incipient body rot.

Railway bars the world over are unutterably awful places. With clients transitory and rushed, the owners can be as rude as they like with impunity. In Italy there is usually a grumpy woman who has to be separately negotiated with and paid before you can return to the counter to get your food, which for foreign travellers especially the English, who tend to find foreign languages so unnecessary – throws an added linguistic hurdle between traveller and sustenance. Prosciutto and *formaggio* still rule, but usually with greater blandness than elsewhere in Italy.

In Catania I watched with glee as the resident loony, a well-dressed but quite obviously disturbed character – he had a suit and slippers on, a classic sign – accosted a Dutch couple and entered into one of those nonsensical 'I like your country' dialogues. They looked pained but being from a country that was once famed for its liberal and tolerant attitudes to all things, including lunacy, they put up with his craziness with admirable aplomb. I looked at what I could eat. Something called a *sandwick*. Something else called a hot dog. But otherwise little that wouldn't have been there a generation or two ago.

I feel mild dread when it comes to the small matter of

biglietti on Italian trains. Italian ticket inspectors work in pairs and are usually highly experienced at sniffing out the mildest of innocent transgressions. You need, to start with, to date-stamp your ticket on one of the machines carefully hidden around the station before boarding the train. Once on the train there are so many combinations of tickets and journeys that you are highly likely not to pass the intense scrutiny of your ticket and be dragged into the guard's cabin for a damned good hiding. You are not allowed on some trains at all with a regular ticket. So beware. On this trip I was asked why I had a 25 per cent reduction. I not only had absolutely no idea why, but also had not asked for one and didn't know that I had got one. I just said I was English. 'Ah,' he said. 'OK then.'

When I bought the ticket in Catania, the man behind the glass seemed particularly keen to hear me say the word 'apricot' in English. For as well as my backpack, I was carrying a small punnet of my Mount Etna apricots and refusing to let them out of my sight.

Milazzo is the main port of Sicily for all departures to the Aeolian Islands, so you might have expected a bit of a buzz at the station. But no. No taxis. No bus. No buzz. And no port. That was a few kilometres away. But this was a perfect day for the hydrofoils that swish across the sea to the islands: the water was flat and glassy, the air hot. And Lipari turned out to be less bleak, more fertile than I thought it would be. It is the biggest of the Aeolians, the insular hub where hydrofoils and ferries zip in and out all day long, disgorging and swallowing passengers at modest cost. As my hydrofoil drew up alongside the harbour walls, a small tribe of over-weight boys jumped into the water, splashing and shouting fairly amiably. I waited, made a few calls, found some-where to stay that had a television – it was World Cup time: allow a writer an occasional luxury – and watched the boys. Another hydrofoil approached, and two of them seemed to be in imminent danger of being scaffed completely.

'*Aliscafo! Aliscafo!*' their friends shouted. Still no response. The crew took little notice, as if they chewed up thousands of small boys every day. But the boys made it out of the water, and were then seriously berated by a wiry old fisherman of whom they took even less notice than they had of the *aliscafo*. Later I began to get the impression that there was an evil tubby gang at work in Lipari. The *aliscafo* warriors. They had perfected, it seems, a lucrative scam for extracting money from each shipment of apostles of the sun. They asked for a euro to be cast into the sea, whereupon they said they would dive down to retrieve it and return it to its owner, standing there marvelling at their skills. Except that they never actually found the coin again. Or not until the generous fool who had fallen for the trick moved on, when they dived in again and came back a euro richer.

Walking along the main street, Via Ambre Solaire it could have been called, I saw more evidence of the evil gang. Sitting outside almost every one of the shops that sold Liparian pumice stone and obsidian in neat little packages was another tubby boy with his own range of obsidian and pumice, offered at less than half the price. Maybe somewhere in Lipari a tubby Don Fagin was controlling all this. But it seems that the days of abject poverty in Lipari are long gone. Waistlines have expanded among the young and old.

I set off to see the town, starting with the Aeolian Museum which proudly tells anyone who is interested the long history of the islands, though in the melting heat nobody seemed the slightest bit attracted by the rows of pots and arrowheads. Lipari's volcanic mineral, obsidian, was once its most valuable resource: sharpened into cutting tools it contributed to a lively trade and brought great wealth to the island, but as so often around these parts, corsairs, Saracens and general insecurity caused its decline, despite the chunky fortress built as defence. I checked out Lipari's most venerable restaurant, Filippino, where Carlo Rosselli and the other malcontents once gathered for the occasional meal. Occasional it must have been, for it has the look of a restaurant rather than a trattoria, and charges hyperinflationary prices. I had a gut feeling here, and chose not to eat in Carlo's shadow, preferring to find somewhere else, and somebody who could talk trattoria with me and bring a little light into my Aeolian culinary darkness. What was the answer to this little culinary conundrum, I wanted to know: when the poor become richer, do they stand by their *cucina povera*? And do the rich ever feel satisfied by such culinary poverty?

The Aeolian Islands are physically remote, but their soil is actually quite fertile, almost indecently so, for they are all variations on a volcanic theme. Most are now fairly dormant, with one notable exception: Stromboli. Lipari has terraced fields cut into the hillside, ideal for hardy drought-resistant Mediterranean plants. The lack of water on all the islands is critical, however. Rainfall between June and August is scarce, so few crops thrive. *Orzo* (barley), hardier than wheat, was used to make bread and is still preferred by older Aeolians, but other than that grains were few and far between, and pasta – this is a province of Sicily, after all – was brought in from out-side.

People tended to use plants that grew quickly. Beans, chickpeas and even *cicerchia*. *Cicerchia* are interesting little bundles of protein, a sort of variation on a chickpea, and I have come across them in at least three separate areas – the Marche, Tuscany and here – and each was convinced that they were the last producers of the plant. *Cicerchia* are undergoing a renaissance in Italy, where old varieties and long-lost crops have a certain cachet. Once grown by the Romans on quite a large scale, they fell out of fashion and were replaced by the *cece*, the chickpea, which on balance was more adaptable and more productive.

By the sixteenth century, Italy was being introduced to a whole variety of New World crops: tomatoes, potatoes – but the one that really caught on in the Aeolians was the prickly pear, hardly a cash crop but admirably suited to the blasting dry summers. In this case, it was simply the invasion of a foreign species, for they are not the sort of plant that is cultivated. They are impossibly difficult to handle, with nasty, brutish, hair-fine spines, but when you get to their centres they are quite delicious. In a curious case of culinary colonialism, the prickly pear was introduced into the hills outside Asmara in Eritrea, which was briefly an Italian colony under the Fascists. The Italian legacy is limited. A few taxi drivers still speak Italian and drive incredibly ancient Italian cars. A road was built that still connects the capital with Massawa on the Red Sea, and the hills have been overwhelmed by millions of these prickly pears, which thrive there just as they do in the Aeolians. The Eritreans still like to wander off and eat prickly-pear ice cream when they take a break from fighting the Ethiopians.

Canny Aeolian cooks don't just rely upon what they grow, but pick and pluck what they can from the wild. The king of all hillside survivors in the Aeolians is the caper bush. It is said that the finest capers of all come from the Italian island of Pantelleria, so far to the south that it is practically African, and sadly one that I have found no reasonable excuse to visit. But here on Lipari capers flourish, and give their own characteristic piquancy to food.

More bizarre is the Liparian fondness for a plant that has never quite made it into the Italian culinary heritage but is fondly sought out by cats. Yes, it's a type of catnip. The islanders call it *neputa*, and the plant is a close cousin of one of the most rabidly invasive of all culinary plants, mint. So, when your cats have finished disporting in the catnip, you might feel tempted, one hot sunny day, to make *neputeddata*, a classic piece of Aeolian *cucina povera* if ever there was one.

Neputeddata

Put a little olive oil in a frying pan and add some of the tastiest cherry tomatoes you can find, a chopped onion, a couple of chopped garlic cloves and the leaves stripped from 3 sprigs of neputa. Cook for 15 minutes, then season and transfer to an ovenproof dish. Crack one egg per person on top and bake in a hot oven (200°C) for 2 minutes. Serve with a further sprinkle of neputa.

Like Ischia, this is not an ideal location for cows or sheep, so once again it is the rabbit that has become the meat frontispiece to the island's cooking. They have a dish, *coniglio all'agrodolce*, that uses rabbit with *vinu cuotto*, cooked wine (*vino cotto* in Italian), a source of sweetness in the food of all the islands.

I asked around for trattorial inspiration, and managed to find somewhere that didn't look like it was going to rob me blind. I think I should add another mild negative to Lipari's profile, for it is, contrary to what you might believe and to what I had imagined, a remarkably noisy little town. *Aliscafi* come and go, and the usual waspish three-wheelers, taxis and scooters zip around tiny roads at a non-tiny pace. Eating at A Sfiziusa is equivalent to eating on the edge of a busy motorway, but then I did ask if I could eat outside. Good spaghetti was what they were known for, so spaghetti was what I chose and they served me a dish of perfect poverty: spaghetti with a *sugo* made from fresh sardines, olives, capers, garlic and olive oil, finely chopped and lightly cooked. Elsewhere on the island such culinary purity becomes a little more luxurious. One of the classic dishes that people now associate with the Aeolians is *ravioli di cernia*, ravioli filled with the flesh of the *cernia*, a large grouper-type fish we would call wreck-fish in English. This has little to do with traditional cooking and is an upstart in the Aeolian repertoire, more suited to the tastes of the tourists than the people of Lipari. It wasn't until the 1970s that the islands began to become developed for tourism with the full baggage that this brings, for which they must thank the mighty *aliscafi*. They're cheap, fast and efficient, and arrive and leave on time.

Aeolian cooking is not as closely related to the sea as you might expect. Fish is usually dismissed as something you roast, *pesce arrosto*. No one I spoke to got much beyond that. Sea urchins, *ricci di mare*, the most sublime of all seafood, are eaten, as they should be, raw, and purists even look down on the profanity of *spaghetti al ricci di mare*. These spiny, prickly creatures grow abundantly here, but since we are talking gonads, the only edible part of the creature, they should be eaten when they are full and ripe, in the spring and early summer. After that, leave the urchins be. Let them relax and fatten for the next season.

The Liparesi pride themselves on their *dolci*, made according to recipes handed down through the generations. This is creative cooking where women show off their culinary skills, for even if the basic recipe remains unchanged, shaping and embellishing the *dolci* allows the occasional flight of fancy, an excellent way for one family to impress another, such as at an engagement party. At the heart of *dolci*-making on the island is the sticky brown liquid that is still very much part of home cooking: *vinu cuotto* made from the long, gentle stewing of wine must, clarified with ashes and left to cool for two days before being bottled ready for use. In the Marche you can buy their *vino cotto* equivalent neatly bottled. They call it *saba*. The Tuscans have their own version, *sava*. But here in the Aeolians, *vino cotto* has remained resolutely part of *la cucina casalinga* (home cooking). Like a precious adolescent, it hasn't quite been allowed out yet. It is widely used in Sicily, which is the culinary mamma of the islands. Aeolian variations are slight.

I sensed a distinct fondness for *spichitedda*, twisted and studded with an almond. And for *gigi*, specially made at carnival. The finest, most creative of all *dolci* are called *nacatole* or, in Sicilian, *nacatuli*, which can be made in any shape that takes your fancy. Tradition has it that these are made for the *fidanzamento* and loving mammas drop the profoundest of hints by making them in the shape of little hearts and babies. Ah, that's really sweet.

Nacatuli

This recipe was kindly given to me by Ivana Merlino of Lipari.

FOR THE PASTRY
1kg type 00 flour
250g lard
250g sugar
3 eggs
1 teaspoon water

FOR THE FILLING
1kg shelled almonds
800g sugar
150ml fresh mandarin juice
3g cinnamon

Make the pastry in the usual way and divide it into two. Leave it to rest for 1 hour in a cool place, then roll each piece to 1cm thickness. Combine all the filling ingredients. Cut identical shapes from the pastry with a cutter, so you have tops and bottoms. Place a small amount of filling on the bottom layer. Cover with a top layer of pastry and seal the edges, then mark the edges very finely with the end of a fork. Be as creative as you like. There are usually holes cut in the top layer so you can see the filling, so if you like cut out small holes before you put the top layer on. Continue until all the pastry and filling are used up.

Bake at 150°C for 20 minutes or longer until done.

Suspecting that the Aeolians are blessed with the sweetest of teeth, I was introduced by my enthusiastic mentor, Ivana, to the *ne plus ultra* of Liparese sweetness and light, *mostarda*. This is found all over Sicily. It is made from boiled-down grape must mixed with starch and left to dry in the sun. There is never ever a hint of the fieriness we get in our mustard, which, by the way, is *senape* in Italian. In the north of Italy, however, you will find another – this time distinctly fiery – version of *mostarda*, in this case a multicoloured mix of candied fruit cooked in a syrup to which mustard powder is added. Cremona is the city most renowned for its *mostarda*, and here, and elsewhere in the north, it is famously served with *bollito misto*, hardly the sort of thing you cry out for in the hot Mediterranean summer.

Ivana, who got very excited about Liparese *mostarda*, gave me her recipe, and I pass it on to you.

Mostarda

1 litre black grape must
100g cornflour
1 tablespoon each of chopped toasted walnuts and almonds
1 dessertspoon wild fennel seeds
zest of 3 big oranges

Boil half the must with all the flour until it becomes like cream. Add the nuts, fennel seeds, orange zest and remaining must, and continue to boil until that too reaches a cream-like consistency, then pour into metal tartlet tins to cool. Traditionally, the *mostarda* was poured into *formelle* with intricate floral patterns on the base and left in the sun to dry for a day or two.

I wondered why it was that such a dish seemed to engender so much misty-eyed romanticism yet was never seen outside people's houses. An American long-time resident of Sicily, Mary Taylor Simeti, who wrote about *mostarda* and even made the stuff, said: 'Well, the problem is it doesn't taste very nice.' I saw her point. I nibbled some and, well, it was OK, but much like the English and their blubbery bland sausages, the truth is that its popularity is in more than the tastebuds. It's back to that old culture thing again.

So Lipari has kept to its culinary roots, despite the change from perpetual poverty to relative wealth for most of the islanders. Restaurants have introduced a few exotic dishes and caused a mini gold rush as fishermen hunt the elusive *cernia*, but Aeolian food is not about being de luxe. The tourists leave, and the islanders still dream of their *nacatuli*.

STROMBOLI

THE SUN IS SETTING. STROMBOLI IS QUIET. SOME OF THE biggest bees I have ever seen are swarming on the roof above me. The apricots are ripening – here, too, they taste sublime. The caper bushes are flowering. A thing that looks like a locust has just crashed into the wall. Oh, and a bee has landed on my laptop, perchance to read, or just to be.

I had promised myself a last island-hurrah, with time to write and reflect a little, in the remotest part of Italy I could find. Stromboli: the word rolls off the tongue beautifully. Stromboli. Of course, it might have been my growing obsession with Italian Neo-realism that made me want to come here. OK, it was. The great Italian director Roberto Rossellini had made a film on the island in 1949 with Ingrid Bergman: the Neo-realist classic *Stromboli*, billed by the American press as 'Flaming volcano! Flaming emotions!' By day, Bergman acted. By night, she found time to make infamous *lurve* with the maestro. She had once seen a film of his showing to an empty cinema in America, one of the few that dared encourage active brain-work, and wrote to Rossellini to say that if he ever wanted to use a Swedish actress who could speak English then he should call her up. They met, fell in love and began an affair that was to provide grist to the puritans and hypocrites of Hollywood for years to come. The picture of a frantic Ingrid Bergman scrambling up the awesome, bare slopes of the volcano with nowhere to go filled me with inspiration. I fondly imagined that the island would be full of sensitive paranoiacs and troubled priests.

Bergman played a Lithuanian refugee called Karin who thought that the only way she could leave the refugee camp on the mainland was to marry the first Italian fisherman who paid her any attention, little thinking that he might come from an obscure, constantly erupting volcano in the middle of the Mediterranean. When she arrives, she announces the immortal lines: 'Is it always active?' and shudders when she learns that it is.

Stromboli: gently steaming and spitting fire. While the town of Stromboli has happily sloughed off its poverty and entered the mucky world of tourism, on the other side of the island is the minuscule community of Ginostra, altogether less sure of itself. Some thirty-strong in the winter, its population positively explodes in the summer as people are drawn by its rather notorious remoteness. There is no electricity, but there is peace and quiet. But is all well in this Italian version of the end of the world?

Without wishing to be a serial killjoy, I should add that ferries and hydrofoils now drop by every day, disgorging their passengers onto a waiting dinghy that speeds them into what is claimed to be the smallest harbour in the world. Unless, that is, there is a raging storm, or even just a swell, in which case you will have to get off at Stromboli, wait and pray – or walk around the volcano. However, the sea is mostly benign in the summer, so persevere and you'll get there, *inshallah*.

So you arrive, to be greeted by a mule and its human minder. Walk up the long winding path to Ginostra, past

'Flaming volcano! Flaming emotions!' cried the publicity for Rossellini's Neo-realist classic Stromboli. *The island produces sublime apricots and capers.*

the other mules lugging crates of this and that, and don't get too upset if you see one of the mules enjoying a thorough thrashing on the way. I asked one of the mule minders for directions to where I was staying. He scowled, pointed and grunted. I grunted back. It's a fine thing, remoteness.

I had chosen well. I had decided at the very last minute that instead of printing out a paper copy, I would riffle electronically through the work on my laptop. So where better to go than a remote island with no electricity? I can say nothing in my defence. Except that I had started this particular journey by going to the wrong airport, and instead of turning purple in the face and attacking innocent ticket-sellers, I just laughed.

My room looked out onto the sea, across to the distant hump of Panarea. Inside all was perfectly white, cool and breezy, with glorious azure blues around the windows and along the paths. But the soil, the ground and almost everything else was a dark, ominous black. Volcanic cinders littered the paths and massive volcanic rocks were scattered along the coastline. The port is roughly hewn from these gigantic jet-black volcanic boulders, which are covered in the most astonishingly lurid sponges and sea anemones. June was uncomfortably hot even for the Ginostresi and there was much fanning and moaning in spite of the blessed shade. But it seemed fitting to be so steamy at the foot of Stromboli. You might think the awesome presence of a volcano would make everyone twitch and jump, but after a while you too will forget all about the boiling mass of magma beneath you.

Life was never easy in Ginostra. There are no roads, no cars, no buses, no water. Lovely. In the old days clothes were washed in the sea; winter rain was all they had in the way of water and it was cannily stored in thick-walled wells. In the war Ginostra was left to its own devices, and people can still remember the awful, endless, merciless hunger. In the 1960s things began to change. A group of Germans arrived from Stromboli after the local priest found their radical ways a little too much to bear. Ginostra was more welcoming, and thus began the village's golden age, when the inwardly fearful Ginostresi joined the world of free love and exotic, strange people.

The arcane purity of Ginostra is still in the living memory of the older inhabitants. I was intrigued. How on earth did they survive in such isolation? What did they think about the outside world? Talk to Assunta, I was told. She knows it all. So off to meet Assunta Lo Schiavo, who lived fifty metres up the hill. I asked if I could come back later and talk. She didn't seem too keen, but the one thing you learn quickly is just to plough on regardless.

'*Buona sera, signora! Buona sera, Signora Assunta!*' I said on my return.

She beckoned me to sit down, shuffled on her seat, drew breath and began a diatribe that quite caught me off-balance. The gist of the problem was this. Some years back, an Italian food writer (*boo, hiss*) had the audacity to use her recipes without acknowledgement or thanks, so I shall now say, loudly and proudly, that Assunta told me I could use her recipe, and damn those foul cheating food writers who never name their sources. I promised her that I would send her a copy of the book and credit her, and when I pointed out it would be in English, she looked only mildly perplexed.

A few generations ago over eight hundred people lived in Ginostra, surviving, if not thriving. With its church, its young and its old, Ginostra was a fully formed community that lived off the sea and the fertile, volcanic soil. Capers, olives and vines thrived on the rich but arid volcanic soils and gave the islanders the means to survive.

Assunta told me that her father once owned over two thousand caper bushes in the hills, but they had since been abandoned. Come spring and early summer, caper-picking from these spiny, low-slung plants used to keep everyone busy for weeks on end. *Capperi* don't ripen all at once so the little ones, *capperini*, were kept to one side and packed separately. Covered with sea salt and left to mature for five weeks or so, capers gradually turned from a fresh to a darker green, ready to be stored and sprinkled on practically everything the people ate, from pasta to fish. Boats would sometimes stop by from the mainland and exchange potatoes and onions for capers, for this was a community that bartered rather than bought and sold. But caper-picking seems to have lost its attraction. So has picking olives. And so indeed has absolutely everything apart from worshipping at the altar of tourism.

Assunta used to cook for those pioneer tourists who came to Ginostra, exercising her Ginostrese cunning to work a few culinary miracles when necessary. Rabbits were once caught in their hundreds, but even they have had a cataclysmic time of it since a deadly virus infected the local population and killed most of them off.

The local marine rabbit turns out to be the *totano* or flying squid, *Ommastrephes sagittatus*, easy prey for even the dumbest of fishermen. Assunta's granddaughter told me how they had seen one the day before that was almost as tall as she was, and reached as high as her nose. *Totani*-fishing is a simple business: you can attract them by shining a bright light and running a series of hooks into the sea from a line that touches the sea floor. This doesn't work when the moon is out, so choose a cloudy night.

Stromboli rises steeply from the sea with the acuteness of a teenager's pimple, so you can find fish that are usually caught well off the coast with relative ease. One of the weirder finds is the *spatola*. This curious fish is half-tapeworm, half-conger eel, with a beautiful, svelte silver skin and a fearsome set of teeth. We call it the scabbard fish in English; it has a dedicated following in Portugal, in particular on the island of Madeira, but you often see it twisted around on its body in the markets of southern Italy and Sicily.

In Ginostra both *totano* and *spatola* are served with pasta, *totano* more successfully because it combines well with a thick tomato *sugo*. It's a rare treat to see their little tentacles reaching through the sauce and trying to strangle the pasta. The *spatola* has a rather feeble, watery taste, so it isn't the most exciting thing on the island to eat. You might even come across the fish they call *aguglia*, which in Latin has the glorious name *Belone belone belone*. Green-boned, needle-nosed, the *aguglia* is billed as a mini swordfish but in fact is nothing like swordfish at all, more mackerel-ish, and is known in English as garfish. *Aguglia* means needle, and the fish's sharp beak does indeed look remarkably like a needle. Far more than a gar.

Once the sea was thick with a creature even more

remarkable and intriguing: *tartarughe*, turtles; *tartuchi* in dialect. Loggerhead turtles once swam freely around the islands, free, that is, to be fished, trapped and caught whenever possible, for their arrival coincided with the leanest months on the island – January and February – and got Ginostrese juices flowing. Assunta became positively wild when I mentioned I had been talking about turtle earlier on. '*Madonna, ch'era buona!*' she said. On clear winter days, just after a storm, turtles in their hundreds would flop languidly on the sea's surface. You can imagine the excitement. '*I tartuchi! I tartuchi!*' You could see them from the village, and off people would rush, down to the sea, squeezing past the rocks, out into the ocean. This was in the days when Mediterranean tourism was but a dream, but the beaches where the turtles had laid their eggs for millennia were soon to become heavily developed, the sand to disappear under concrete. Estimates suggest there are barely two thousand breeding females left, where once there were hundreds of thousands.

Gaetano Merlino is one of Ginostra's most successful fishermen. He told me of what life was like back in the 1960s when he was young and fishing *tartarughe* was almost more thrilling than the electrifying prospect of German girls keen on free love. 'I am a very natural man, a very funny person,' Gaetano kept telling me, one blistering afternoon, as I listened to his life story. There was a man – 'I think he really loved me,' he said – who despite his crippled hands knew how to fish for turtles. Gaetano would row them both out to sea, as silently as he could, for if a turtle heard you, splash!, it would swim down into the depths. Slipping silently up behind one, Gaetano would warily grab its back flippers – for a turtle has a nasty habit of biting a hand that fishes it – and overturn the beast, leaving it to thrash ineffectively, caught by the wiles of *Homo sapiens*.

At the gloomiest part of every winter, this glut of turtle

would arrive. Never sold, it was handed around the village, bartered for this and that. Every woman knew how to prepare and cook a turtle. Gaetano's mother, Assunta . . . all of them knew just what to do.

'The smell was horrible,' Gaetano said, 'so strong it stayed in my nose for weeks. Horrible! I can remember it still.'

Assunta told me how she used to cook it. 'First you cut off the head, then all the meat from the shell, and the flippers. They're good to eat. Boil them all in seawater, then cut the pieces up into smaller pieces, and scrape all the meat from the flippers. Fry the meat in oil with some onions, garlic, parsley, almonds, capers, and then a little *vino cotto*. This was the best way. *Tartarughe agrodolce. Madonna, ch'era buona!*'

You can imagine the ladies of Ginostra scampering back to their kitchens with their turtles, chopping and bashing, and the smell of turtle hanging heavily in the air. I told Assunta, almost embarrassed, that I had not yet tasted the *vino cotto* that appears in the island's cooking so often, even added to turtle. One evening, as the sun was setting gloriously, Assunta invited me for a drink, and brought out a bottle to taste. It was as dark as gravy browning, with the unctuousness of molasses plus a little grapiness. I showed her a book I had found with a recipe for *sfinci di fichi d'India*. She swore this recipe was hers, but agreed to let me reproduce it so long as I gave her due acknowledgement. This I was happy to do, I said as I took my leave of her and the island.

Sfinci are another of those things that Sicilians, and in particular Aeolians, get sentimental about. In the wrong hands they are leaden, but well made they are excellent. As you might expect there are a thousand variations on the basic principle, which is this. *Sfinci* are fried pastries combining flour, lard and something else. So you find *sfinci i cucuzza*, for example, made with the flesh of yellow pumpkin. In Ginostra, where they have to be extra resourceful, *sfinci* are made with the flesh of prickly pears. Picking these is a challenge thanks to the abundant, fine spines. Assunta told me they wrapped vine leaves around the fruit before twisting it off the main stem.

Sfinci di fichi d'India

This recipe for prickly pear sfinci *was given to me by Assunta from Ginostra on pain of volcanic death if I failed to credit her. If you are about to set off to harvest* fichi, *arm yourself with a bunch of vine leaves or gloves to protect you from their prickles. Serves four.*

3kg prickly pears
30g fresh yeast
50ml warm mineral water
white sugar for the yeast and for sprinkling
salt
500g white flour
oil for deep frying

Peel the prickly pears carefully, then pass the flesh through a sieve. Mix the yeast in a large bowl with a little warm mineral water. Add a sprinkling of sugar and leave for 10 minutes. Add a touch of salt and the sieved prickly pears, then slowly add the flour, working it with your hands until you obtain a thick, stretchy dough. Leave to rise for an hour in a warm place.

Heat the oil for frying. Pull off a chunk of mix, roll it into a ball and, using a slotted spoon, put it into the hot oil. Fry the *sfinci* one at a time, sprinkling each with sugar when done and serving immediately.

You read that Ginostra has no electricity. Once again, this isn't entirely true. Generators whirr and cause more than a little neighbourly friction. Not everyone has one, but they have arrived and somehow I feel there will be no turning back. It is one of the many issues that divide the little community. Are they to have light bulbs and televisions blaring like everywhere else? Or do they hang on to that rare purity, real and undeniable, and become a living social fossil? As I was told by one of my wise storytellers, Ginostra is neither fish nor fowl.

PART THREE
MAINLAND

AMALFI

A LITTLE WAY TO THE SOUTH OF NAPLES THE PLAIN BECOMES
a mountain that drops vertiginously down to the breath-
taking Amalfi coast where some of Italy's loveliest towns
cluster together in an impossibly tortuous way. These days
Amalfi is one of the favoured destinations for middle-aged
tourists on a grand tour of frumpiness but it has just about
managed to avoid becoming completely soulless. In the
hills above perches celestial Ravello with its ridiculously
beautiful views, unbeatable on a glorious, sunny, sky-blue
day, where Wagner was inspired, and Gore Vidal con-
tinues to be, looking out from on high to the sea far
below. It is a truly spectacular place. A little further along
the coast is Positano. And yes, it too is hopelessly pretty,
but seems to have modelled itself on a mildly snotty
French Riviera resort. Svelte bronze characters try to
interest not-so-svelte white characters in buying inappropriate skimpy dresses and brightly painted bottles, destined
to be stuffed away in some urban drawer.

I hung around Positano and ogled and marvelled at its
beauty, and stopped for a coffee at the magnificently
named Chez Black. But it was off-season and I was on

another gastronomic blind date, waiting for a man I knew only as Peppe.

Peppe arrived. I piled into his car, which was tiny – here tiny is wise as the roads are serpentine – and rapid, and listened to a crucial match of *calcio* on the radio, not quite what I was expecting but captivating nonetheless. We launched ourselves skywards, up past Positano Wanderers' own football patch, and on to a little place called Montepertuso.

The hills are particularly rich in springs, which once allowed the ancient maritime republic of Amalfi to thrive, make pasta, mill wheat and even make paper. If you walk up the Valle di Mulini, dodging the naff displays of dried chillies – natural viagra, they like to call it – the piles of lemons and their grotesque cousins the citrus, you'll come across a funky, refurbished museum that brims over with mad enthusiasm for paper. It's an odd story. Instead of using copious amounts of papyrus or sawing up bits of wood like everyone else, the basic raw material for Amalfi's fine, voluptuous paper was pure white cotton cloth, which was precisely what the Amalfitani apparently once wore.

Greeted at the door by a Dutch girl who wishes you a good morning in perfect English or a *buon giorno*, depending on your look, you are passed on to a guide, a young Amalfitano wearing an incongruously smart suit and black shoes, with a real passion for paper. You soon realize the word 'medieval' has special significance here. Everything is medieval. The cloth masher, the well where mashed cloth is mixed with spring water, the walls, the tiles, everything but the outrageous upstart from the middle of the eighteenth century, a machine that managed to mash the local population out of a job but increased the production of paper enormously. Today the springs still gurgle but only one working paper mill remains in Amalfi, filling the nichest of markets with its lovely, soft, pure white paper.

At the spring on the Montepertuso road we stopped to fill our bottles, to wash and cool ourselves down. I had always liked the idea of a semi-paradise where water sprang from the ground and maidens frolicked, and Peppe was under strict instructions from his friend and mine, Gennaro Contaldo, to lead me springwards to this gurgling paradise, whatever it took. 'Madonna! I could show you places that nobody knows about where I used to go when I was little,' Gennaro had told me in London once. Born locally in Minori, he had long tempted me with stories of his younger days on this bucolic coast. 'There are springs where people still come to fill their bottles with water. It tastes so beautiful. Water is like a jewel. And look what we have to use here,' he said to me, knocking an unsuspecting London tap on the head.

This spring had the added bonus of a shrine: a Madonna, flowers, lights and women looking like extras from an Anna Magnani movie. Right above it is the site of one of the more subtle battles between the Virgin Mary and her old foe, the devil. Each was challenged to make a hole in the mountain. The devil tried his best but failed while the Virgin Mary watched, serenely drifting by on a holy cloud. Then whoom! there it was, a hole in the mountain and the mountain became Holy. It's so easy when you're a virgin.

If Montepertuso seems a calm and tranquil place, carry on a little further up the mountain until you get to the apogee of calmness, the minuscule, one-track village of Nocelle, only recently linked to the outside world by an asphalt road, *grâce à* munificent Brussels. Nocelle makes Montepertuso seem hectic. A few houses surrounded by a deafening tranquillity. Here Neapolitan is spoken rather than Italian, a living language with its own poets and heroes, a language that has youth, old age, a life and a future. And as we passed by, everyone without fail stopped to talk to Peppe in Neapolitan. It sounded like a mix of Portuguese and rubber. One old smiling figure who

walked towards us, talking volubly, was well known to
Peppe. So well known that we went with her to her home
for coffee, my four-thousandth cup of the day, and to catch
up with the *calcio* on the radio in her house. Let me introduce you to Filomena Cannavale, a woman fit, lithe and
eighty-something.

Filomena's house is where I want to live, to sit, to
write, to be, to die. Yes, I know it is occupied and
Filomena has the prior claim, but of all the places I have
seen in Italy it was the most captivating and exquisite. It
is no Palladian mansion or medieval castle. No crisp, neatly
designed house with a brilliant blue swimming pool. In the
kitchen was an old stove, a square basin and, of course, a
wood-burning oven. The bedroom was empty apart from
a solid wardrobe and a modest bed. The walls were burning white and the window opened inwards to reveal with
a theatrical hurrah a view of such beauty as to bring a smile
to the face and make the most hardened heart burst with
adrenalin. Below, olive trees, lemon trees and terraces
stepped down all the way to Positano itself, a toy town far
away on the edge of the sea. The house had been dosed
up with a bit of modernity: a shining and incongruous
bidet and a shower. And on the other side, a cow stall,
where cows once mooed and pooed the day away and fed
the family with milk and cheese, and a pig sty where
piglets had their own upper level to stop them being
squashed by their mother. There were still a few perky
chickens and one of the neighbours was harbouring a
gaggle of Christmas escapees, turkeys with their machine-
gun gobble. It was utterly enchanting.

Filomena showed me the gnarled old beam across
the kitchen from which she once swung her children in the
crib. From time to time, she said, she made bread, using
the yeast that grew on top of the old wine, the *cresciuta*,
as a starter. And there was wine from the vines below
stored in huge glass jars. If you tire of the saltless bread of

Tuscany, then head down here, for under the influence of ancient bread-making traditions and the wood-fired oven, bread both here and in Naples is thick-crusted, slightly sour and quite lovely.

Sometimes I wish there would be a gerontocratic revolution, where the ancient ones would rise up and make us study polenta and pig slaughter, cheese-making and how to preserve your vegetables *sottolio*. And then I remember Mao Tse-tung. However, the art of preserving food through the winter really was a matter of life and death once. I asked Filomena if she could still live up here as she always had.

'Of course I can. I don't need supermarkets. I don't need them at all, and there aren't any up here. I grow my vegetables, I have my chickens. There's all this fruit that grows,' she said, pointing to the fig tree, the almonds and the lemons outside.

But not many people live as Filomena does. Winter still moves to spring, planting time to growing time, but living off the land has turned into a dream for the rich and lost its appeal for everyone else. Here is a way of life that is sustainable, but there are not many *contadini* left up here to sustain it. In the full heat of summer, the roads below stack up with thousands of people quite unaware how close they are to such timeless calm. The contrast between Positano with its St Tropez persona and the hills above with their peace and tranquillity is almost shocking. The choice between the two lifestyles is stark, but I must say, with my mobile telephone on my heart, that I can think of no more beautiful a place to live out this cultural battle.

Filomena could see that I was love-struck. She beckoned me to stand on her roof with her. I did as I was bid and stepped right up to the edge, and smiled as she burbled on about this and that, me playing the entranced foreigner to a T. I could not leave without asking her a question.

'Filomena,' Peppe said. 'William would like to know what you would eat for your last dinner. If you were going to die tomorrow and you could choose anything in the world, what would it be?'

'*Pasta al forno*,' she replied with barely a moment's hesitation. 'I'd cook it in my wood oven, use my tomatoes to make the sauce and get some ricotta from the village. And the pasta would be made with my eggs, and the water from the spring. *Buonissimo!*'

Pasta al forno

This dish is essentially cobbled together from leftover beef ragù that has been cooked long and slow. Serves four.

400g rigatoni
20g butter (for the dish)
3 hard-boiled eggs, sliced
1 uncooked Neapolitan sausage, sliced
1 buffalo mozzarella, sliced
leftover beef *ragù*, enough to cover the pasta in the dish
50g breadcrumbs
100g grated Parmesan
salt and pepper

Cook the rigatoni until *al dente*. Generously butter an ovenproof dish then line with a layer of pasta. Cover this with layers of hard-boiled egg, pasta, sausage, pasta, mozzarella, pasta – until the dish is filled. Cover with beef *ragù*. Top with breadcrumbs and Parmesan, check the seasoning and bake in a moderate oven (160°C) for 20 minutes. Serve at once.

But all things must pass, and fighting the temptation to tie her up immediately and move in, I walked down the hill with Peppe, back into the hectic evening buzz of Montepertuso, where a gaggle of wizened faces greeted us. A fresh, muscular American was asking directions. He was about to be all manly and set off on the path along the cliff edge as the sun was setting. They thought him a little unwise since he had no torch, nor did he have anywhere to stay. I thought he should go for it and sleep out but the gaggle tutted and ummed him down to the bus back to Sorrento, where he would be safer but less blessed.

Among the wizened were Raffaele, slightly gloomy, with Vincenza beside him and opposite her Aniello, who sprang to life when we began to talk about food. Peppe told them what I was up to, and they all started to talk about what they liked to eat. They, like Filomena, wanted to eat anything that grew in the ground here at Montepertuso, but when it came to a dish for the eternal afterlife the consensus was that it should be *minestra maritata*. You need a pig first of all. A home pig, no doubt a happy pig, led out full of trust and caught by the sharp treacherous knife. The vegetables they grew. The stock they made with the ear, the chin and the pig's thin front legs. From the hills they would collect eight different kinds of herbs and vegetables. This was *minestra maritata* in its purest form, and this was how they wanted to eat it.

By now the sun was setting and there was a chill in the air, so we drove back to Positano and the bright lights, down the busy bends, stopping once more at the spring to sip a little water and to call Gennaro on my trusty *telefonino* and toast his health.

'Everyone has a mother,' Peppe said later, being particularly wise and reflective. 'And with the first food you eat, the smell of your mother's breast or something, you start a sort of bank of memories that stay with you for ever. And that's all part of the difficulty many of us have about food. How can we equal the food our mothers have made? And that's not the only problem. Just watch television. There are adverts for chocolates, pizzas, all sorts of things we thought we'd never ever eat in Italy. But we do. There's even a McDonald's in Napoli.' But the fear that Italy's cultural heritage is being engulfed by fast food and American ways hasn't quite reached the neurotic levels of France. Not yet. I suspect that Italy is culturally strong enough to ward off the invasion in any case.

Tempted by this band of perfect mothers, what do many men – and some women – do? Why, stay with Mamma, of course. These are the country's growing band of mammistas. You meet them everywhere, content to stay put and have their shirts and skirts ironed and their pasta made the way mamma has always made it. The downside? For one, the birth rate. Italy has one of the lowest in Europe. They still seem to like the bit that goes before the mucky business of birth and nappies, however. It's fine to have the fun, but where? Dotted around the country are hot lurve spots where what has been called the Quivering Car Syndrome is well practised. So don't worry if you see lines of groaning cars with sunblinds blocking the windows. It's all in a good cause.

I didn't like to interrupt Peppe's reveries, and didn't suggest he got on the next flight to England to see that things are even worse over there. Many of our mothers also put in hours of hard work, but our kids eat crisps and crappy pizzas by the ton. And what did the mothers eat when they were young? Crisps and crappier pizzas. The bland leading the bland. But the warriors are about in Italy. Globalization is a big issue here, and fighting for our gastronomic and cultural rights is Slow Food.

I had begun to wonder whether the whole Slow Food movement was just another Piemontese plot. With their head office in Bra, near Turin, the ancient seat of all

Piemontese duplicitousness, was Slow Food aiming for gastronomic domination? Would we see history repeating itself? The core of the movement consists of the regional groups and the presidia. A presidium acts as a forum for the producers of a particular endangered food to come together, organize and enter into the network of enthusiasts and followers, creating new markets, lobbying anyone who needs to be lobbied and, crucially, both funding and helping to raise money so that the producers can continue to function.

Among the stiff peaks of the Costa Amalfitana, Slow Food was well established and managed definitively to cure me of my cynicism. The story that first grabbed my attention was this. A type of prawn known as the *gamberetto di Crapolla* swims in pathetically small numbers around the coast of Sorrento and Massa Lubrense. You can tell it by its long beak-like proboscis and the gentle yellow striations along its red body. Although they were once sold and eaten locally, in recent years they have become mixed in with all the other prawns caught locally and almost lost to the world. Most of the *gamberetti* are caught using a *nassa* made of wood in the inlet of Crapolla. This is admirable for many reasons, one being that they taste quite delicious. The *nassa*, or trap, is made by the fishermen as it has been for generations, keeping this droplet of marine culture alive and active. It is biodegradable, unlike the plastic equivalents that clutter up the sea floor for hundreds of years if accidentally lost. The word *nassa* appears in various linguistic forms all over the Mediterranean and I have occasionally seen artisanally minded fishermen chit-chatting away while making them in ports far and wide. In the south of France *nasses* once served to catch the small rockfish that are used to make bouillabaisse. So it gladdens my marine heart to see these prawns still pursued in this way, and beginning to be given their own little story: a prawn that has been saved by the gallant locals of the Slow Food movement.

But I do have one problem with Slow Food. How on earth does any punter come along and know about these monumentally obscure things without reading the Slow Food magazine avidly and being part of the movement? It seems a tiny bit elitist to me. I mentioned this to a few of the enlightened enthusiasts, who told me that the presidia don't just act as gastronomic focus groups but raise much-needed funding to help protect gastrodiversity. So why not, I wonder, have a label that you can use to help spread the word?

Having a little of the green warrior in my blood, I know that there is an insidious and pervasive belief in the north that the south of Europe is deeply irresponsible in all matters environmental − the converse being that the north is wise and wonderful. This is in spite of the fact that in the UK we are way behind in organic agricultural production and import much of it from Italy, and that the North Sea is one of the world's most seriously over-exploited seas, fished almost beyond the point of recovery.

The second threatened food I came across was only marginally less obscure than the *gamberetti*. The day after I had fallen head over heels for Nocelle, I scuttled back like a lovelorn dog, glanced skywards, dabbed my eyes a little and continued up and round the eternally bending road. This time I was heading up into the Monti Lattari and Agerola, on a road you can easily take if you are coming down to the Costa Amalfitana from Naples. I was on the trail of a cheese, the much-lauded *provolone del monaco*, made from the spring milk of a race of cow called the Agerolese. It is a brown cow and not the freest milker in town, significantly out-uddered by the ubiquitous Friesian. These cows are descended from a cross created in the nineteenth century by a retired Bourbon general, Paolo Avitabile, who, seeking the calm of the Monti Lattari after a long stint working abroad, arrived home with four Jersey cows and promptly interbred them with the local stock to start the *razza* Agerolese, which thrived up in the hills. Milk, like water, has an infinite variety of minerals, traces of this and that which give it its particularity. Part of what makes it special is the cows' diet — in this case mostly spring hay — and another part is the cow herself, in this case the Agerolese.

In the past when famine lurked, the cheeses were important reservoirs of fatty food, and, unlike the fresher ricotta and mozzarella-type cheeses that are also made up here, were long-lasting. The *provolone del monaco* is rather rotund and is made using rennet from a goat and milk from the Agerolese cows heated to a particularly high degree for a cheese, which gives it a characteristic texture. The *provolone* is left to ripen in the same caves where generations of others have been left, so the microflora get to work and add their character. It is surprisingly sharp to taste, an exquisite nibbling cheese.

These days there aren't many Agerolese cows left, for the Friesians dominate here as elsewhere. Things evolve, and Friesians give higher yields. But to the rescue comes good old Slow Food, trundling along with one of their magic presidia. Contact is made, a group is formed and the network of enthusiasts starts the long process of revival. *Viva* Slow Food.

I stopped outside the Cioffi family's *caseificio* in Agerola looking for some *provolone del monaco*. The road ran along right outside the front door. The odd car stopped, picked up something and drove on. I spied one cheese looking rather forlorn in the corner, unlabelled and covered in a thin skin of grey mould. This just had to be *provolone*, and so it was. Meanwhile, warm, pure white, sweet-smelling piles of ricotta were being wrapped, packed and dispatched to God knows where.

'Excuse me. Is that a *provolone del monaco*?' I asked.

'*Sì, signore.*'

'Where is the Monaco that this cheese comes from?' I asked.

Laughter. 'It's not from Monaco, it's *del monaco*, from the monks. They used to ripen the cheese.'

A subtle thing, language, unsubtle in the hands of a novice.

'Meet me by the fountain in Amalfi at eight.' These were my beautifully simple instructions, and since Amalfi isn't overrun by fountains, I settled down and waited for a long-time expat resident, a friend of a friend who had kindly arranged for me to spend a morning engrossed in mozzarella.

'I'll have a copy of the *Sunday Times* under my arm,' she said, reassuringly. I was in the right place at the right time, but looked on in amazement as endless middle-aged women carrying the *Sunday Times* walked by. When we finally met up, I with my *Guardian* and she with her *Sunday Times*, we sat down over a morning's cappuccino in the shadow of Amalfi's beautiful duomo. More accurately, rather than mozzarella I was in pursuit of *fior di latte*, which is nothing more than mozzarella made with cow's milk. Here in Amalfi, buffaloes have trouble being buffaloes. There are few low-lying swampy areas where they can hang out, and the springs and fountains are strictly off-limits.

Further down the coast, on the flat plain around Battipaglia, are some of the prime buffalo-mozzarella-producing areas of Campania, where malarial swamps were once abundant and buffaloes thrived but little else did. These days you would be hard pressed to imagine that this dry, noisy plain was ever swampy or malarial at all. We must thank the wonders of modern chemistry and the munificence of the Americans who blasted the swamps with DDT to rid them of mosquitoes, allowing successive post-war Italian governments to build a network of hideous industrial zones, and the farmers to plant endless fields of artichoke, for which Paestum, a little further down the coast, is justifiably famous.

We set off to meet the Bottones. Fernando Bottone had spent much of his long life making cheese. His family ran a small shop in Amalfi while he stayed up in the hills, at Scala. When I walked into their *caseificio*, a chunky slab of curd was already steaming quietly away in the background. There is always an aura of calm about cheese-making. I am more used to the hysterical screaming you get either at home or in a fish market. But I love the infectious quiet as the warm milk slurps and moves gracefully around the cauldrons. Cheese-making is magical. However many times I watch the milk slowly warm and gently solidify as the rennet is added, I never fail to marvel.

The warm and rubbery mass — the coagulate, *quagliata* in Italian — is the mother of all cheeses, and in its infinite variety provides us with the raw material for the thousands of different types of cheese, some with obscure un-pronounceable names and others quite banal, that is our cheese heritage. This cheese, *fior di latte*, is one to eat *rapido*. Neither mozzarella nor *fior di latte* keeps very well, especially in their raw, unpasteurized form.

MOZZARELLA LAW

Keep fresh unpasteurized *mozzarella di bufala* or *fior di latte* for no more than two days. Eat it preferably on the same day. Keep the cheese in its container in the saline water — the *acqua di governo* — it should have been packed in until you get home, then transfer it — if you're going to commit the sin of keeping it — to a glass container.

Other versions of the cheese have names that refer to specific weights and sizes: Ciliegina, 25g; Bocconcino, 50g; Aversana, 500g. *Mozzarella di bufala Campana* has achieved DOP status (*Denominazione di Origine Protetta*), so look on the label. The word 'mozzarella' is derived from the verb *mozzare*, to cut off.

I asked Fernando what was the secret of a good cheese, a crackingly original question for a cheese-maker, I admit. 'The milk,' he said, stopping a while to stir the cauldron of warm milk in front of him with a giant wooden paddle. 'And the bacteria,' he added. 'The best cheese we make here is from unpasteurized milk. It doesn't keep long so you don't see it much outside Campania.' And it was true – when you tried his best against his pasteurized, the unpasteurized was tastier.

If you know the right place to go, you can buy real buffalo mozzarella as well as the *fior di latte*. Both are shipped over by plane and sold in some of our burgeoning farmers' markets. Even the supermarkets, bless, are selling it now, although they are all long-life and blander versions of the original. I told Fernando we could get excellent mozzarella at home now. He laughed.

'We once made *fior di latte* in England. It didn't really work though. The cheese was too hard. I think the milk was too rich. It has to be just so.' Stir stir.

'*Organoleptico*,' I said, using this ugly, untranslatable word I had become rather fond of, which refers to the specific taste and mineral content of a food.

Fernando looked at me strangely. He was about to destroy one of my most cherished stereotypes: that cheese-makers are calm people who like to listen to Mozart and are particularly fond of sheep. He started telling me what he thought of England, which was immensely refreshing for me who had spent months thinking about Italy, struggling through books and tracts and websites in a language that was almost new to me. I told him about my book, about Mazzini, and we got all political.

'Why is it,' he asked, 'that the more democratic the

country, the worse the food? Where are the most democratic countries in the world? Sweden, Denmark, Norway.
Have you ever tasted Danish mozzarella? It tastes of
nothing.' He had a point. Had I ever tasted Dutch
aubergines, tomatoes, peppers? Indeed I had. All of them
perfect, shiny, but astonishingly tasteless.

Fernando liked England, but what had his eagle eye
noticed? He loved the oak trees he had seen in Sussex. And
the *porcini* that sprang from the ground. But what about
the English, I asked almost defensively.

'Warriors! You can see it in how the children behave.'

He had a point there too. I fondly thought of my son
who at that moment was probably beating the shit out of
his sister. Yes, I told him, we in Britain had our *mucche
pazze* (mad cows), our enormous agribusinesses, our foot
and mouth and our mutated chickens, but there was
revolution afoot. We had become profoundly distrustful of
governments that told us our beef was safe to eat as mad
cows were being surreptitiously destroyed. Or that the
nuclear waste from Sellafield was causing no harm. Or that
our trains will one day run on time.

His wife called us. Enough of this. It was time for
Fernando to supervise the *fior di latte*. A machine gurgled
into action, steaming and hissing its nozzle into a vat of
water. I remember seeing cheese being made high in the
Alps in Switzerland. The light of the morning sun fell onto
a huge steaming copper cauldron of delectable Alpine
milk. There was no sound but the swishing of the milk
and the gentle mooing of the cows outside. Two men set
about the work, swooshing and stirring away until the
curds had set, lifting them out in a giant cloth, using
hands, teeth, everything, and gently plopping them down
on a wooden counter.

Europe is generally less tolerant of wood when it comes
to food, especially cheese, so there are battles and
simmering wars between those dedicated to preserving the

taste of food and the culture of food and those intent on making food as clean, anodyne and characterless as possible. Wherever you go, walls can be scrubbed and everyone can wear the same silly euro hat. But Fernando, the master of the magic, still presided here in the hills of Scala. He chose the milk. He chose when the curds were ready, and watched over the process every day.

The *quagliata* was placed in the machine, which mixed it slowly, accompanied by an unhurried electric hum. Next to it water was heated and when it was just hot enough it was poured over the *pasta*, the mass of curd, which then slowly began to change. More of the magic. More water, the mass becoming even more elastic. Silence reigned. I was transfixed. A hand dipped into the pure white cheese, pulled it and stretched it, testing it to a level that had been learnt long ago. Into another machine. The mass was cut and chopped and out plopped the cheese, uniform and ready to be wrapped. Artisany.

AL DENTE

IT SOUNDS A MARVELLOUS IDEA THAT MARCO POLO TREKKED
back from the Far East with the recipe for dried pasta, but
would this claim stand up in court? As it happens, we have
Boccaccio's description of a town called Bengodi where
true experts on the matter once lived, and we were
fortunate to attend the trial that tried once and for all to
resolve this intractable problem . . . who really did invent
dried pasta?

> There was a mountain made entirely of grated Parmesan
> cheese, with people on top of it, who did nothing but
> make maccheroni and ravioli, cooking it in chicken broth
> and throwing it down, so whoever caught the most, had
> the most to eat.
>
> Novella CXXIV of Calandrino, in Boccaccio's *Decameron*

'Please be upstanding! All rise! The Court of Gastronomic
Obscurity is in final session. All rise! All rise!'

The delegates shuffled their papers, murmuring lightly,
and obediently rose to their feet. The judge, a tiny but
authoritative Tuscan professor (Mazzini), now crooked

with age, wheezing, wrinkled and barely audible, stumbled in, guided by two burly Italian bodyguards, and took a seat on the dais. He tapped the microphone gently, almost lovingly, ready to try to bring to an end this most contumacious dispute. *Carabinieri* stood around the edge of the courtroom, admiring themselves in each other's polished dark glasses. The air was tense, fetid even. Journalists sat with pencils poised. The inquiry was drawing to a close. The whole world wanted an answer to this simple, almost innocuous question: who invented dried pasta?

On one side of the courtroom stood the Etruscan delegation, staring once more at the warm sheep's liver in front of them, sweating, brows furrowed. The muscular Romans next to them bristled. The sullen Greeks played with their geometry sets. The Arab delegation, incongruous in their carefully ironed Palermo T-shirts, looked smug. Marco Polo stood in chains, sucking a mint.

'I cannot say . . . I must allow time . . . I must . . . I must . . .' The judge's voice was feeble now. And no one, be they Etruscan, Arab, Roman, not a single one of them could understand a word of what he said. The scribes and technicians were silent. The computer operators froze.

The judge tipped forward slightly and whispered to the clerk: 'I must have an espresso, quickly.' The clerk sent a message out to the caffè next door. 'Another caffè, *rapido!*' The rush the judge felt, the quickening heart, made him think of one thing only: a cigarette. But he knew that if he popped out now for a fix of nicotine, history would damn him for ever. In front of him were the tired blades of wheat. Exhibit A, *Triticum durum*, the *grano duro*, piled in the same thick glass bowl that each delegation had spent months, years staring at with varying degrees of desperation. Next to it, blades lined efficiently side by side, was *Triticum aestivum*, with its bowl of sparkling white flour: exhibit 00. Dull, unhulled, unmilled, sad exhibit C,

emmer, *Triticum dicoccum*, collected dust at the far end of
the table, almost totally ignored. These props had been all
that was needed to keep the delegates and their posses of
lawyers in business for over fifty years. No country but
Italy, the cynics would say, would ever have allowed due
process to become such an arduous procession.

It seemed so long ago that the Etruscan delegation had
arrived, speaking their impossible tongue and arguing with
their peculiar devotion to fact and fantasy. They had
stubbornly insisted that the stucco relief found at Cisra did
indeed show that they used rolling pins and pasta cutters,
but the judge preferred the explanation that they were just
the parts of a game. Neither had he been impressed by the
grains of hard emmer and barley found in their ancient
pithoi among the olives and the vines. Where was
the *Triticum durum*, the vital ingredient, the source of
Italy's finest golden *semolina*? The English lawyer had been
seen to heave inwardly at this point, thinking no doubt of
school dinners and blobs of unctuous jam, never quite
understanding how semolina could have played such a
noble role in the annals of Gastronomia.

The Etruscans had survived a calculated attempt to
blacken their character and question their veracity. Few
really knew anything about them. They referred to their
many gods, and caused upset and confusion in the courtroom by having their *netsvis*, liver diviner, on hand at all
times. A sign of obvious weakness, according to the
Christians and the worshippers of the Prophet seated
nearby in the courtroom. The clerk had had to explain
carefully where Etruria was, and that their land once
stretched from the River Arno right down to the Tiber
before they succumbed to the growing Roman Empire and
disappeared down a historical S-bend.

The Greek and the Roman delegations had bored everyone with their interminable disputes and each one's claim
that the dish they knew as *laganum* or *laganon* was theirs

and theirs alone, and used the purest semolina made from hard wheat and water. They were both right, which caused the judge to lapse into focus group mode, calling for consensus and wisdom in an attempt to counter the casual, addictive bickering that ran through the courtroom day after day. Despite their very best endeavours, the Roman delegation was publicly belittled when the Greeks proved irrefutably that the Romans' beloved *laganum* was derived from the Greeks' very own, equally beloved *laganon*, the original dish made from a thin strip of dough that was used in soups and baked. But neither managed to convince the judge that they had dried this paste, had stored it and traded it and perfected it. And this was the issue in this court of lore.

For convoluted and exceptional reasons the court then allowed a presentation by a man of the highest fame, Marco Polo, the son of Venetian patricians, born in 1251, who had known the world when it was largely unknown, and had travelled freely throughout much of Asia with the authority of the great Kublai Khan, the ruler of much of China, Mongolia and Tibet. He had finally returned to the Christian world after twenty-four years away, barely able to speak his native tongue, having recorded all he had seen with typical Venetian thoroughness. But he proved to be a slightly unwilling witness. For Marco Polo had never suggested that he had brought dried pasta back with him from China. Others had done that. True, he had seen the Chinese eat copious amounts of noodles, and they reminded him of the vermicelli that was eaten by the Genovesi. What he had also seen was a curious form of pasta eaten in Java made entirely from fruit, but this wasn't what the inquiry was interested in. When his contribution proved to have been based on the fantasy of unnamed others, the judge wished him well and ordered him to be transported back into the historical ether.

When the Sicilians took the stand the courtroom fell

into an awed silence. Word was that they had put together a formidable case, despite the mutual hostility of many in their delegation. An unseen force seemed to be acting behind their backs, keeping them all remarkably subdued, even fearful. Some had had gruesome and bloody horses' heads delivered to their bedroom doors. Others had received mere verbal threats. Others still had witnessed family members being killed. 'Violence and honour,' people mumbled, 'violence and honour.' In the end, this peculiar combination of Saracens, Normans and Sicilians agreed to present to the court their reasoned argument on condition that they could sip coffee and lemon *granita*, while their minders insisted that they be guarded by an exceptionally large contingent of fierce men who muttered continually about *omertà* and carried postcards of Corleone.

Sicily had developed into a culture that was truly different from the rest of the Italian peninsula. The Arabs had brought Islam as their faith. They practised a highly refined system of agriculture, irrigating the earth and bringing it to life as they had done for generations in their parched native land across the Mediterranean. They brought with them rice, *cuscus* and *limunya* – lemons – unknown to the Greeks who had ruled the island before them. The Romans looked on with considerable interest, and showed them their own larger, ungainly *cedri* almost with a sense of embarrassment. But it was the long thin dried strands of pasta they called *itriya* that sent a real frisson among the assembled delegates.

The Saracens hadn't wanted any native Sicilians to plead their case at all and looked down upon them as unsophisticated brutes who drew pleasure from eating raw onions. To the Saracens, little about the island was refined. But much of the land was rich and fertile. Wheat grew well, and they had brought their own variety whose grains had a hardness and resilience that no native plant could match, which was ground and milled to a gloriously golden rough powder that kept well, important to a people who had lived with such an unremittingly harsh climate.

Their star witness, Abu Abdullah Muhammed Ibn Idris, was called to the stand. In 1138 he had been asked by Norman-born King Ruggiero to write and record all that he saw on the island, and while visiting Palermo, then called Termini, he had been to a 'settlement called Trabia, a charming place with abundant water all the year round and several mills'. And it was here, he wrote, that a 'quantity of *itriya* is produced that is sufficient to provide not only for Calabria but also the Muslim and Christian territories, where numerous cargoes are sent by sea'.

When the man they called Idrisi left the stand, the Palermo delegation called for fresh *granita* in quiet celebration.

The judge called Idrisi over to the dais.

'We know you have travelled far and seen this thing you call *itriya*. You tell us it was made from wheat and water. But can you show us what you saw? Do you have some of this *itriya* to hand?'

'Not only do I have some to hand, your honour, I have some ready to cook. We must all wash. It is time to eat. Come, follow. All is prepared,' Idrisi told the judge.

A little way from the courthouse, the normal bustle of the Trattoria da Maria where the Sicilians had been wining and dining during the long years of the inquiry had been silenced in preparation for this grand finale. Piles of dried *itriya* lined the counters and hung from the rafters. The judge looked up, touched the thin, loose strands and muttered sotto voce but almost triumphantly: 'Why, this is *maccheroni!*'

He cleared his throat, and speaking strongly for once he began: 'Friends, Etrurians, Romans, Greeks, Sicilians, Saracens and countrymen! I have listened for years to your endless speeches, your words of passion, your stories, your hatreds, and above all your pride. And to me, to my

old sclerotic mind, we now have the answer before us.'
The judge paused to reassemble his teeth. 'Let me say that
in the opinion of this court it is the Saracens, and their
compatriot Sicilians, who have convinced me of the
veracity of their argument. It is now clear to me that *itriya*
was first known in medieval Sicily, and I therefore award
the honour of invention to the Sicilian delegation.'
And the Sicilians threw the pasta at the delegates, drunk
on the strong red wine. Whoever caught the most had the
most to eat.

* * *

Ciceri e tria

*Chickpeas and pasta. This recipe is a distant echo from
the days in the tenth century when the Arabic word
itriya was used. Puglia, where the recipe comes from
(www.cantinedellisanti.com), is one of the few areas in Italy
that still grow durum wheat. (Most of the wheat used in
Italian pasta-making is imported from North America.)*

*Soak dried chickpeas overnight in water with salt and a
dash of bicarbonate of soda. In the morning rinse the
chickpeas under running water, then transfer them to a large
saucepan filled with water and add parsley, celery, onion,
tomato and half a glass of olive oil. Cook over a high heat,
every now and then skimming the foam from the top. On a
large wooden surface put wheat flour with some water in the
centre and knead to make dough for the tria, which are like
tagliatelle only cut short, to the length of a finger. Fry half
of this in olive oil and cook the rest in abundant salted
water, draining it al dente. While the pasta is boiling,
make a soffrito by gently frying onion and garlic in olive
oil. Unite the chickpeas and the boiled pasta, taking care
not to drain off all the water, then add the soffrito and
continue cooking on a high flame for 10 minutes. Remove*

from the heat and stir in the fried pasta and a good chilli.
The mixture should be neither runny nor dense. This dish
should be eaten hot, but is also pleasant cold. For best
possible results the chickpeas should be cooked in a terra-
cotta pot — la pignata *— like in the old days.*

Maccheroni, heavenly maccheroni, the less you are cooked
the more perfect you are.

Gennaro Colombo

If history really has given us a definitive answer to this
gastromystery and we can say with certainty that dried
pasta was an Arabic invention and the myth of Marco Polo
has finally been put to rest, then we can begin to fine-tune
our appreciation of dried pasta. Crucially, you will need
teeth, for dried pasta in Italy is served *al dente*. Many non-
Italians haven't quite got used to the concept of *al dente*.
We who are trained to eat rather soft, dull, toothless stuff
from an early age feel uneasy at food having any bite to it
at all. Others familiar with the phrase get it horribly wrong
and serve food that is simply uncooked. *Al dente* is the
middle ground between crunchiness and sloppiness. It is a
fine balance. With pasta, a resistance to the tooth, the
stage immediately post-crunchiness, is what is called for,
especially when you use the best 100 per cent durum
wheat pasta, which even in its finest, choicest manifestation
is hardly bank-breaking. So throw away those packs of
filled pasta, those spirals of slop that we see everywhere.
Welcome to the wonderful world of *al dente*.

Although I'm personally not too keen on the idea, there
are quasi-scientific formulae around that could help you,
me even, cook pasta 'correctly'. And there are some
totally unscientific methods too, the best of which is
perfectly simple but unsuitable for those who disdain stains
on their beautifully painted ceiling. This method works
particularly well with spaghetti, which, by the way, is what

maccheroni is now generally called. What we in the English-speaking world know as macaroni isn't *maccheroni* at all, but short squat tubes that in Italian would be called either *maccaroncelli* or *mezzani*. We have developed our own little way with macaroni, which is to bake them with a strong English cheese sauce, which works well. I love macaroni cheese, but I never think of it as Italian food.

First, the unscientific method. Take a strand of spaghetti and throw it to the ceiling. If it stays there, it's done, and has just the right amount of stickiness to it. If it's over-done, it'll slide off and splat you in the face, so beware. If it isn't done enough, it will also fall off. Easy. But you might feel you need a little more precision. You need to cook pasta in ten times its volume of water. A standard portion of 100g of dried pasta needs a litre of water in which to cook. That's quite easy, so for more than one person you'll need a fairly large pan. When the water comes to the boil, add the pasta. Bring it back to the boil and cook for a further two minutes. Then turn off the heat, cover the pan and leave it for the amount of time suggested on the packet. This technique is almost fool-proof, and results in pasta that is both richer in nutrients and tastier. Ah – but it isn't really foolproof at all, for the water, being an inconstant part of the equation thanks to the chemicals within it, will cause the pasta to vary slightly, and even I cannot quite bring myself to boil pasta in spring water. If you feel you can, then I'm sure you'll have as perfect a medium as it is possible to find. Of course, you might feel that the end result is nothing more than undercooked pasta. But I am a dedicated follower of authenticity, so let's do it the Italian way.

Although Italy's fondness for eating pasta *al dente* is consistent throughout the country, certain areas tend to manufacture and use dried pasta, while others have a preference for fresh pasta, often made with eggs and a softer type 00 flour. And for once it's not simply a north–south divide. For dried durum pasta, the real experts are almost always to be found around the ports, which were after all the centres of trade for wheat. As early as the thirteenth century the Genovesi ate *maccheroni-cum-spaghetti*, which was made using the hard wheat shipped in from Sicily. You could always recognize Genovese spaghetti by its utter straightness, unlike Neapolitan *maccheroni*, which was dried on hooks and kept its curved end. Ancient trade routes meant that Sicilian wheat was milled to make Genovese pasta, and the Ligurian climate proved ideal for drying the pasta.

Around the Bay of Naples huge demand for *maccheroni* called for enormous amounts of durum wheat. In 1833 Ferdinand II, King of the Two Sicilies, was a recently married, strikingly ugly monarch with mild liberal tendencies. In the early days of his reign, when still enthusiastic about the business of being a king, he decided to visit Torre Annunziata, a town that is now a grimy suburb of Naples but was then the source of some of Naples' finest *maccheroni*.

The visit proceeded with due pomp and the king set about learning a little more about the Neapolitans' favourite food. Not long before they had been known as *mangiafolia*, leaf-eaters, but *maccheroni* had since become the citizens' most highly valued street food, with the great advantages of being available all the year round and being virtually imperishable. Eaten on the streets, mostly with cheese and with little elegance, it was bought by the poor from stalls and stands throughout the city. This mucky street-eating had proved a popular subject for postcards sold to the many Europeans visiting the city on their Grand Tour.

The king was taken through the factory to see the pasta being kneaded and was horrified to find that this was done not by pairs of strong Neapolitan hands but by odorous Neapolitan feet. The idea so upset his royal sensibilities

Maccheroni, *bought by the poor from stalls throughout Naples, was eaten on the streets.*

that he immediately called on his advisors to find someone who could invent a machine to do the job of the labourers, who had for many years been producing what was by all accounts the best dried pasta in the peninsula. Engineers and experts of many kinds huddled together to choose the best man to create a pasta machine and after much prevarication the job was given to Cesare Spadaccini, who diligently worked away in his workshop in Naples. A year later he was ready to show his royal client the fruits of his labour. And what had he come up with? Nothing more than a bronze man, a machine that faithfully reproduced the action of human feet. This managed to keep the monarch's attention engaged and he eventually agreed to finance a top-of-the-range pasta factory. But it didn't last long. More pressing matters took his interest, such as bombing Messina, and after a while he refused to fund the factory any longer. It was closed down and fell into disrepair.

With so many Neapolitan emigrants in the US and such a massive amount of prairie land given over to wheat production, it was hardly surprising that so much of the wheat used in pasta-making came, as it still does, from North America. The last bastions of *grano duro* cultivation in Italy itself are Puglia and Sicily. However, there was once another source of the ultimate *Triticum durum*, the star in the hard-wheat firmament: Taganrog. Boatloads of this excellent Ukrainian variety arrived from the Crimea during the pre-Revolutionary days of the nineteenth century, but Lenin's little men quickly put paid to the exports, while Stalin, wise old central planner that he was, took the path of mass starvation instead for his grateful comrades. You can still find the odd company that sells Taganrog, most of which is now grown in Argentina. (There's a stable alternative for you.)

Since producing dried pasta calls for mills, driers and shiploads of wheat, it tends not to be the sort of thing that one can make at home, so making sure you've bought good quality dried pasta calls for a little understanding of the surprisingly complex business of its manufacture. Wheat is the first fundamental, and the first process is milling the hard grains into a finer granular form, called *semola*. Modern stainless-steel rollers are efficient but generate heat, which can alter the taste and composition of the grain, so although mechanization is not at all looked down upon, the slower the process the better the end result.

Semola and water are mixed together to make a *pasta* – remember that the word *pasta* means 'paste' so it can be used in a number of contexts – which is then shaped. Although there are machines that can extrude pasta into a thousand forms, if you want the best check out the die: the *trafile*. Modern machines mostly have Teflon dies that allow the pasta to slip easily and quickly past, but the very best pastas are made using bronze dies. The reason is this: Teflon gives a smooth surface to the pasta, too smooth for any sauce to stick to, but bronze dies give a rougher edge, and the sauce sticks to the pasta just enough to combine the two in perfect gastronomic harmony.

Then comes the equally important business of drying the pasta. Again there is a difference between pastas that are dried slowly and those that are dried quickly. Slow-dried pasta is more supple and tastes better. The very best was said to come from the hills around Naples, particularly Gragnano, where the wind blew up from the bay onto the chestnut-covered hills behind the town – an ideal wind to dry pasta. You pass through Gragnano on the way to the Amalfi coast. It is not a desperately attractive town, but it still has the rump of a pasta industry that produces some of the highest-grade dried pasta in the country.

Minori lies two towns to the east of Amalfi at the foot of a valley that once positively effervesced with springs, and it has always had a reputation for making excellent pasta. The water powered the mills, and in the past wheat was both shipped in and grown on the mountain plain that lies between Gragnano and the coast. Although Minori's business has changed over the years, it has somehow managed to keep the reputation for making the best pasta around. This the town has done quite cannily – by continuing to make the best pasta around. The mills that once worked may have been silenced. The mules no longer tramp endlessly up the two thousand steps to Ravello, but Minori has a pasta saviour to hand in the shape of Signor Antonio Rocco, or Tony, as he likes to be called, who spent many years working in London at the Bistingo. (In the heady days before Italian restaurants in London had learnt that people were more than willing to pay £15 for a plate of pasta. Remember them?) Minori isn't exactly huge, so you will find Tony's shop, Il Pastaio, easily enough. And within a seagull's sniff of the sea, his machines whirr and his rollers roll and through his hands comes some of the best pasta I have ever tasted.

I drifted into the shop, speaking like a harlot in Harvey Nichols. 'Tony! I've got some people coming round at the weekend. You couldn't just knock up some *'ndunderi* for me?'

It's an ominous word, *'ndunderi*. Heavy, sullen. Like the 'Ndrangheta, Calabrese extortionists. To be quite honest, I saw the word on his board and wanted to know what on earth they were. Tony went to his fridge and pulled out what looked suspiciously like *gnocchi*. *'Ndunderi* are indeed as dense as they sound, filling *gnocchi* made from semolina and ricotta. Winter food.

He looked at me slightly sceptically. 'Do you know how to cook them? Where are you going after this? You can't keep them long, you know.'

So I promised not to maltreat them, and asked how best to serve them.

'On your way back, stop off in Furore and buy some *pomodorini*. When you get home, you make a *sugo* with them. You boil the *'ndunderi* for about seven minutes. They need a little longer than *gnocchi*. Add a bit of *Parmigiano*, not too much. That's it!'

I followed Tony's instructions to a T. I drove up the hill to Furore, and did indeed see dangling from the odd wall or two vinous bunches of tomatoes, small, cherry-size. They are called *pomodorini al piennolo* and are used throughout the winter as you would fresh tomatoes. From September right through to March these *pomodorini* gradually shrivel and with flavours duly intensified make the perfect, authentic sauce to go with your *'ndunderi*.

'Ndunderi di ricotta

This is Tony's 'ndunderi recipe. It goes well with a fresh tomato sauce. Serves four.

250g fresh ricotta cheese
3 egg yolks
2 tablespoons of grated Parmesan or pecorino cheese
salt and pepper
200g plain white flour

Mix together all the ingredients to form a supple dough. Leave to rest for an hour. Roll the dough by hand into a rope about 2.5cm thick and cut it into 2cm lengths. Roll the *'ndunderi* down the face of a curved grater to shape and pattern them. Cook in boiling salted water for at least 5 minutes, testing them as they cook.

Like so much in Italy, pasta made in one region can differ considerably from that made in the next. The names alter too, often evocative and at times obscure. Who knows these days that the pasta called *ziti* takes its name from the Neapolitan for 'bride'? Words and shapes trip off the tongue. The Minoritani have their *'ndunderi* (which means 'hit' in Neapolitan), their *scialatielli* and their *fusilli*. Puglia, Naples, Piedmont — just about every part of Italy has its own little world of shapes and sauces which in each and every case reflect a little of the people and how they have adapted the basic ingredient to their own ways.

As an exercise in using original local material, there is nothing finer than *ravioli al limone*, which Tony said I should try and promised to make.

'What about the ravioli, Tony? How do I serve them?' I am but an ignorant London boy, Tony, after all.

'That's easy. Boil them for three minutes. Add a bit of butter and some mint. Give some to Gennaro.' They are actually pretty easy to make. Use a standard ravioli recipe, make the filling from fresh ricotta, drained if it is particularly watery, and grated pecorino, with the lightest touch of lemon, freshly grated nutmeg and salt. And while I was out and about chasing prawns and elusive cheeses, Tony got to work and made me packets and piles of pasta. When I got back to England, exceptionally well laden, I tracked Gennaro down and left him a little rootsie bundle to gladden his heart: lemon ravioli, a chunk of *provolone* and a bottle of Montepertuso spring water.

PISA

SPEND TOO LONG IN LIVORNO AND EAVESDROP ON TOO MANY conversations and you might start to believe that every single Pisan is devoid of a brain. But just as not all Livornesi are wild revolutionaries, not all Pisans are entirely brainless. After all, Pisa is a university town of some repute, though it has to be said that most of the students are not from Pisa at all. You can hardly fail to have heard that they once built a tower, and that its construction didn't go entirely to plan. But was this Pisan stupidity, or could it have happened to the best of us? Pisa is an ancient Tuscan city, once briefly a significant maritime power, but it was never, unlike the others, actually on the sea. Hmmm. Oh, and their great culinary speciality is tiny newborn eels for which they are no longer allowed to fish. So what does this tell us about the Pisans?

Tuscany is the homeland of *campanilismo*, which originally expressed the idea that nothing of any interest happens outside hearing distance of your village church bell. Over time, this has evolved on many levels. First, there is the loathing that hundreds of towns and villages have for each other. We know about the Pisans and the

Livornesi, but quite a lot of hate is also beamed Florence's way. The Senesi and the Florentines don't see eye to eye. Grosseto doesn't like the Florentines either. And so on. Every small village seems to have its own particular bête noire, and they spend hours, years, fine-tuning this institutionalized slagging off of each other.

The next level down is *campanilismo* within the city walls. There can be no finer place than Siena on the day of the Palio to see just how far this can go. The city was once divided up into military districts called *contrade* and each summer they compete, as they have done for hundreds of years, in a wild bare-backed horse race around the city's Piazza del Campo to win the *palio*, the silk banner, for their *contrada*. Lurking somewhere in all the excitement is the communal memory of when the Senesi beat the *merda* out of the Florentines at the Battle of Montaperto in 1260.

The Palio is a peculiarly Italian event, where fierce loyalty finds easy expression. The races vary in their seriousness. The donkey Palio in Alba is one of the more relaxing, but even this is linked to an ancient enmity with Asti. It is certainly a good deal less vicious than the Senese Palio, the grandmaster of them all. The Pisans have their own, rather less bloody, less orgiastic version, the Palio di San Ranieri, where the city's four *quartieri* compete against each other in a display of mock-medieval heroics. But this is Palio lite, revived in 1935, using of all things fibreglass boats. The boats, emblazoned with the colours of the four sectors of the city – San Martino (white and red) and San Antonio (white and green) to the south of the river and Santa Maria (white and blue) and San Francesco (white and yellow) to the north – try to row down the Arno to the finishing line, then send the 'climber' up the mast of a boat where three pennants are flying. The first to get the blue flag is the winner. The losers get a pair of goslings. This is supposed to celebrate Pisa's great and wonderful victory over the Turks at the naval Battle of Lepanto in 1571. When the Florentines were in charge of Pisa, as they were for many hundreds of years, the Pisans were not allowed to celebrate this great battle and had to make do with other, more lowly events laid on by their Florentine masters.

Throughout much of the twelfth and thirteenth centuries, a far more serious rift pitched towns and districts and factions and families against one another. This was the eternal conflict of the Guelfs and the Ghibellines. These are odd words linguistically, and you would have to be an expert in medieval German history to know that they are derived from two battle cries – '*Hie Welf!*' and '*Hie Waiblingen!*' – used in the equally obfuscating German dispute between the Bavarian dukes of the Welf dynasty and the Hohenstaufen dukes of Swabia, whose hearts were firmly attached to the castle of Waiblingen, italianized as Ghibelline.

The dispute centred on the role of the Pope and that of the Emperor of the Christian Empire, the Holy Roman Empire as it was at times called, but deeper down it was the fundamental issue of whether communities should by and large be allowed to rule themselves or whether they should be told how to do so by an emperor. As feudal centres evolved into cities and towns, Italy, which was at the heart and soul of the conflict, lived through hundreds of years of great uncertainty.

Florence, the city of Dante, the civilized centre of Tuscany and some would say of Europe itself, was deeply divided by this endless bloody conflict. Theoretically the papacy supported more communal power and thus was more likely to be supported by artisans and lower-order aristocrats. The emperors had more support from the aristocracy. The empire's chief protagonists were Frederick I, Barbarossa, who lived from 1123 to 1190, and his grandson, Frederick II. While Barbarossa was forever on the move, Frederick II made Sicily his power base and was a strict master of the growing cities of the south. In the north things were different. Cities had become powerful and rich, building defensive walls, creating laws and raising armies to defend themselves against attack. Venice, the immensely powerful Serenissima, as she was known, looked to the east for her wealth and had as leader a doge, an elected member of the merchant elite, rather than a king. So did Genoa, but Florence, although it was eventually to become a grand duchy, was a self-contained, even mildly democratic city that was perhaps the most deeply troubled by the Guelf wars.

With the cities in the south far more closely controlled by the emperor, you begin to see a pattern. You could almost say that the south didn't have much chance to rule for itself but was ruled in the interests of others for at least two thousand years. Perhaps this is why there have long been so many undercurrents of impenetrable groups and secret organizations, such as the Mafia, the 'Ndrangheta and the Camorra.

Pisa's glory was closely connected with the successful conquest of Sicily by the Normans in the eleventh century. Pisa had supplied King Roger of Normandy with troops and ships to conquer the Saracens, ending a unique and unusually rich period of Islamic rule that had radically influenced the island. Land had been irrigated. Lemons, aubergines and fennel had arrived. Sherbets were made with the snow from the mountains. Scholarship flourished. There is still a little wistful longing in Sicily for those theoretically paradisical years of tolerance and wealth.

Then along came the Christians, and Palermo was looted, much to the delight of the merchant adventurers of Pisa. Their influence had spread far. The Balearics were conquered, as were Corsica and Sardinia. You can still see the ancient fortifications the Pisans built above Cagliari in Sardinia, as well as a few emphatically Tuscan-style churches dotted around the island.

In 1068 Pisa defeated Genoa, and their golden age, brief and distant, started in earnest. You can see a scene of this conquest carved into the bottom of the Leaning Tower, showing two Pisan vessels sailing past Porto Pisano at the mouth of the Arno, long before it silted up and the Medicis built Pisa's great modern rival, the arch-villainous city of Livorno.

While Pisa was strong, the city felt it important to cock a snook at Florence. How better to do this than to construct the biggest bell tower in the world? Thus began the story of the *torre pendente*, the Leaning Tower. In 1172 a good Christian lady known as Widow Berta of Bernardo left 60 soldi in her will for the purchase of stones to build a bell tower alongside the cathedral. We know that the design was radical. Never before had a round tower of such height been built in Tuscany, with all the very particular problems such a structure has. But it isn't the design that has given the lean. It's all down to a curious combination of geology and prevarication. The leaning started almost as soon as the building work began. In 1174, the tower had been built up to its third storey when work stopped, possibly because of its lean, or because of the need to focus on defending the city from the Florentines.

War, pestilence and even a touch of famine followed, all of which allowed the tower to settle on the clay beneath its foundations, which hardened and gave it a little stability. The tower was dormant and bell-less until 1272, when one Giovanni of Simone took matters in hand and added three more storeys and the bells. Pisa could listen at last to the chiming of the bell tower in the Piazza dei Miracoli. By 1284 the tower was already forty-eight metres high, with an ever-increasing lean.

The first of many inquiries into the source of the leaning was convened in 1298, but it wasn't until 2001 that a definitive solution was found that not only arrested the lean but also understood it, and preserved it, for who would travel thousands of miles to see the Upright Tower of Pisa? What would they do with all those leaning beer mugs, leaning wine glasses, lights, pens and other knick-knackery of supreme bad taste?

And despite slipping into almost terminal decline after their defeat by the Genovesi at the Battle of Melora in 1284, Pisa became one of the world's oldest university towns, was subsumed into the Florentine Republic, and then under the Medicis became part of the Grand Duchy of Tuscany, where it remained until the Tuscans with almost indecent haste decided to jump onto the Piemontese unification express under the royal House of Savoy in the nineteenth century.

While food in Sicily, for example, has been a positive riot of influence from outside, in the *campanilismo* heartland of Tuscany it has remained remarkably unchanged: hams and pulses, sausages, and Italy's finest beef from the Maremma, the swampy coast that runs south from Pisa towards Rome. Tuscany has also managed to retain its one-pot classics: dishes such as *zuppa pisana* and *ribolitta* that were originally cooked in a single pot over a fire. Tuscan cooking is to this day essentially a regional brand of *cucina povera*, though richer in meat than many others, and richer in some of the most excellent pulses to be found, too. Pisa, to an extent, reflects this.

Say 'cee' to a Pisan, a middle-aged, corpulent Pisan for preference, and watch the effect. It is pronounced 'che' as in Guevara but has no other similarity to the man of the staring masculine eyes and iconic posters. What we are talking about is little more than water and slime. *Cee* is the immature version of the European eel. While over the hills on the eastern coast sits Italy's greatest eel city, Comacchio, there once used to be a flood of tiny immature elvers that swam up the Arno too, only to be greeted by endless rows of men with fine-meshed nets and eel traps waiting to catch the city's most beloved fish. But, sadly, like the esteemed Cuban revolutionary, *cee* are now a thing of the past. The Arno is too polluted. The eels have been overfished. Their ancestral swamps are industrial wastelands. Pisa has been a cosmopolitan city for so long now that it seems to have lost its culinary soul as it fills up its *pizzerie* with Italians from Lombards to Sicilians, and tourists from Taiwanese to Tasmanians.

Dedicated gastronomes might be advised to give Pisa a miss. I struggled to find not only somewhere to eat *cucina pisana*, but somewhere to eat. If you are doing the classic tourist thing you may be dragged into a dodgy trattoria where you will feel at home sipping a *cappuccino* in the afternoon, which is not the done thing, or even sitting down for breakfast, which is certainly not the done thing. If you have worked up a medieval appetite by climbing the ancient helter-skelter, a.k.a. the Leaning Tower, why not seek out Da Bruno, a venerable Pisan restaurant just outside the city walls?

Da Bruno is a serious restaurant, a sort of relaxed serious but serious nonetheless. That is not to say cloche serious. There are a few restaurants in Italy where deviants think that cloche-lifting epitomizes good taste when we all know it is quite unsuited to the gutsiness you would expect here, for Pisa is after all in the heart of Tuscany. Da Bruno is the sort of restaurant where once Chianti would have been served in *fiaschi*, which I say uncritically for I truly loved them. When I was young we had one in my family that was used as a table lamp and lasted for at least ten years, then faded and melded into the background along with our Vauxhall estate.

If Da Bruno was in London, it would have a sweet trolley. Blissful things, sweet trolleys, and a marvellously English interpretation of Italian food, offering virtually nothing that is Italian. When bored, see if you can name twelve things that would once have appeared on the sweet trolley.* Middle-aged businessmen, attracted by the bonhomie, come in droves to Da Bruno, where the food is good and solid if a little unexciting. One of the dishes they have perfected over the years is *zuppa pisana*. This dish has long been cooked by Pisan mammas to good effect and uses two key Tuscan ingredients. The first is Tuscan bread: saltless, as we have learnt. The other is *fagioli*, far more than just dried beans, for in the hills behind Pisa grow some of Italy's very finest.

Zuppa pisana

Enough for eight to ten people.

1 large onion, chopped
1 clove garlic, chopped
100g pancetta, diced
olive oil
1 green cabbage, shredded
3 courgettes, sliced
1 leek, chopped
1 stick celery, chopped
1 carrot, chopped
50g tomato purée
1kg fresh borlotti beans
500g dried borlotti beans, soaked overnight
1 ham bone
1 sage leaf
1 slice of Tuscan bread per person, pulled into bits

---

* Trifle, orange in caramel, Black Forest gâteau, figs in syrup, profiteroles (of course), cheesecake, out-of-season tasteless strawberries, crème brûlée – that's as far as I've got.

salt and pepper
1 mild chilli, chopped
1 handful flat-leaf parsley, chopped
a few leaves fresh basil

In a large saucepan, fry the onion, garlic and pancetta gently in a little olive oil for 5 minutes. Add. the vegetables, tomato purée and a little water and cook for 1 hour.

In another pan, put the borlotti beans, both fresh and soaked, the ham bone and the sage leaf. Cover with water, bring to the boil and then cook gently for about 30 minutes until the beans are done. Don't add salt.

Drain the beans and add to the soup along with the bread, and taste and adjust the seasoning. (Remove the ham bone.) Add the chilli and cook for a further 30 minutes, then add the parsley and basil and serve.

Food stop number two showed me being carried away by a streak of Livornese *campanilismo*, for when I walked in on a cold and dreary February evening, the trattoria I had chosen was completely and utterly empty. When I said something along the lines of 'Well, it looks like you can manage a table for one,' the waiter looked at me disdainfully and said that all the tables were booked. I laughed uproariously and moved to sit down. He lurched forward and said: 'No, sir, the restaurant is full tonight. You must book in advance. Sorry.'

So I walked briskly out and sought refuge in the local Sardinian, where I ate some delicious *casu marzu*, wormless rotten cheese, and saw people smile. It was quite a relief.

The odd thing about Tuscan food is this. The rich cities, Florence, Siena, Lucca and Pisa to name but four from a long and mighty list, had a rich elite who travelled widely and whose influence was felt as far away as France. Catherine de' Medici, an enigmatic, fascinating woman who was shipped off to marry Henri, Duke of Orleans, and who, after years spent twiddling her thumbs in France, eventually became queen, was said to have travelled with a whole coterie of chefs and retainers from home. She introduced the French to the delights of frangipane, ices and sorbets, sugar, and quite possibly spinach. So the story goes, though it is almost certainly one of the great culinary myths that there was a sea change in eating habits in the French court when she arrived. The fourteenth-century Neapolitan cookbook *Liber de coquina* mentioned Lombard *tourtes* and *crustades* and in France King Francis I had already shown interest in Italian culinary ways, so quite a lot of exchange across the Alps was already going on. Catherine de' Medici has perhaps been credited with too much, though the fondness for sweet things was certainly down to her, for the Florentine court had become used to voluptuous cane sugar brought in by the ever-industrious Venetians.

And yet, while France went on to develop a whole culture of *haute cuisine*, Tuscany's rulers appear to have been as narrow in their food tastes as they were broad in their distaste for other communities. To this day Tuscan food is remarkably unrefined. It tends to rely on the excellence of prosciutto, salami and fagioli to make such fundamentally simple dishes as *ribollita*, a twice-cooked bean soup, or *pappa al pomodoro*, bread with tomatoes.

I might as well break it to you gently but there are other reasons why I was staying in Pisa, beyond simply tasting their good, solid food. For here it was that Mazzini, my friendly corpse, my ghostly companion, quietly breathed his last. Wheezed his last, it seems, for the cigars finally got to him. And he died not in a rest home for incurable romantics but in a house that belonged to the Rossellis, to my great-great-uncle, Pellegrino Rosselli, and his wife Giannetta.

The story had come full circle. Since seeing the photograph in Turin on 12 September 2001, I had reflected and genuflected in Genoa and Livorno, relived the thrills of the Republic of Rome and sympathized with Mazzini in his years of exile in cold and foggy London. I had completed the exercise of stalking the ghost of Mazzini, quite used by now to his ethereal presence across my table.

Decades of smoking cheap cigars and living in London hadn't given him Queen Mother-like longevity, but as he puffed and wheezed his way around Europe, still plotting, still eluding the authorities, he decided to spend more time with one of his favourite companions, Giannetta Rosselli, daughter of Sara Nathan, whose matronly bosom, among many others, was also said to have succumbed to Mazzini's charms. The Nathans and the Rossellis had close connections through marriage and the world of banking. Some of the family settled in Clerkenwell, London, an area rich with Italian émigrés, where Mazzini first lived when he arrived in the city. The two families set up a stockbroking firm together and struggled hard over its name: Nathan Rosselli. It seems they could offer the Republicans ways to channel money, and might have helped finance some of the Mazzinian ventures over the years from the relative security of their London base. After Mazzini's death they were to fund a school in Rome in his name, open to the poorest, most hard-pressed Roman families.

By 1872, the authorities were slightly less jumpy about Mazzini's presence. He was an old man, and the country was now united under a monarchy. It seemed that Mazzini's great Republican dream was dead in the water. Tuscany had practically forced itself into the union with the House of Savoy, voting in a closely controlled and apparently overwhelmingly convincing plebiscite. Mazzini was a disappointed man, and he wrote: 'I smoke perennially, I am sorry to say, but what can I do? I write unwillingly, through a sense of mere duty, without a spark of enthusiasm and smoking is a mere diversion to the soul's fog which is coming heavy on my head, like a leaden cap.'

That year Mazzini arrived in Pisa from Switzerland, looking drawn. Every evening he walked slowly outside, watched the world go by and the children play, and then wandered back to the Rosselli house in Via Maddalena. The neighbours politely asked after the kindly old gentleman, and were told that he was an Englishman, a doctor, John Brown. When his cough worsened, Giannetta called the local doctor to get him some medicine, and they spoke amiably enough, but passionately, of Italy. Mostly in English, for he didn't want his cover blown.

'You seem to love Italy, Dr Brown,' the doctor was heard to say.

'Love Italy? Love Italy? No one has ever loved Italy more!' replied Mazzini.

He had reason to be dispirited. Garibaldi had refused to meet him in his final years, convinced that he had contributed to the failure of the Roman Republic and the uprising in Palermo in 1860. The Italy that had emerged was little more than an extended Kingdom of Sardinia. The papacy remained. Mazzini's dream of a democratic republic had come to naught. It wasn't until 1946, after the catastrophe of the Second World War and the country's Fascist interlude, that Italy finally became a republic and the Italians ditched their asinine royal family.

On the morning of 18 March 1872, Mazzini's condition deteriorated. The family gathered around his bed: Sara Nathan, Pellegrino and Giannetta Rosselli. He dipped in and out of consciousness, until his fever quickened and his rambling became incoherent. Later that afternoon, Mazzini suddenly sat up and spoke clearly, his face shocked: '*Sì, sì. Credo in Dio!*' Yes, yes, I believe in God! And fell back on the pillow, dead.

The word soon spread around Pisa, full as ever with students whose own Republican dreams of independence had been inspired by this honourable Italian hero. They asked that the university be shut in his honour but the authorities refused, so the students took to the streets. His funeral procession in Pisa wound along the Lungarno, followed by a hushed crowd some 80,000 strong, but the indignities suffered by Mazzini in life were to be nothing compared to what would happen to his body in death.

Mazzini had asked that he be buried alongside his mother in Genoa, but his friend and fellow Republican Dr Bertani felt that the body should be preserved, embalmed, in order to become a veritable saint for the saintless Republicans. Bertani called on the expertise of the strange

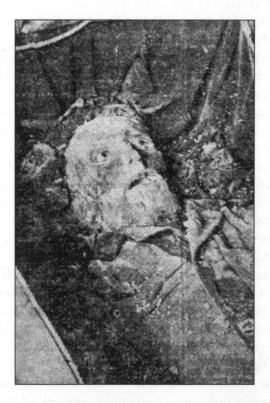

Mazzini's embalmed corpse was displayed as recently as 1946.

Dr Paolo Gorini of Lodi. Gorini was a master of mummification and had perfected a way to preserve bodies, and bits and pieces of bodies. You can see his handiwork in the Gorini Museum in the Old Hospital in Lodi. And odd it is, too, to see ancient eyes staring out at you. You will not, however, see Mazzini's. His body was preserved in a grand and classic mausoleum on the hills above Genoa at Staglieno, which you can still see. Two years after his death, his mummified corpse was shown to the public and attracted the curious and the reverent. Even as late as 1946, the year that Italy finally became a republic, his body was being disturbed and shown to a select few, looking quite tortured and distinctly unrestful.

The London ladies railed at his mummification. In a heartfelt letter to Giannetta Rosselli, Jessie White Mario, a formidable activist in her own right and a dedicated Mazzinian, wrote: 'Write me something. Think what it must be not to have seen him – heard his voice and known it was the last time . . . tell me of his last hours. I do not wish to see the beloved man embalmed . . . I could not bear it.' And neither could the Rossellis. It was very distasteful. But despite their protestations, Bertani had his way and Mazzini's body slowly decayed, intermittently witnessed by reverential Italian citizens. Not a fitting end for a great Italian hero.

AFTERWORD

IT WAS THE CHIPS THAT DID IT. I WAS IN PARIS. SIX OF US HAD travelled to the land of the giant baguette, the city of the welcoming waiter and the guillotine. We had all got up horribly early in the morning, along with hordes of other cosmopolitans, to get on the morning train at Waterloo to celebrate a friend's birthday. It was one of those that casts you nearer old age than middle, and makes being young a distant dream. Going to Paris for the day seemed as good a way as any to soften the blow.

As we settled down to a fabulous meal sitting outside the Palais Royal, the sun shone, happy Parisians strolled by and all seemed well. It was almost refreshing to be able to understand every word, although I wanted to answer in Italian. My, my. Paris. Where I had lived off and on for two years and visited once a week for ten.

We had barely made it in time. We had been warned that we would eat nothing if we arrived after the gastro-nomic witching hour of two. The train had lumbered out of London as slow as Stevenson's *Rocket*, and then we were left outside *le tunnel* for fifty minutes, gasping for fresh air as the train's electricity was cut for unknown reasons.

Sangatte, people mumbled. Immigrants. We wondered whether they were scraping from an inbound train the remains of a tragic character pursuing a mad dream to join a land that prides itself in being civilized but has forgotten how to treat those who need it most. England's green and pleasant land.

From the Gare du Nord we rushed off in a taxi down to the Palais Royal. And it was almost refreshing to be served by a typical Parisian waiter. Grim, clock-watching and rude. The menu came. We considered. The waiter took the order. The only time we saw him again was when he assured us that another salad was quite out of the question. His underlings, happily, were charm itself: smiling, solicitous and professional.

Ah, how sweet. They used the word *tian*. The starters came. I had been tempted by what they called a *buisson d'escargot*. A bush of snails. It came with a regular pattern of neat snails wrapped in what appeared to be home-made shredded wheat and sitting in a creamy sauce, which looked rather like the thing that French restaurateurs name *cappuccino* that has nothing to do with coffee but is a frothy soupy liquid served in a coffee cup, a profound culinary irritation. The first time I ate this I was with a plain-speaking Scot who referred to it as dog sick, and it lost its appeal after that. The girls ordered steak with a béarnaise sauce and *frites*. The steak arrived with eight *frites* piled in an Escher cube, one on top of the other. Good chips. Good sauce. But why not just a good old pile of chips? Why so much cream? Why chives sticking out of plates, and dribbles of jam like the devil's ejaculate over the strawberry tart? And it dawned on me that I no longer had *le feeling* for this kind of food. Take me to Italy, my body screamed. Fly me quick to the nearest congested no-frills airport. Give me a slice of pure prosciutto. Let me stand by a blazing wood-fired oven and see the *farinata* bubble before my eyes, served sizzling in pure white waxy paper. Let me nibble on an apricot from Etna, and sip from a glass of *granita del gelso* stained with mulberry juice so laughably purple you want to bathe in it. This is food with a purity and simplicity that French food so seldom has. You cannot make good Italian food without good ingredients, but here in France, where food is so fiddled and mixed, even the finest chefs have been known to work their magic on the most ignoble industrial chickens.

There is no need for frippery. No need at all, *mon vieux*. Take me back to Piazza Mazzini, even if no one can quite remember who Mazzini was. Let me listen to musical Neapolitan, and watch the beautiful streets of Rome come to life, and glance up through the roof of the Pantheon into that crystal stark-blue sky. Just let me soak in a little more. Take me back to Italy!

SLOW FOOD

You will need fortitude, a ticket to Turin and a toothpick to appreciate just how far the Slow Food movement has come over the years. Once every two years, the citizens of Turin play host to an enthusiastic swarm of international devotees who pour into the city to visit the Salone del Gusto, the Salon of Taste. I joined them, swarmed and was massively inspired by what I saw.

Since this is an international exhibition, with an international pavilion, there is a sprinkling of distinctly un-Italian exhibiting. One of the few English exhibitors was an old friend from Cornwall, Nick Howell, the county's last remaining producer of salted pilchards, *salacche inglesi* in Italian, whose main market has for generations been Italy. At the Howells' fascinating Pilchard Museum in Newlyn you can still see how pilchards have been salted, pressed and packed over the centuries, and shipped off to the long-established markets in Italy. As a very special treat, visitors are encouraged to nibble. Invariably in England mouths pucker and sounds of disgust along the lines of 'eugh' issue forth. Here in Turin the reception was rather different. With nary a sign of a wrinkled nose or puckered lip, the Italians jostled for the plate of samples, wielding their sharpened toothpicks. A few said how the very particular taste of the *salacche inglesi* gave them Proustian flashbacks of their youth by reviving the inimitable taste of them served with polenta.

The huge, slightly undisciplined enthusiasm the Italians had for the cheeses, the thousands of *salsicce*, the hams and the wines was genuinely inspiring and infectious. Cannily, as you stepped into the salon at pavilion number one, you were immersed in some of the Slow Food's presidia, the groups that act as the means to bring life to produce which, without Slow Food, might have faded away into the collective memory.

The movement started back in 1986 when a leftist activist from Bra in Piedmont, Carlo Petrini, reacted to the opening of McDonald's in Rome by creating its antithesis, Slow Food. While not quite McDonald's nemesis, Slow Food has become an extraordinarily effective movement, transcending its roots in the north of Italy to find followers in five continents and over 60,000 members.

During the writing of this book, I came across Slow Food in every part of Italy I went to. Yes, it is true, they annoyed me by being slow to respond to my requests for help and, yes, part of me thought it all a bourgeois plot, but then when I had calmed down and thought about it, I realized that they are doing what needs to be done, and what I feel deeply and passionately is right.

One of the most depressing things I come across is children with little experience of the sense of taste. Children are eating in monochrome. My kids' friends come round and have no idea what a date is, and loathe anything that is unusual and different. They are being brought up on food controlled by companies who need to generate high demand to survive, which they do with loud packaging, loud advertising and by producing food that is as far removed from anything living as possible. The multinationals thrive and offer us what all European post-war governments have seen as the cure-all, the sine qua non of progress — cheap food.

And in the name of cheap food we have developed extraordinarily sophisticated methods of getting pigs to grow and chickens to mature as quickly as possible, of growing potatoes that are perfectly round but tainted with chemicals. Heavily industrialized countries like Britain have lost their food markets to shops that are ironically called supermarkets. We have, frankly, lost the culture of taste, the culture of food. But like a punch-drunk Goliath, the consumer has risen and begun to remember that food is about more than eating. Food is produced. It was once closely attached to time and place.

Italy plays a curious, central role in all this. It is a young country, where regions and regions within regions have preserved an extraordinary richness and diversity of foods and wines still closely linked to place. Stepping through the doors of the Lingotto, the old Fiat factory in Turin that hosts the biennial Slow Food Salone del Gusto, brings you into immediate, almost shocking contact with the fightback against the industrialization we no longer want. The Italians, with their inimitable, lovely attachment to everything that is truly sensual, are the very best guardians of this revival, and the very best guides, taking us firmly by the hand and reminding us of the story behind food, of the experience of taste, and showing us that we should not and must not allow so much of our cultural heritage to be ironed smooth and neutralized by bureaucratic diktats and the unwarranted fear of bacteria.

Spend some time with Slow Food. They are doing the right thing.

http://www.slowfood.com

FURTHER READING

For those of you who would like a more detailed account, look at fairly formative in-depth studies or thoroughly written books. On the broad historical side, a classic general History of the Italian People (Penguin 1991) is on a brilliant book, and so is Luigi Barzini's *The Italians* (Penguin 1964). On the Risorgimento, too long to recount here, Lucio Sponza's book is worth a read, particularly much as can a Christopher Duggan (Oxford 2007) *Francesco Crispi* ... as is the ... Denis Mack Smith (Italian 2002)... For learning ... omit only material ... Denis Mack Smith ... Christopher Duggan (Penguin 1980)'s *Italy in the Twentieth Century* and *The Force of Destiny: A History of Italy since 1796* (Allen Lane 1996). For those interested in Italy, a good introduction is Paul Ginsborg's *Italy and Its Discontents* (Bloomsbury 2001). Staying novels, I would choose *The Leopard*, the classic exquisite work of the Sicilian nobleman Giuseppe Tomasi di Lampedusa (Harvill Press 1958), and also from Sicily, anything by Leonardo Sciascia but particularly his collection of short stories *The Wine-Dark Sea* (Granta 2001), a marvellous gentle work even in translation.

FURTHER READING

For those of you who would like a more detailed, serious look at Italy, here are a few books I thoroughly recommend. On the broad history of Italy, Giuliano Procacci's *History of the Italian People* (Penguin 1973) is a brilliant book, and so is Luigi Barzini's *The Italians* (Penguin 1968). On the Risorgimento, any book by Professor Denis Mack Smith is worth a read, particularly *Mazzini* (Yale University Press 1996). G. M. Trevelyan's *Defence of the Roman Republic, 1848–49* (Orion 2001) is a classic. In addition, I would recommend Martin Clark's *Modern Italy 1871–1995* (Longman 1996); Denis Mack Smith's *Modern Italy: A Political History* (Yale 1997); *The Bourbons of Italy* by Harold Acton (Prion 1998) and Terry Coleman's *Nelson* (Bloomsbury 2001). Among novels I would choose *The Leopard*, the classic, exquisite work of the Sicilian nobleman Giuseppe Tomasi di Lampedusa (Harvill Press 1996) and, also from Sicily, anything by Leonardo Sciascia but particularly his collection of short stories, *The Wine Dark Sea* (Granta 2001), a marvellous poetic work even in translation.

INDEX

Val d'Aosta · Piemonte · Lombardia · Trentino-Alto Adige · Veneto · Friuli Venezia Giulia · Liguria · Emilia-Romagna · Toscana · Marche · Umbria · Lazio

MILAN · Vercelli · TURIN · Alba · GENOA · Verona · Mantua · Venice · Comacchio · Bologna · FLORENCE · Pisa · Livorno · ROME · R. Po · R. Tiber

1. Val d'Aosta
2. Piemonte
3. Lombardia
4. Trentino-Alto Adige
5. Veneto
6. Friuli Venezia Giulia
7. Liguria
8. Emilia-Romagna
9. Toscana
10. Marche
11. Umbria
12. Lazio
13. Abruzzo
14. Molise
15. Puglia
16. Campania
17. Basilicata
18. Calabria

Caprera · Fertilia · Alghero · Orgosolo · SARDINIA · Arborea · Carbonia · Carloforte · San Pietro